P9-BZX-184

Third Edition

Choices and Constraints in Family Life

Maureen Baker

OXFORD
UNIVERSITY PRESS

OXFORD
UNIVERSITY PRESS

Oxford University Press is a department of the University of Oxford.
It furthers the University's objective of excellence in research, scholarship,
and education by publishing worldwide. Oxford is a registered trade mark of
Oxford University Press in the UK and in certain other countries.

Published in Canada by
Oxford University Press
8 Sampson Mews, Suite 204,
Don Mills, Ontario M3C 0H5 Canada

www.oupcanada.com

Copyright © Oxford University Press Canada 2014

The moral rights of the author have been asserted

Database right Oxford University Press (maker)

First Edition published in 2007
Second Edition published in 2010

All rights reserved. No part of this publication may be reproduced, stored in
a retrieval system, or transmitted, in any form or by any means, without the
prior permission in writing of Oxford University Press, or as expressly permitted
by law, by licence, or under terms agreed with the appropriate reprographics
rights organization. Enquiries concerning reproduction outside the scope of the
above should be sent to the Permissions Department at the address above
or through the following url: www.oupcanada.com/permission/permission_request.php

Every effort has been made to determine and contact copyright holders.
In the case of any omissions, the publisher will be pleased to make
suitable acknowledgement in future editions.

Library and Archives Canada Cataloguing in Publication
Baker, Maureen, author
Choices and constraints in family life / Maureen Baker.
– Third edition

Includes bibliographical references and index.
ISBN 978-0-19-900537-6 (pbk.)

1. Families – Textbooks. I. Title.

HQ519.B34 2014   306.85   C2013-902372-0

Cover image: Mike Jessen/Picture Press/Getty Images.com

Oxford University Press is committed to our environment.
This book is printed on Forest Stewardship Council® certified paper
and comes from responsible sources.

Printed and bound in Canada

1 2 3 4 — 17 16 15 14

Contents

9 Constraints on Personal Choices 199

List of Tables and Boxes

Tables

Boxes

Preface and Acknowledgements

Many young students seem to believe that they can create their own "personal biographies" or freely develop their own individual lifestyle and domestic relationships. Although I agree that more personal choices are available now compared to a few decades ago, I argue in this book that many of the old constraints on relationships continue and some new ones have been added. Current knowledge and controversies about intimacy, the nature of marriage, cohabitation, and family life are examined from the fields of sociology, anthropology, cultural studies, psychology, gender studies, and social history. These research findings are compared with some of the concerns of politicians and representations of personal and family life in the media.

Over the past few decades, the study of personal and family life has changed in terms of the basic assumptions behind the field, the issues being researched, and the practical relevance of the research. In my view, new life has been breathed into the sub-discipline by paying greater attention to gender relations and domestic work as well as issues relating to cohabitation, same-sex relationships, the creation of personal identity, new reproductive technologies, fathering, and public discourse about parenting and family responsibilities. I show that while innovative family patterns have developed in recent years, some of these "new" patterns are really variations on older themes. In addition, a number of battles fought in the 1960s and 1970s relating to gender equity and work/family balance continue unresolved into the twenty-first century.

A number of colleagues have assisted with the development and preparation of this book. Back in the early 1980s, Professor Lorne Tepperman from the Sociology Department at the University of Toronto encouraged me to edit my first book about families by recommending me to a publisher. Lorne also recommended me to author the first edition of *Choices and Constraints in Family Life* with Oxford University Press. I am very grateful for both suggestions. Second, I would like to thank the staff at Oxford University Press, especially Mark Thompson (developmental editor) and Richard Tallman (copy editor), who helped guide my revised manuscript into the third edition. Although I live in Auckland, New Zealand, and my publishers operate from Toronto, the process ran very smoothly using electronic mail with all three editions. Third, I would like to thank my partner, Dr David Tippin, for his continuing support throughout the preparation of this book and all my other academic projects.

Maureen Baker
University of Auckland, New Zealand
January 2013

1

Variations in Family Life

Learning Objectives

◎ To understand the different ways that families and family policies have been defined.

◎ To explore some historical changes in marriage and family life.

◎ To investigate the ways that family experiences vary by gender, ethnicity, and social class.

◎ To understand some cultural variations in family and marriage systems.

Introduction

Compared to a few generations ago, some aspects of family life have changed considerably. For one thing, our intimate relationships now involve more personal choices about partners, sexual behaviour, and living arrangements. In the twenty-first century, more of us believe that we have the right to choose our partners without interference and that whether or not we cohabit, formalize our relationships, or produce children should be our own decisions rather than something we might be pressured to do by family members, religious leaders, or legal requirements. Many people also feel that they should not be forced to remain with their partner if that relationship proves unsatisfactory.

In this book, I argue that intimate relationships are certainly influenced by our personal preferences but to a large extent our "choices" are shaped by family circumstances, the attitudes and behaviour of our friends, and events in the wider society, such as downturns in the economy, labour market changes, technological innovations, media representations, and new ideas about human rights or personal entitlements. Consequently, patterns are noticeable in family life, including rising rates of cohabitation, the formalization of same-sex relationships in some jurisdictions, fewer births of which more occur outside marriage, higher rates of separation and re-partnering, and more step-families. In fact, similar trends in family and personal life are apparent in most Western industrialized countries (Lewis, 2003; OECD, 2011c).

At a time when more of us insist on making our own choices about partners and children, many people also expect government or public agencies to safeguard their human rights, to protect them from violent relationships, to help them manage problem children, or to supplement their inadequate household incomes. New public expectations have heightened controversies about who is responsible for protecting and supporting vulnerable family members and those in need. Public debates have also questioned the validity of new forms of marriage, sought solutions to declining fertility and the enforcement of child support after separation, and examined new ways of interacting with immigrants whose family practices diverge from the majority.

"Child poverty" is growing in many countries despite political promises to reduce or abolish it, and this poverty is aggravated by higher rates of marriage breakdown as well as labour market deregulation (UNICEF, 2005). Especially in the **liberal states** (or Canada, Australia, New Zealand, the United Kingdom, and the United States), policy-makers continue to search for ways to reduce this poverty. However, they are also concerned about maximizing personal responsibility for family well-being and reducing income taxes and social spending—and one set of goals seems to counteract the other. Nevertheless, controversies over relationships and family obligations permeate both public policy debates and private conversations.

This book aims to understand how relationships, family practices, and family policies have changed over the past decades in Western industrialized countries but especially in the liberal states. It also aims to differentiate between *actual* changes and the misconceptions voiced in political speeches or perpetuated in the media. Discussions of social research will reveal that our personal choices about intimate partners, having children, dissolving relationships, and maintaining contact with parents and siblings are influenced by our family and friends, our cultural upbringing, our socio-economic circumstances, the social policy environment, and political and economic events in the larger society. This means that the nature of family and personal life is always changing, although some aspects have remained remarkably stable.

The studies and examples used to illustrate the arguments in this book are derived from several different countries but focus particularly on Canada and the other liberal states (Esping-Andersen, 1990) because these countries usually expect individuals to rely on employment earnings and the assistance of household members and voluntary organizations for well-being. Relatively ungenerous state assistance is made available only when people cannot cope. However, by examining relationships and families in various countries, eras, income levels, and cultural circumstances, we are better able to understand the diverse factors that influence personal choices about love, sex, marriage, and family formation.

Defining Families

The word "family" is used in various ways in popular usage, referring in different contexts to our parents, siblings, spouse, and children, as well as referring to all the relatives sharing a household and the larger group of relatives with whom we may or may not maintain some contact. Social scientists usually feel the need to clarify the meaning by adding qualifiers such as **nuclear family** (husband, wife, and children sharing a household with no other adults present) or **extended family** (husband, wife, and children sharing a household with other relatives such as grandparents, aunts, or uncles). Most academic and policy definitions focus on the structure of family households—whether it is nuclear or extended, and whether it contains one or two parents. They also emphasize the legality of the relationships—whether partners are married, in a civil union or civil partnership, or cohabiting—rather than considering feelings of love or obligation, or shared activities.

Early social scientists called the family a **social institution**, emphasizing the rules and expectations that guided family patterns and interaction. They stated that the family consisted of at least two adults (one female, one male), united by marriage, living together, pooling their resources, sharing intimacy, and producing and raising children (Murdock, 1949; Goode, 1964). Over the years, this definition has been challenged as ideological, outmoded, and over-emphasizing the heterosexual nuclear family. Increasingly, academics and ordinary citizens argue that the structure of families or the legality of their relationships is less meaningful and has fewer implications for their daily lives than the services that household members provide for each other or how they feel about these relationships. Consequently, both researchers and advocacy groups suggest that definitions should be broadened to encompass caring and enduring intimate relationships regardless of their legal or blood ties (Cherlin 2010; Luxton, 2011; May, 2011).

Governments, however, are particularly concerned about who shares a dwelling, whether or not couples have formalized their relationship or share a "marriage-like relationship," and the legal relationship between adults and any children living in the household. This information tells state officials who should be held accountable for financial support, care, and protection. They are particularly interested in whether households contain one or two adults, how much income is available to support the children, whether families require state income assistance, and whether vulnerable members are "at risk." The state develops specific definitions of family for planning and policy purposes and is unwilling to allow people to create their own definitions, especially when making decisions about entitlement for social benefits or immigration status. However, advocacy groups persistently pressure the state to expand or clarify its definition of family. Many governments have recently responded by including same-sex couples and by acknowledging stepfamilies and the extended family arrangements of immigrants or indigenous peoples.

The fact that families are ancient institutions with many structural variations provides opportunities for social scientists to note patterns and trends over time and to identify factors promoting change, or at least associated with change. For example, social researchers try to understand how couple relationships and reproductive choices vary with socio-economic transformations such as industrialization, urbanization, the expansion of the service sector of the economy, widespread migration, the global economy, the computer revolution, and a growing individualistic and consumer-oriented society. Researchers and theorists study how these societal trends influence attitudes and behaviour, as well as public discourse, or the way people talk about sexuality, marriage, reproduction, parental responsibility, and divorce.

Despite evidence of diversity, "the family" is still being discussed in some circles as though it were a single institution that means the same thing to everyone. However, considerable evidence shows that family life has always varied— parents remarried, children lived with step-parents, and family members in the past shared dissimilar views about the nature of their home life and personal relationships. Canadian sociologist Margrit Eichler (1988, 2005) argues that before the 1980s, both the academic and policy portrayal of North American families resembled the nuclear family (with male breadwinner and female caregiver) rather than any other family configuration. Assumptions about family life were conservative and often based on the views of one member, without acknowledging gender differences or variations in viewpoint between children and parents. Academics and policy-makers also normalized the experiences of young, white, middle-class families in which two heterosexual parents and their biological children shared a household without other relatives, and the parents maintained a gendered division of labour.

Opponents of same-sex marriage still promote this nuclear family model even though most people no longer live in these kinds of households in OECD countries (Cherlin, 2010; Coontz, 2005; Giddens, 1992). A growing percentage of the population lives alone, some people never marry or reproduce, many couples separate, parents re-partner, children live with step-siblings, and children grow up and leave their older parent(s) in childless households. Although social research now emphasizes the multi-dimensional nature of family life, this diversity is not always incorporated into public discourse or social policy debates.

In many government analyses, a "family with children" refers to a heterosexual couple or lone parent sharing a dwelling with never-married children. These children could be their biological offspring, the children of their partner, or adopted children. A lone-parent or sole-parent family usually refers to one parent who shares a dwelling with her (occasionally, his) never-married children, without another adult present in the household. Although governments sometimes call these units "lone-parent (or sole-parent) families," in fact they are typically "lone-parent households," because the father usually maintains some contact with his children even when he lives apart. Consequently, other researchers use the concept of "post-divorce family" to encompass both the non-resident father (who often lives alone or with a new partner) and the mother-led household containing their children. More descriptive terms, such as same-sex families, blended families, or stepfamilies, can help to clarify vague definitions.

The most prevalent definition used in policy research is the **census family**. There are cross-national variations of this term but Statistics Canada, for example, has redefined this unit as:

> a married couple and the children, if any, of either or both spouses; a couple living **common law** and the children, if any, of either or both partners; or, a lone parent of any marital status with at least one child living in the same dwelling and that child or those children. All members of a particular census family live in the same dwelling. A couple may be of opposite or same sex. Children may be children by birth, marriage or adoption regardless of their age or marital status as long as they live in the dwelling and do not have their own spouse or child living in the dwelling. Grandchildren living with their grandparent(s) but with no parents present also constitute a census family. (Statistics Canada, 2006)

This definition reflects the legal changes for same-sex couples but also socio-demographic trends in the country. However, the structure of census families has also changed over the decades, as Table 1.1 shows for Canada, Australia, and New Zealand, with fewer couples in 2006 living with children, more cohabiting, and more households led by lone parents than in 1986. Since the 2006 figures were published, the Canadian census from 2011 shows a further increase in the percentage of "common-law" couples and one-parent families (Statistics Canada, 2012a). In 2011, 16.3 per cent of children aged 14 and under in Canada lived with common-law parents, compared to 12.8 per cent in 2001. If we look at all households in Canada, the gap between those without children and those with children widened in 2011, with 29.5 per cent comprised of couples without children and 26.5 per cent comprised of couples with children. A further 27.6 per cent of households contain only one person (ibid.). In addition, of all the couple families with children in 2011, 87.4 per cent were "intact" families while 12.6 per cent were stepfamilies (Statistics Canada,

Table 1.1 Percentage of Census Family Types, 1986 and 2006

% of All Census Families	Canada		Australia		New Zealand	
	1986	2006	1986	2006	1986	2006
Couple families with children in household	52	41	56	45	53	42
Couple families without children in household	–	43	30	37	33	40
% of couples not legally married	7	16	6	15	12	18
One-parent households	13	16	8	16	14	18

Statistics Canada (2008a) "Census Snapshot of Canada—Families", *Canadian Social Trends*, 39. Catalogue no. 11–008; AIFS (2008); Qu and Weston (2008); Research New Zealand (2007: 9); Ambert (2005); Statistics New Zealand (2004); NZ 1991 Census, Table 13, Family Types 1986–1991.

2012c). If policy-makers acknowledged these changing family patterns, the social programs they create or restructure might look quite different.

Some cultural or religious groups prefer to live in extended family households consisting of parents and/or siblings, as well as their spouses and children. These groups argue that the "census family" is only one family structure (essentially the nuclear family or a one-parent household) and that to assume this is the normal arrangement misrepresents sources of caring and social support in their lives. This definition also creates problems when they want to sponsor family members as immigrants, especially their unmarried adult daughters or married siblings. Using a nuclear family definition could also create a problem if a large group of extended family wanted to visit a sick household member in hospital but were denied access because they were not "close family." Assuming that the normal family is nuclear also implies that the family relationships of same-sex couples are different and less valid, and it deprives them of certain social benefits such as the right to be considered "next of kin" in medical emergencies. Issues of entitlement are always contentious, but clear definitions of "family" are essential for establishing eligibility for social benefits or designing the government census or research projects.

In this book, I use the plural term "families" to reinforce the idea that variations have always been apparent and that families were never as uniform as some people have implied. Generally, my definition of families is similar to the Canadian census definition plus the extended family (with grandparents or aunts/uncles), yet I acknowledge that definitions need to be more specific for some purposes, especially those relating to the eligibility for social benefits. Therefore, I often use adjectives with "family" to clarify the specific meaning (such as "step-family"). However, we need to keep in mind that definitions of family and of marriage have changed considerably over the past century.

Historical Changes in Marriage and Families

Before colonization in the eighteenth and nineteenth centuries, the indigenous peoples in what are now North America, Australia, and New Zealand used a variety of family systems and practices, but most lived in tribal villages in extended family groups, placing high value on ancestry, reproduction and tribal loyalty. Some of the tribes were nomadic or semi-nomadic, some were **matrilineal** (tracing family descent from the mother's family), and some arranged marriages, but few gave priority to the nuclear family household or believed that the land could be owned solely by individuals. When their territories were colonized, the Europeans settlers typically expected the indigenous tribes to adapt to European values and family practices, which gave centrality to the patriarchal nuclear family household, private property, and Christian values. These values were typically enshrined into family law and social policies in all the liberal states, with only a gesture made to the previous indigenous cultures.

Among the early Europeans who settled in North America, Australia, and New Zealand, legal marriage was not as widespread as it later became in the twentieth century (Funder and Harrison, 1993; Baker, 2001b). The early European fur traders in Canada, for example, created liaisons with indigenous women, who helped them survive in a harsh environment and provided them with the protection of their own kin group, sexual relations, companionship, and a temporary home and community. Yet these relationships seldom led to legal marriage, as the men often moved on, leaving the women and their children with their own kin group. Even when European men legalized their marriages with indigenous women, the children of these unions were not always accepted as social equals in the colonial community (Bradbury, 2005).

Historically, both the church and the state in Britain, France, and their colonies viewed marriage as an economic and sexual partnership between husbands and wives that involved mutual dependency in the common endeavours of earning a living and raising children (Funder and Harrison, 1993). Particularly in agrarian and cottage industry-based economies of the

Box 1.1   Early Indigenous Families

When Europeans settled in Upper Canada (now Ontario), Native family life changed because their livelihood and culture were systematically undermined. The culture and legal systems forced upon them were foreign and in many ways contradictory. For example, family law brought from Europe by both the French and the English was patriarchal. Despite the matrilineal descent patterns of the Huron, Canadian law stated that Native women and their children lost their "Indian status" when the woman married a non-Indian. This law was not changed until the 1980s (Nett, 1988: 95).

When treaties were signed between indigenous people and the English, reserves were sometimes established on infertile land that could not support the traditional lifestyles of Native people. Yet colonization changed men's roles more than women's (Castellano, 1991). Especially for those First Nations people who were migratory hunters and gatherers, such as the Ojibway, the transition to sedentary life was difficult. Men whose education from infancy was directed to preparing them to assume the roles of hunter, warrior, and visionary saw their opportunities to use these skills shrink with urbanization, industrial development, and eventually environmental degradation. Women as farmers, gatherers, and homemakers retained much of their traditional role despite cultural change (Castellano, 1991).

Source: Baker (2001b: 42). Reprinted with permission of the Publisher from *Families, Labour and Love* by Maureen Baker © University of British Columbia Press 2001. All rights reserved by the publisher.

eighteenth and nineteenth centuries, marriage and family relationships were critical for economic and social survival. Most men and women (both indigenous and colonial) worked long hours and needed a domestic partner (or at least another household member) to help grow and prepare food, to make shelter and clothing, to protect and care for the home, to raise children, to earn money for household purchases, and to care for them when sick or frail. They also needed children to form a domestic labour force or to work around the household and contribute to the family economy.

The roots of family law in English-speaking jurisdictions are found in English common law, while the French **civil code** provides the basis for family law in the Canadian province of Quebec. Under both of these legal systems, the husband and father initially retained authority over his wife and children, and a wife had the legal status of a minor child. Women did not acquire political or civil rights until late in the nineteenth century—or later, in some jurisdictions—and a married woman could not acquire or sell property on her own, but was expected to depend on her husband to control it for her. By today's standards, these former marriage laws were sexist but they were also Eurocentric, largely ignoring the traditional customs of the various tribes of indigenous people (Baker, 2001b: 183). Some of these tribes arranged marriages, used marriage systems that prioritized the mother's family, accepted a less gendered division of labour between partners, and were the guardians of tribal property rather than the owners of family land.

Early English common law viewed marriage as a heterosexual and gendered work partnership but not a partnership of work equals. A wife tacitly agreed to provide her husband with sexual intercourse, children, and domestic services in return for a home, protection, and economic support. The man was the legal head of the household, representing the family's interests to the larger community and making major decisions such as where they would live and at what living standard. Until the late nineteenth and early twentieth centuries, husbands also controlled their wives' income and property, voted on their behalf, and retained guardianship of any children resulting from the marriage. Women gained the legal right to vote in national elections in New Zealand in 1893, in Australia in 1902, and in Canada in 1918; but in Quebec, married women were not permitted to vote in provincial elections until 1940 or to become the legal guardians of their own children until 1964 (ibid.).

Historically, marriage was based on the public claim that marital roles were complementary but equal, although legal evidence indicates that the courts did not equally value women's unpaid contribution to marriage upon separation or divorce (Funder, 1996; Greenwood, 1999). Despite these inequities, young people typically anticipated marriage and parenthood because they were viewed as **rites of passage**, or synonymous with adulthood, maturity, respectability, and authority within the community. They also anticipated sexual relations, which were socially approved only within matrimony in European and colonial families, but economics and social status played a large role in the pairing process. In poorer families, parents wanted their sons and daughters to marry higher status or wealthier persons who would raise their standing in the community or help them out of debt and bring productive land into the family. They wanted a child to marry a partner who was kind but who was also an industrious, strong, and healthy person who would bring grandchildren to the family and who would be able to care for them in their declining years.

Ideal family systems in the past differed considerably from reality, as they still do today. Even when chastity before marriage was considered an essential virtue among Europeans, many young men frequented prostitutes or had secret sexual liaisons. Married men and, less often, married women had secret affairs, but without reliable contraception, premarital pregnancies in colonial society were disguised with hasty marriages, adoptions, or backstreet abortions, and extramarital pregnancies were passed off as children of the existing marriage or terminated with an illegal abortion. Even before the eighteenth century when European marriages could still be arranged by parents, many children probably persuaded their parents to arrange a marriage with people they already knew and wanted to marry. Many married partners grew to love each other deeply after sharing their lives, even when their marriage was partially arranged. Despite the fact that the male head of the household had considerable authority over other family members, there were undoubtedly fathers and husbands who were sensitive to the wishes of their wives and children.

In the first half of the twentieth century, most unmarried young people in both urban and rural areas continued to live with their parents or relatives, and few adolescents or young adults shared accommodation with friends or lived alone before marriage (Nett, 1993: 216). While living with family, most young people paid "room and board" and engaged in unpaid chores to help cover household expenses. If they lived apart from their parents to attend school or earn money, they usually boarded with relatives or lived in supervised residences or boarding houses with little autonomy or privacy. Working long hours without much leisure time meant that young people had few opportunities to party, to date widely, or to develop more than one intimate relationship before they married for life (Bradbury, 2005). Furthermore, social rules reinforced by the church permitted men and women little opportunity to spend time alone together in public or in private, unless they were engaged or married. Those who lived in remote areas would also have had few opportunities to meet suitable partners.

In recent decades, remaining single has taken on new meaning, but a slightly smaller percentage of the population now reaches middle age without marrying, compared to a century ago. Although it is difficult to find statistics that are exactly comparable, we know that 10 per cent of Canadian women in 1900 had never married by the age of 50 compared to 7 per cent of women who had never been married by the ages 50–54 in 1996 (Dumas and Péron, 1992; Beaujot, 2000: 103). Data from the 2006 census indicate that the percentage of never-married women aged 50–54 was about 10 per cent (Statistics Canada, 2012a; VIF, 2010: 35). In many countries, marriage rates increased until the 1970s and then declined again as more people began to cohabit in the 1980s and 1990s. Current marriage and partnership rates remain slightly higher than in 1900 and more never-married people cohabit or have had sexual experience than in 1900.

Several factors lie behind the larger single and celibate population a century ago. Despite the importance of marriage for social status and economic survival, social rules discouraged people from marrying if they fell in love with someone considered to be an inappropriate marriage partner—such as a person already married or one from another religious or cultural group. Others failed to marry because they were running the family farm or caring for elderly parents and experienced few opportunities to meet potential partners. Early in the twentieth century, more people lived in remote rural areas and small communities and most did not travel as far from home for education or work. Consequently, many could not find a suitable partner within their home communities. Others entered religious orders that required celibacy, a choice that might have been made by some women who preferred a career over marriage and children. In addition, two world wars, by killing thousands of young men, created a shortage of eligible males, and some women were not content to marry anyone else after losing their fiancés in battle.

Generally, marriage and child-rearing are encouraged by family, friends, and state officials because they are seen as synonymous with maturity, heterosexual identity, and social responsibility. In addition, marriage and reproduction are thought to help individuals retain permanent employment, remain law-abiding, and develop stable relationships and communities. In early settler societies such as Canada, the United States, Australia, and New Zealand, unmarried men were viewed as a threat to community life because they had higher rates than married men of heavy drinking, gambling, and other anti-social activities (Bradbury, 2005). Sexually active but unmarried women were also assumed to threaten **family values**, although at the same time chaste women were stigmatized as virginal, unwanted, and limited in their life experiences. Ironically, single women in the nineteenth century had more legal rights and better employment opportunities than married women, even though their occupational advancement and social freedom were restricted more than men's. However, legal marriage and child-rearing continue to provide respectability and social status both to men and to women, and to encourage them to spend more time at home within their nuclear families.

Securing a marriage partner was essential for young women partly because they were excluded from most employment and were less likely to inherit the family farm or business. Even if they found wage work, women earned considerably less than men and most employed women were unable to fully support themselves and/or their children. Generally, the woman needed a husband to earn sufficient money to run the household, to perform heavy chores around the house, to "cherish" her, and to provide her with children (who raised her status within the family and community). Similarly, few men could survive without a wife to cook, clean the home, launder the clothes, grow vegetables, provide him with regular sex, and raise the children, and housework was very time-consuming and laborious before electricity, refrigeration, and imported food. Wage labourers normally worked long hours each weekday as well as Saturday mornings, and farmers worked every day. Before the 1930s, few employees were entitled to paid holidays. The banks and food stores were closed by the time most men finished work, leaving little opportunity to run personal errands after work. Wealthy men could afford live-in servants, but most needed a wife to manage the household.

Young people met their potential spouses at school, in their neighbourhood, at their church, or through their siblings and other relatives. Sometimes they were introduced by friends or family members, and occasionally they were "set up" by friends on "blind dates." They also met partners at dances, parties, and other social functions, but these were usually community activities attended by a variety of age groups, where the activities of young people were closely monitored by adult chaperones to ensure that no "unseemly conduct" occurred. These activities were based on expectations of heterosexuality, as intimate relationships among same-sex couples were either illegal or not condoned.

Christian beliefs and practices required that the community, as well as the church, recognize potential marriage partners as "legitimate" both in Europe and in the European colonies overseas (Baker, 2001b). This meant that marriage partners had to be legal adults, could not be close relatives, and could not be simultaneously married to someone else. However, colonial settlers could easily leave spouses behind in Europe or Britain but the church (and later the state) presided over wedding ceremonies to ensure that unions were legal and registered. In early Christian doctrine, the status of marriage had already been elevated from a private contract between individuals to a religious sacrament deemed to be indissoluble and beyond the scope of human will or law (Fletcher, 1973). Marriage contracts, unlike business contracts, were seen as sacred or blessed by God, and lasting until the death of one partner.

During the Christian wedding ceremony, a woman used to promise to "love, honour, and obey" her husband while he promised to "love, honour, and cherish" her (ibid., 186). Until the 1960s, a Canadian husband had the right to establish the couple's legal residence or "domicile" and he was expected to provide his wife with the "necessaries of life"; but the husband had the right to decide what was necessary (Dranoff, 1977: 25). In contrast, a wife was expected to live wherever her husband chose to live, maintain their household, care for their children, and be sexually available when he wanted. In recognition of these services, women were entitled to "dower rights" or the right to one-third of his property under common law should the marriage dissolve. In civil law, the wife could retain the property brought into the marriage, but her husband controlled it for her. In both forms of European law, the marital roles of men and women differed.

Growing dissatisfaction with the restrictions of marriage and concerns about gender equity encouraged some spouses to separate, and by the 1960s more couples were applying for divorces. Backlogs of applications and concern about the outcomes for children and sole mothers provided a strong impetus for family law reform, including laws relating to divorce, child support, and custody. In the 1960s, divorce was still legally complicated but reformers had successfully argued that the marriage contract could be broken with proof of a "matrimonial fault" or a violation of the marriage contract. This usually meant providing proof of "adultery," but grounds were extended to physical cruelty, imprisonment for a specified period, homosexual acts, and later to "marriage breakdown." In many countries, marriages can now be dissolved by mutual consent, provided that partners sign legal documents to verify irretrievable marriage breakdown, which is discussed in Chapter 7.

Over the centuries, governments have reformed family laws to make them more equitable for women and children but they have not necessarily become more sensitive to the many cultural variations among indigenous peoples and immigrants. As we will see in this book, legislating changes to accommodate or counteract individual and cultural practices remains politically contentious, and governments cannot easily control certain forms of behaviour. Increasingly, relationships and family life are influenced by personal choices rather than relying so much on legal requirements, community standards, or family obligations.

Family Policies and the State

This book discusses various **family policies**, which are defined as official decisions to implement state-sponsored social programs, services, regulations, and laws that specifically affect families with children. These policies might relate to reproductive health, family well-being, or the maintenance of family income. They could also enforce financial or caring obligations among family members, protect vulnerable family members from harm or neglect, or enable the integration of earning and caring. Family programs do not have to be delivered directly by the state but they must be mandated or regulated by the state to be included in my definition. Therefore, programs contracted out to voluntary agencies or subsidized by public money could be included, such as child welfare services contracted to the Children's Aid Society or to an indigenous tribal group. Employer-sponsored programs for maternity/parental leave or for family responsibilities also are included in the definition of family policy because governments often require employers to provide these benefits or their provision is required by international agreements among countries (Baker, 2006).

When academics or politicians talk about the **state**, they usually are referring to legislative and executive bodies (such as Parliament and government departments) as well as the publicly funded agencies (such as child welfare) and institutions (such as the police and courts) mandated to implement or enforce these policies. When studying family policies, the concept of **welfare state** refers to the social services and income support programs designed to improve the social and economic well-being of families and to regulate and control family and personal life. Researchers and theorists studying the development of welfare states have shown that nations differ in the ways they think about the nature of family life and social provision, the kinds of programs they actually create, and their preferences for funding and delivering social programs.

Welfare states were generally developed between the 1940s and 1970s, when social and family life differed substantially from the present, but new social programs continue to be established and existing ones are restructured. Although most social programs have been amended since they were developed, a few still imply that intimate relationships and paid employment remain stable throughout life. Some public discourse about families also suggests that most people live in nuclear family units consisting of a breadwinner father who supports "his dependants" in full-time paid work and a homemaker mother who cares for the children at home or works part-time. The couple is often assumed to be heterosexual, legally married for life, and living with their two or three children who are biologically related to both parents (Eichler, 1997). However, most people no longer live this way. State involvement in family life continues to change over time because policy ideas and the actual social programs originate from different governments with varying agendas, and ideas about human rights and the role of the state in family life evolve over the years. In addition, policy reform tends to be incremental and developed from previous programs, because in a democracy it is easier to modify existing policy than to introduce major reforms.

As well as noting changes in family law and policy over the decades, academics have compared social provision among countries and the philosophy underlying it. A number of categorizations exist, but Canada has typically been linked with the other English-speaking countries labelled as "liberal" or

Box 1.2   Three Features of Nineteenth-Century Welfare

Margaret Little, in her landmark study of the regulation of single mothers in Ontario during the twentieth century, describes the disorganized, judgemental, and pinchpenny rationale of early welfare provision that even today is part of the welfare system.

> Nineteenth century welfare in Ontario was characterized by three important fea-
> tures that have cast a long shadow over welfare debates well into the twentieth
> century. First, welfare took the form of a haphazard *mélange* of public and
> private administration with no organization or government body assuming full
> responsibility. Except for local governments, the state resisted direct disburse-
> ments to the needy and instead helped to finance and regulate institutions such
> as orphanages, houses of industry, and prisons. Other types of welfare varied by
> community, but generally took the form of haphazard distribution of food and
> clothes. Second, both public and private welfare administrators believed that
> welfare should distinguish between the deserving and the undeserving poor,
> providing a minimal existence for the former and denying the latter. . . . Third,
> welfare administrators adhered to the principle of "less eligibility"; it was
> believed that assistance should always remain below the lowest wage, thus
> assuring that welfare would not be too appealing.

Source: Little (1998: 1–2). Margaret J.H. Little, 1998. *No Car, No Radio, No Liqour Permit. The Moral Regulation of Single Mothers in Ontario, 1920–1997.* Toronto: Oxford University Press, p. 1–2.

"residual" welfare states, meaning that in these countries individuals and families are normally assumed to be responsible for their own economic and social well-being (Esping-Andersen, 1996; O'Connor et al., 1999). Parents are held responsible for the care and support of their children both when they live together and if they separate, and spouses are expected to support and assist each other during marriage. When state benefits are made available, they are relatively ungenerous and well below minimum wages, even below accepted poverty levels.

In contrast, the **social democratic states**, such as Sweden and Denmark, view the well-being of family members (especially children, sole parents, and the frail elderly) as a social responsibility as well as a parental or family one, and place more importance on redistributing income, preventing poverty, and promoting gender equity. **Corporatist states** such as France and Germany—so called because they involve business, labour, and the state working together as corporate entities to create **social insurance** programs—are financed through employer and employee contributions, and are designed to replace lost wages due to unemployment, sickness, work-related injury, or retirement (Esping-Andersen, 1990). These social insurance programs were developed by trade unions, employers' groups, and government to share the cost of income loss, and they continue to be managed by representatives from these three groups.

Some theorists have argued that Australia and New Zealand should not be included with the liberal states but should instead be classified as "wage earners' welfare states" (Castles and Shirley, 1996). These countries used to be different because their trade unions and governments sought to ensure that (male) wages were high enough to support families at a comfortable level through centralized bargaining and restrictions on immigrant labour. State assistance was also provided for home ownership, but the basic income support programs targeted to low-income households were less important to family well-being than these other factors. Increasingly, however, Australia and especially New Zealand have come to resemble the other liberal states through a series of welfare and labour market program reforms in the 1980s and 1990s (Lunt et al., 2008).

Social support for families with children clearly varies cross-nationally (Hantrais, 2004; OECD, 2005b). However, important differences are also apparent among the various jurisdictions of the same country. Federal states like Canada and the United States have decentralized many laws and social programs, which are designed and administered at the provincial or state level. In Canada, for example, the federal government retains jurisdiction over some income support programs (such as Old Age Security, Canada Pension Plan, and Employment Insurance), federal tax concessions for families, maternity/parental benefits, and divorce law. The provinces have jurisdiction over marriage law, **maternity leave** provisions, social assistance, and social services such as child protection, child-care services, health-care services, and education. They also control the division of matrimonial property upon separation of spouses, and laws pertaining to the implementation of child custody, **access**, child support, and spousal support (Guest, 1997; McGilly, 1998). In addition, some Canadian provinces, such as Ontario, allow municipalities to create and administer child-care provisions and income support for some categories of welfare recipients.

Divided jurisdiction within a federal state permits inconsistencies to develop among different regions and inhibits the creation of national programs in matters of provincial jurisdiction (Baker, 2006). This means that the welfare state might not be internally consistent in its goals or in eligibility rules for benefits, even within the same country and the same kind of social policy. In addition, some jurisdictions might provide generous social provision for retired people but restrict support for children or employed mothers. This suggests that studies of "the" welfare state might fruitfully be broken down into jurisdictions as well as particular policy areas, such as employment benefits or family-related programs.

Gender, Class, Ethnicity, and Family Policies

State involvement in families has always varied by gender, social class, and ethnicity, as well as by jurisdiction. Women's access to social provision has been shaped by their relationship to men and children, their incomes, by different views about suitable roles for women and mothers, and by prevalent models of the typical family (Lewis, 1992; Sainsbury, 1993). Men are still assumed to be the main breadwinners and women the primary care providers within the liberal and corporatist welfare states, and parents normally are seen as fully responsible for their own children. In addition, men tend to receive more generous benefits through paid work rather than parenthood, while women gain their entitlement mainly as mothers and wives. In contrast, the social democratic states tend to view both marriage partners as earners and carers (Leira, 2009). They see the well-being of children as a joint responsibility between parents and the state, exemplified by the provision of affordable child care and generous social provision for leave for family responsibilities.

Historically, liberal states have treated low-income wives and widows as more deserving of state income support than never-married or separated mothers. If women became lone mothers through premarital pregnancy, separation, or divorce, they used to be offered minimal benefits (Ursel, 1992; Baker and Tippin, 1999). These benefits were sometimes delivered in discretionary ways by welfare officers rather than being seen as legal entitlements. The recipients were thought to require close scrutiny concerning their maternal and moral behaviour to ensure that they were truly eligible and not defrauding the taxpayers (Swift, 1995; Little, 1998). In contrast, wives and widows often became eligible for more income support through the husband's work-related social insurance entitlements as well as his private insurance policies. Now, the benefits available for lone mothers vary less by their route to lone parenthood, but married women and widows are still more likely to gain access to private insurance or pension funds acquired through their male partners' earnings (Baker, 2011c). Furthermore, welfare-to-work programs encourage mothers parenting alone to depend less on the state and more on their own earnings but also on their friends and family, which often requires them to provide reciprocal services (Cooke, 2011).

Men typically receive benefits from employers or the state as earners rather than husbands or fathers. Work-related benefits may be sponsored by employers but some are financed through social insurance programs, such as Canada's Employment Insurance. Receiving such benefits involves less investigation into recipients' personal lives and higher payments based on the contributions from employees and employers (Sainsbury, 1996). As more women enter full-time paid work, they also become eligible for employment-related benefits, but women earn lower average wages and make lower contributions to social insurance programs, and therefore receive lower average benefits than men. If they privately insure their earnings or their lives, the payments also reflect lower female earnings as well as their longer life expectancy.

State intervention has also varied by social class and ethnicity. Welfare workers have been permitted to investigate the family circumstances and living conditions of impoverished families even though such investigations would be considered an infringement of privacy for those with higher incomes. For example, a lone mother living on social assistance might be visited by social workers searching for evidence of another adult living in her home who might be considered a potential breadwinner (Baker, 2007; Little, 1998). The state has been most interventionist with visible minorities and indigenous peoples. In the past, impoverished but much-loved children from indigenous families were considered to be "at risk" of maltreatment, disease, and lack of education by well-intentioned missionaries and government officials (Baker, 2001b; Edwards, 2011). Consequently, these children used to be removed from their parental homes and placed in residential schools run by churches or the government, often against the wishes of the children and their parents. Since the 1960s, these practices have ceased because they are considered racist and psychologically damaging, although the "Sixties Scoop" in Canada and the "stolen generation" in Australia resulted in thousands of Aboriginal children from impoverished or allegedly dysfunctional families being placed in foster care and adopted into non-Aboriginal families (Dickason, 2006: 229; Summers, 2008). Today, income support programs and local schools have been developed, efforts are made to keep children from "problem homes" within their own communities, and local child welfare services are sometimes managed by the indigenous people themselves.

Researchers have also studied family life in different cultures, investigating the connections among family structure, patterns of authority, marriage systems, descent and residence rules, and how cross-cultural variations relate to systems of economic production, religious beliefs, and other cultural patterns. Academics have questioned whether or not the nuclear family is a universal group, whether men are always family "heads," and what difference it makes when the marriage system permits more than one spouse at a time. One of the central questions has been whether the nuclear family with free-choice marriage is a product of industrialization, urbanization, and westernization. If so, will families begin to look more similar around the world if westernization and global culture expand? In the next section, some of these issues will be outlined as I discuss cultural variations in family patterns.

Cultural and Historical Variations in Families

Family Structure

When people in Western industrialized countries live in family households, they usually form nuclear families consisting of a husband, wife, and their children sharing a dwelling without other relatives present. Some academics assume that, in the past, most households in both Western and non-Western societies consisted of extended families in which several generations shared a residence. They believe that more people came to live in nuclear families with the pressures of **industrialization** and urban migration between the seventeenth and nineteenth centuries.

In France, Frédéric Le Play (1806–82) studied changes in the rural European "stem family," an extended family consisting of parents and one married son who would eventually inherit the family property. He lamented the rise of the "unstable" nuclear family and the demise of patriarchal authority caused by industrialization and modernization. Friedrich Engels (1884) also saw the nuclear family as the product of industrialization, theorizing about the ways that society and family structure were transformed from the times when people lived in large hunting-and-gathering clans or kin groups through to private nuclear families in the industrial cities of England. American sociologists Parsons and Bales (1955) were also concerned about the loss of the extended family, which they felt provided more effective authority, household labour, child care, companionship, and economic security than the nuclear family.

Social historians have demonstrated, however, that nuclear family households were always the most typical living arrangements both in Europe and among the European colonists (Laslett, 1971; Goldthorpe, 1987). One reason that this living arrangement persisted is that life expectancies were much shorter than today and many parents died before their children married. In the colonies, extended family households were even less common among Europeans because many of these settlers had left their parents and older relatives behind when they migrated. Canadian sociologist Emily Nett (1981) contends that it had never been a widespread practice for married couples to live with their parents at any time in the Canadian history of European settlement. Class differences are also apparent as lower-income families with British backgrounds were more likely than richer settlers to share accommodation with parents and children, especially in times of financial need, separation, or widowhood.

Despite the prevalence of nuclear families in the English-speaking countries, extended families continue to be more prevalent among many indigenous peoples (Baker, 2001b). In addition, extended families continue to serve as living arrangements and support groups in parts of Africa, South Asia, and the Middle East. They have become slightly more prevalent in high-immigration countries such as Australia, Canada, New Zealand, and the United States as they accept more immigrants from countries with extended-family systems. In Canada, the percentage of three-generation households increased from 1986 to 1996, mainly as a result of increased Asian immigration, but only 3 per cent of households included three generations in 1996

(Che-Alford and Hamm, 1999). According to the 2011 census, about 2.5 per cent of people aged 15 and over lived with relatives in family households that could approximate an extended family (Statistics Canada, 2012a). This suggests that most Canadians consider living alone or in nuclear families more acceptable and feasible, and that many cultural groups alter their traditional practices after migration.

Practical constraints also shape family structure and living arrangements, as well as cultural considerations. Immigrants with few economic resources and limited skills in the host country's official language are more likely to share accommodation than wealthier immigrants who can afford separate housing, those who can communicate more effectively, and those able to find employment (Thomas, 2001). Furthermore, living with relatives is not necessarily permanent but could involve sharing accommodation with adult siblings until separate housing can be located or financed. Living with relatives is more prevalent among female immigrants, those with lower education and incomes, and recent arrivals (ibid, 21).

This suggests that gender, social class, and culture (as well as personal choice) influence whether immigrants continue to live in extended families. Immigrants often attempt to integrate into the new country by giving up some aspects of their cultural practices. This means that the family demography of the second generation tends to look more like that of others born in that country (Albanese, 2009a). In other countries, especially in rural areas or those with few Western influences, cultural traditions strongly shape marriage and family patterns, and the decisions of elders might override the personal choices of youth.

Authority and Lineage

Most family systems around the world designate a "head" to make family decisions and represent the group to the larger community and state authorities. In both Western and non-Western societies, the oldest male typically is the family head, and this system, called **patriarchy**, has a long tradition that permeates laws and practices around the world. In the liberal states, families were legally patriarchal in the past, but these countries have reformed their laws and practices and no longer assume that men officially lead the family (Kamerman and Kahn, 1997). In fact, Western states have been pressured to eliminate most remnants of patriarchy and to create legal equality between men and women, both within the household and in the larger society. However, vestiges of patriarchy are still apparent, such as the traditional practice of fathers "giving away" their daughters to the groom during some marriage ceremonies.

Matriarchy is an authority system in which women are granted more authority than men, but such systems are rare throughout the world. At the time of European contact, the Iroquois tribes of North America were described as matriarchal because women's power in the economy, politics, religious ceremonies, and family life exceeded that of women in French and English cultures, as well as women in other Native tribes (Brown, 1988). In the 1930s, the American anthropologist Margaret Mead referred to the Tchambuli people of New Guinea as matriarchal because women seemed to run the economy and make most practical decisions while men were engaged in cultural pursuits (Mead, 1935). Working-class black families in the Caribbean and the United States have been called matriarchal or at least **matrifocal families** because so many of these households are led by lone mothers while the fathers live elsewhere, or the mother/wife is the pivotal figure in many of these two-parent families (Quinlan, 2006; Smith, 1996). For a society or family to be considered matriarchal, women must hold considerable respect, decision-making authority, and control over household resources (Sanday, 2002).

Some sociologists and anthropologists have argued that laws and unwritten rules guide behaviour within and between families in all societies. Family law designates certain categories of people as "out of bounds" for sex and marriage but cultural traditions also govern family behaviour. For example, patterns of descent may determine where newly married couples live, how they address family members, what surname their children will receive, and from whom they inherit. When people marry, they may also be encouraged to grant more importance to their relationships with one set of parents or siblings, as we will see in the next section.

Marriage Systems

In many cultures, marriages are arranged by elders, as we will discuss in more detail in Chapter 4. In these arrangements, a close intimate relationship between the couple is not a priority because marriage represents a union between extended families rather than individuals. Young people are encouraged to want to marry in order to acquire adult status, to augment their position in the community through parenthood, to gain satisfaction from watching their children mature, to continue the family name, and eventually to become respected elders within their family and community. In cultures where the inheritance of wealth and the continuity of kin lines and family name are important, arranged marriages or partially arranged marriages remain widespread. Young people sometimes appreciate family assistance with the difficult task of finding a compatible life partner who meets their relatives' expectations. They may justify parental assistance by the high divorce rate among Western or free-choice marriages, which suggests that young people who make their own decisions often make ill-informed ones that they later regret. Furthermore, many immigrants and indigenous people guard their family practices as part of their cultural identity that they are unwilling to shed.

It is still legal in many parts of the world for a man to marry more than one wife at a time if he has the resources to support them. In the 1990s, three-quarters of the world's societies still preferred **polygyny**, or multiple wives for one husband (Saxton, 1993), although the percentage actually living in these unions was lower. Polygyny continues to be practised in some African countries as well as some in Southern and Western Asia, especially those using Islamic law. In sub-Saharan Africa, about half of married women aged 15–49 were in polygynous unions in Benin, Burkina Faso, and Guinea, and over 40 per cent in Mali, Senegal, and Togo in the 1990s (UN, 2000: 28). Wealthy men are more likely than those with fewer resources to take on more than one legal wife (Broude, 1994).

Polygynous unions tend to be associated with patriarchal authority and wider age gaps between husbands and wives. They are more common among rural and less-educated women, as well as those who do not formally work for pay outside the household (UN, 2000: 28). Multiple wives, who are sometimes sisters, may resent their husband taking a new partner, but they may also welcome her assistance with household work, child care, and horticulture, and may value her companionship in a society where marriage partners are seldom close friends. Furthermore, the husband's second marriage typically elevates the rank of the first wife, who then becomes the supervisor of the younger wife's household work. However, family conflict can occur among the children of different wives, who may also see less of their father than children from monogamous marriages (Al-Krenawi et al., 2008).

Polygamy refers to the practice of having more than one spouse at a time, but polygyny is much more prevalent than **polyandry**, which is marriage between one woman and several husbands. When polyandry does occur, the husbands are often brothers (fraternal polyandry) and the practice may relate to the need to keep land in one parcel (Ihinger-Tallman and Levinson, 2003). However, most societies prefer polygyny because more children can be born into marriages with multiple wives and this could be important if children are the main source of labour for the family or community. Also, the identification of the father is particularly important in **patrilineal societies** because children receive their father's surname, belong to his kin group, and inherit from him, and married men are responsible for supporting their children. Knowing who the father is would be difficult with multiple husbands, so this is not usually an acceptable form of marriage in patrilineal systems. Most societies have been patriarchal and men more often have the power to ensure that the marriage system suits their own interests.

All westernized countries have prohibited polygamy as Judeo-Christian beliefs promote sexual exclusivity. Some researchers explain these doctrines on the assumption that men would experience difficulty providing adequate financial and emotional support for more than one wife. However, some groups have practised polygamy in nineteenth- and twentieth-century North America, including some Mormons in Utah and British Columbia, but the general population strongly objected and insisted that the authorities put a stop to this practice. In New Zealand, some Maori tribes practised polygyny at the time of European contact, but the Christian missionaries and British settlers opposed the practice and ensured that it did not continue (Baker, 2001b).

Although polygamy is now against the law in all the liberal welfare states, it may continue to exist clandestinely in some communities where a man has one legal wife but also cohabits with other women. Neighbours or state officials might not interfere because they assume that these other women are roommates or relatives rather than wives, or may feel that their neighbours' sexual relations are not their business. In addition, some men who travel for a living have maintained female partners who are unknown to each other. However, this is neither legal nor socially acceptable in Western countries.

Some new immigrants come from countries accepting polygamous marriage. This could lead to problems for immigration departments of receiving countries unless they develop clear policies about how polygamous marriage should be treated in terms of legal recognition, support obligations, and inheritance rights. The receiving country can certainly refuse to permit new polygamous arrangements as well as exclude potential immigrants with existing polygamous marriages. If it permits entry to men with partners back home and refuses to recognize their previous legal obligations, official wives and legitimate children could be left destitute when their husbands emigrate (Beeby, 2006).

Group marriage also continues to exist but in Western industrialized countries it is illegal and socially unacceptable. Historically, it was practised in some utopian communities, such as the Oneida Community in nineteenth-century New York State or more recent communal experiments in the 1960s. In these marriages, more than one couple consider themselves married to one another, and they share resources, meals, child-rearing, and sexual access. However, these arrangements tend to last only a few years, partly due to opposition from the authorities, but also as a result of interpersonal conflicts (Ihinger-Tallman and Levinson, 2003).

People in westernized countries are permitted to marry only one partner at a time, although an increasing percentage of the population divorce and subsequently remarry or cohabit without any social or legal ceremony. However, even when couples initially live together without a wedding, many legally marry later when they make a long-term commitment to each other or when they decide to have children. Both same-sex and opposite-sex couples sometimes participate in wedding ceremonies and celebrations that draw on traditional cultural symbols of virginity, fertility, and patriarchy (Baker and Elizabeth, 2012a; Schecter et al., 2008).

At the time of marriage, most family systems require the exchange of gifts. Time-consuming negotiations as well as traditional practices may guide families when they select these gifts, which may be distributed or consumed in formal ceremonies. Some cultures require families to provide dowries as part of the marriage settlement, which I discuss in more detail in Chapter 4, but these practices are most often retained in rural areas where wives lack formal education or do not work for pay. When women acquire Western education and become self-supporting, they or their families are less likely to participate in arranged marriages, dowry negotiations, or polygamous marriages.

Multiculturalism and Cultural Clashes

Cultural clashes have always been apparent between the family practices of colonists and indigenous peoples of Canada, the United States, Australia, and New Zealand. Now, with high immigration rates from a variety of origins in these countries, more people are becoming aware of variations in family patterns, although they may not accept them as normal, acceptable, or fair. A number of contentious practices relate to the status of girls and women. Female circumcision, for example, is practised in some cultures to discourage non-marital sexual activity among women. However, the United Nations, many Western governments, and women's groups have viewed this practice as unacceptable, a violation of human rights, and a risk to women's health and well-being.

Prenatal screening is routinely done for pregnant women in most Western countries, but in some cultural communities it has included the selective abortion of female fetuses. Males are still preferred in some cultures because they are granted higher status, continue the family lineage, financially support the extended family, and bring wealth in the form of wedding gifts or marriage settlements. Selective abortions are prohibited in Western countries but they continue to occur because abortions can sometimes be performed in private clinics or with less official scrutiny. The United Nations and state authorities have tried to reduce the preference for male babies by attempting to eliminate all forms of discrimination against girls and women, including making the dowry system illegal in some countries.

Another controversial issue has been the veiling of Muslim women, a religious practice that requires women to cover their hair with a scarf when in the presence of unrelated males. Women's arms and legs are also covered with long sleeves and long dresses or trousers, and sometimes their entire bodies, including their faces, are enrobed beneath a burqa. France has outlawed the wearing of religious symbols in state schools, angering the Muslim community by requiring their schoolgirls to remove their headscarves during lessons.

In 2004, two Muslim refugee women living in New Zealand were asked to serve as Crown witnesses in an insurance fraud trial (Devereux, 2004). The women wanted to remain veiled during their court appearance, but the lawyer for the accused man successfully argued against their request. He stated that the court and his client are entitled to see the faces of witnesses in order to help verify their verbal statements by observing their demeanour or body language. The women refused to remove their burqas in court and one claimed that she would rather kill herself than show her face in public. Religious leaders were consulted, who stated that the burqa was not required by the Koran but was simply a religious custom exemplifying female modesty in the company of unrelated males. The New Zealand authorities subsequently asked these women to remove their veils but permitted them to give evidence behind a screen so that the male public could not observe them during the trial.

In Canada, controversy continues over the legality of polygamous marriages and whether men should be prosecuted for having more than one wife. Some claim that prosecution would violate religious freedom, while others argue that the state has already permitted non-marital cohabitation and same-sex marriage, so why should it prohibit polygamy? These examples, as well as discussions about structural variations in family systems, shed some light on the cultural relativity of personal beliefs and family practices. They also suggest a close association between family practices and religion, educational attainment, urban/rural residence, patterns of authority, factors relating to work and economic production in the larger society, and growing individualism in society.

Conclusion

Many scholars argue that family life in advanced industrial societies has become more fragmented and complex with a number of sources of differentiation, including social class, gender, sexual preference, ethnicity, and age (Abercrombie et al., 1994: 326; May, 2011). Young people are demanding more personal choice in their intimate relationships and expecting to create their own "biographies of love" (Beck and Beck-Gernsheim, 1995). In addition, popular culture has become more global and consumer-oriented, and more couples are delaying marriage and reproduction. At the same time, current social conditions in the liberal states are dominated by economic markets that have become internationally competitive, family income is less secure, and more households are falling into debt. At the same time, some liberal states have been dismantling aspects of social provision, arguing that families need to be more self-sufficient and less dependent on state income support.

Keeping this socio-economic context in mind, the chapter has discussed varying definitions of family and family policies, recognizing that these definitions reflect changing living arrangements and legal requirements. The chapter also provided a historical overview of the significance of marriage and family in the past, and outlined some of the cross-national variations in marriage systems and family practices. The chapter argues that both the academic and policy definitions of family need to be broadened to encompass the many variations in family structure and experience. Clearly, family life is conceptualized differently by men and women at different stages of the family life cycle, as well as by people with varying political viewpoints and those living in different eras, cultures, and jurisdictions. Furthermore, perceptions of an acceptable or desirable family life vary considerably, and certain family practices remain contentious, as we will see throughout this book. The next chapter examines some of the theories or explanations of family patterns and prevalent methods used to research them.

Questions for Critical Thought

1. How do extended families differ from nuclear families, and how are they similar?
2. Why are patriarchal families so prevalent around the world?
3. Is there any evidence that expectations about family life and actual family patterns are becoming more similar around the world with urbanization, international travel, and Internet usage?

Questions for Debate

1. Should governments permit immigrant groups to maintain their family practices such as polygamy? Which practices might be less acceptable to the host society?
2. Should same-sex couples be permitted to marry and raise children?
3. Should the state intervene in any aspects of family life? If so, which ones?

Suggested Readings

Cheal, David, ed. 2010. *Canadian Families Today: New Perspectives*, 2nd edn. Toronto: Oxford University Press. This book examines a wide range of topics to introduce the sociological study of families, provides information about various stages and events in the life course, and discusses current issues faced by Canadian families.

May, Vanessa, ed. 2011. *Sociology of Personal Life*. Basingstoke, UK: Palgrave Macmillan. This recent British collection broadens the field of family studies by focusing on all aspects of personal life.

McDaniel, Susan, and Lorne Tepperman. 2010. *Close Relations: An Introduction to the Sociology of Families*, 4th edn. Toronto: Pearson Prentice-Hall. This Canadian text includes numerous studies and statistics on family trends and patterns.

Suggested Websites

Australian Institute of Family Studies
www.aifs.gov.au
> This website provides numerous statistics and research papers on family life in Australia.

Families Commission, New Zealand
www.nzfamilies.org.nz
> This government-funded agency produces many online research reports including New Zealand and international information on families.

Statistics Canada

www.statcan.ca

> Statistics Canada provides numerous statistics about families, households, paid work, and unpaid work.

Vanier Institute of the Family, Canada

www.vifamily.ca

> This privately funded organization based in Ottawa provides educational material, news items, and research on Canadian families. The Vanier Institute also publishes a magazine called *Transition*.

2

Theorizing and Researching Family Life

Learning Objectives

◎ To understand the main theoretical perspectives in family studies.

◎ To differentiate between the basic assumptions behind these perspectives.

◎ To understand how conceptual frameworks have developed and changed over the decades.

◎ To explore the different methods of studying family life.

Introduction

When social researchers study family and personal life, they make some basic assumptions about the nature of human behaviour and social interaction. Initially, they assume that intimate relationships and family practices do not occur in random ways and do not result merely from personal choices or biological urges. Instead, social researchers generally accept the idea that social patterns and trends are apparent because our ambitions, desires, relationships, and choices are shaped by social forces, including the influence of our family upbringing and **significant others** (or those important to us), our socio-economic circumstances, gender, culture, religion, life experiences, and political and economic trends in the larger society. Some researchers focus on the influence of the changing political economy and labour market trends on family life, while others emphasize the ways that family upbringing and interaction with significant others shape our future intimate relationships. Still others concentrate on the impact of ideas and popular culture on current living arrangements, desires, and aspirations. These basic assumptions about the important influences on relationships and family life are called theoretical perspectives or theoretical frameworks. They cannot be proven or disproven yet they help guide our research and make sense of our observations.

This chapter outlines three broad theoretical frameworks that have been used in previous studies to analyze and explain patterns in family and personal life. The first framework argues that social structure (including the economy, policies, laws, and social expectations) influences and constrains family life, and alters our opportunities and intimate relationships. The second argues that psychosexual development and interpersonal interaction shape personal identity, perceptions, aspirations, and future family relationships. The third framework emphasizes the importance of prevailing ideas and cultural images in creating and shaping desires and lifestyles. Understanding these broad theoretical frameworks can shed light on the history of ideas, the development of sociology as a discipline, and the ongoing debates among academics and policy-makers about the crucial influences on social behaviour. The chapter also provides an overview of the various research methods used by social researchers to study family and personal life, as these tend to be shaped by their preferred theoretical perspective.

Social Structure Shapes Family Patterns

Researchers and theorists have argued since the nineteenth century that political and economic transformations in the larger society make a significant impact on the way we live in our personal lives. We already mentioned the research of the rural European family by Frédéric Le Play, considered the pioneer of empirical sociology, who argued that socio-economic changes such as urbanization and industrialization led to the rise of the nuclear family and to the demise of patriarchal authority and hierarchical family relations. Despite the conservative biases in his analysis, Le Play helped legitimize the study of family structure and social history (Gilding, 1997: 46).

Friedrich Engels (1820–95) also studied the impact of transformations such as urbanization and industrialization in the economy on family structure and authority patterns in England. He argued that changes in the political and economic basis of society from feudalism to capitalism altered family life by moving production outside households and into factories. These production changes encouraged a patriarchal family structure in which men, as household wage earners, became the intermediaries between their families and the larger community, while their wives were expected to care for the children and home. As wives played a reduced role in economic production, Engels noted that their status and authority declined because society increasingly measured personal worth by earning capacity (Engels, 1884).

Family research using this "political economy" perspective has continued until the present, emphasizing the ways that labour market restructuring, the growing need for post-secondary education, the rise of computer technology, and the development of a globalizing economy not only alter the way we earn a living but also influence prevalent living arrangements such as the timing of marriage and childbearing. In fact, many of the arguments made in this book are based on the **political economy perspective**. Generally, political economists argue that people's access to wealth, production, and power influences their desires, beliefs, and behaviour. In this approach, interpersonal relations, community stability, and social cohesion are de-emphasized. The focus, instead, remains on the impact of historical trends in paid and unpaid work on family structure, different opportunities or life chances based on social class, and the impact of social policies on family and personal life. Historically, political economists attributed greater importance to **social class** than to gender, sexual orientation, age, ethnicity, or race. In recent years, however, many feminist scholars have used a political economy perspective, acknowledging the importance of gender, race, and class to the kinds of work people are forced to accept and how this impacts on their living standards and personal relationships (Bradbury, 2005; Luxton and Corman, 2001; Bezanson, 2006).

Another structural approach, **structural functionalism**, has argued that the family is the basic social institution of society, containing widely accepted rules, expected forms of behaviour, and hierarchical relationships. The family ideally provides social stability when it offers emotional support, companionship, sexual expression, reproduction, and the socialization of children. This institution also provides important functions for the larger society by maintaining social order and control through the disciplining of children and other family members. The extended family especially offers protection from outsiders, while individuals often relate to the outside world through their family head. Family members usually co-operate financially and help each other through hard times by sharing resources. Finally, people acquire money and property through inheritance from family members, which suggests that social status and wealth are largely established and perpetuated through families.

Early European anthropologists, such as Bronislaw Malinowski (1884–1942) and Alfred Radcliffe-Brown (1881–1955), used a structural functional approach to compare culture and family life in various parts of the world, including the South Pacific and Australia. They studied how family systems were integrated into the entire culture. Later, the American Margaret Mead (1901–78) became one of the first female anthropologists to carry out field research among South Pacific cultures and focused primarily on how cultural expectations and practices influenced girls as they matured into women. The ideas of these researchers were highly influential at the time and widely debated among academics and educated citizens.

Throughout the 1950s and 1960s, American sociologist Talcott Parsons (1902–79) and his collaborator Robert Bales theorized about family life from a structural functionalist perspective. Focusing on the American family, they concluded that industrialization and urbanization produce a smaller and relatively isolated nuclear family that specializes in the socialization of children and in meeting the personal needs of family members (Thorne, 1982: 7). They assumed that the family as an institution has two basic structures: a hierarchy of generations in which children are expected to obey their parents, and a differentiation of adults into instrumental and expressive **roles**. Parsons and Bales made the debatable argument that the wife necessarily takes the expressive role or maintains social relations and cares for others, while the husband assumes the instrumental role or earns the money for the family and deals with the outside world (ibid.).

Present-day structural functionalists acknowledge that **gender roles** have changed and children have gained legal rights and increased their influence over parents. However, some functionalists continue to imply that a certain type of family structure (male breadwinner/female homemaker) was maintained throughout history because it was "functional for society"—it was what worked best. In fact, it may have worked best mainly for heterosexual men or for capitalist producers who could assume that working men had wives at home to attend to their personal needs (ibid.). Some functionalists still talk about "the family" as though there is one acceptable family form rather than many variations. They also believe that behaviour is largely determined by social expectations, rules, and family upbringing and therefore not easily altered through personal choice. Change is sometimes considered to be disruptive rather than normal, and individual opposition to social pressure has been viewed as "deviance." Consequently, the structural functionalists do not deal with social change and conflict as well as the political economists, but neither focuses on the dynamic nature of interpersonal relations or sees the individual as the major agent of social change.

A variation of structural functionalism is **systems theory**, which views the family as a social system in which members are interdependent and any change in the behaviour of one affects the others. The family is also seen as a task-performing unit that is expected to meet the requirements of both the larger society and its own internal needs. The family is also a relatively closed boundary-maintaining unit that closes ranks against outside interference, as well as being an adaptive organization that incorporates new forms of behaviour and attitudes from the outside world. Family systems theory has been influential in several disciplines such as psychiatry and family therapy because it focuses attention on the interrelationships between family members (Braithwaite and Baxter, 2005). This has enabled therapists to assist clients to co-operate in order to enhance couple communication and to work towards positive change. However, emphasizing social interaction leaves no way of explaining why some clients exhibit certain kinds of problems more than others. Furthermore, the analysis cannot adequately explain change over time, is limited to one culture, and often focuses on one family. Viewing the family as an open system takes into consideration the external influences on family interaction but the systems approach does not focus on the social, economic, or political context within which families live.

This discussion suggests that structural approaches may vary considerably. They can emphasize change and conflict (as does the political economy approach) or focus on consensus and cohesion (structural functionalism). However, both versions suggest that personal choices about relationships and family practices are limited by societal constraints such as access to money and power, the enforcement of regulations and rules, and social expectations about behaviour. Structuralists emphasize that we are all born into families that are part of a larger culture with existing social traditions, legal and educational systems, and expected patterns of behaviour. We cannot choose our parents or family circumstances. Some children are privileged from the beginning of their lives while others must struggle to grow up and fend for themselves under difficult socio-economic circumstances. Although structuralists acknowledge that life involves personal choices, they tend to argue that opportunities or "life chances," as well as attitudes and patterns of behaviour, are more often shaped by forces beyond the individual.

Interpersonal Factors Shape Family Life

In contrast to the structural approaches, other social practitioners, researchers, and theorists have focused on early family experiences that shape our personal identity, our attachments to parents and siblings, and intimate relationships throughout life. For example, Sigmund Freud (1856–1939) believed as a result of practising as a psychotherapist that the early years of a child's life are critical for the development of sexual identity, personality, and the ability to form lasting relationships. He argued that children's future relationships are shaped by their early reactions to their physiology and interaction with parents, including the ways they are held, fed, toilet trained, talked to, listened to, and disciplined. Personality development is largely influenced by unconscious motives and repressed emotions but the Western process of socialization involves teaching children to control their selfish urges. Freud also observed that children learn partly by identifying with their same-sex parent.

Freud's psychoanalytic theories have been criticized because his research was based almost exclusively on a European clinical sample, and because he "explained" women's "fantasies" by portraying them as "defective men" who subconsciously envy men's power, symbolized by their penises. He also assumed that socialization takes place only in early childhood, but social scientists later concluded that it continues throughout life. Nevertheless, Freud made a major impact on Western thought and is credited with useful insights into personality development that stimulated a considerable amount of further research and theorizing. Psychoanalysis was initially rejected by early feminists such as Kate Millet (1970), but it was modified and developed by Juliet Mitchell (1974) and Nancy Chodorow (1978, 1989), who used Freudian theory to analyze patriarchal society (Humm, 1995: 102). Judith Butler's early theorizing about gender and sexuality has also relied heavily on psychoanalysis (Butler, 1997).

Another developmental approach was initiated in the 1920s and 1930s by the Swiss psychologist Jean Piaget, who studied systematic patterns of change occurring in children's thought processes as they mature. Like psychoanalytic theorists, Piaget suggested that all children pass through similar stages of cognitive development, but he concluded that they could not learn particular tasks or concepts until they had reached a certain level in their development. He further theorized that children's experiences and interpretations of the physical and social world modify the timing of these stages, as children actively participate in their own socialization (Baker, 2001b). In the 1960s, Erik Erikson (1963, 1968) argued that children pass through stages of development or preoccupation in which they must resolve certain crucial life issues in order to reach maturity. These include developing a capacity for trust, autonomy from parents, initiative, industry, identity, and intimacy.

Psychoanalytic theory and **developmental theory** remain influential but learning theory became a popular way of explaining child development from the 1920s to the 1980s, especially in the United States. Learning theory emphasized the importance of "nurture" in the debate as to whether inherited characteristics ("nature") or social learning ("nurture") plays a more important role in personality and social development. According to learning theory, parents and care providers retain almost infinite potential to shape infants' attitudes and behaviour and to socialize children through rewards or punishments. Children also learn from observing and imitating adults, especially their parents and siblings. These above approaches, which tend to be psychological rather than sociological, downplay the political and socio-economic context of family life. They also suggest that adult behaviour is difficult to understand and modify without some knowledge of the early interaction experiences with parents, siblings, and other family members.

Social interaction is also the focus of **social constructionism** or **symbolic interaction perspective**, which remains prevalent in sociology. This approach assumes that social life is determined neither by social structure nor early psychological experiences but is constructed by individual "actors" who create their own reality through their interactions with others in families, schools, and workplaces (Berger and Luckmann, 1967). This theoretical perspective originated with the work of Americans Charles H. Cooley (1864–1929) and George Herbert Mead (1863–1931), who separately studied childhood socialization, how children develop an identity, and the importance of family interaction in this process. They noted that, early in life, parents communicate with their children through words but also through gestures, facial expressions, and tones of voice. Symbolic communication alters behaviour as individuals interpret these messages about themselves and their world. Within this interpretive perspective, the ways that children and young people understand non-verbal communication from significant others are more important than parental rules or social expectations for the development of personal identity and future relationships.

How people treat us and react to us can be influenced by the image we project, including our demeanour, dress, posture, and speech, which sociologist

Erving Goffman (1959) called the "presentation of self." This approach, also called an interpretive theory, focuses on the "social construction of reality" and argues that the interpretation of other people's reactions to us is critical in shaping our personalities, as a strong association exists between the development of self and what we believe others think of us. In addition, part of growing up and becoming a social being requires developing the ability to look at the world through the eyes of others and to anticipate a particular role before taking it (anticipatory socialization). According to this theory, socialization takes place throughout the life cycle rather than only in early childhood.

Research based on symbolic interactionism often centres on what individuals and society perceive to be real or important, such as what constitutes a good relationship, a worthwhile life, or a social problem (Giddens, 2006: 152; Holstein and Miller, 2006). Researchers using this perspective analyze how people come to these conclusions. They argue that it is not enough to observe people's behaviour but that we also must understand why they behave that way, how they interpret their own actions, how they *feel* about what they do, and why they feel this way because perceptions shape behaviour and relationships. This framework could be seen as the precursor of post-structuralist theory, which is discussed later in this chapter.

Social exchange theory, which uses economic analogies from cost–benefit analysis to explain human behaviour, is also related to symbolic interactionism. The German sociologist Georg Simmel (1858–1918) argued that all human interactions involve some form of social exchange even when they appear to be altruistic, and he emphasized the importance of reciprocity in everyday life. His work was translated into English during the 1950s and became influential in American sociological theory. In 1961, the American sociologist George Homans (1910–89) accepted the structural functionalist idea that values and norms govern behaviour but argued that people also attempt to minimize costs and maximize benefits when interacting with others.

Within social exchange theory, the anticipation of a "reward," such as social approval or emotional security, is the main motive behind social behaviour. All interpersonal behaviour, including deciding on a dating or marriage partner or accepting a particular household division of labour, is assumed to involve a process of negotiation and bargaining (Scanzoni, 1982). Social exchange theory has been used to explain why some relationships break up and others last. When one partner feels that he or she contributes more time or emotional energy to a relationship, feelings of resentment may develop and he or she may start looking elsewhere for gratification.

Theoretical approaches that focus on social interaction can provide insights into the dynamics and satisfactions of relationships but cannot explain the historical or cultural change in family patterns. Nevertheless, the social constructionist approach is widely used in sociology and gender studies, suggesting that perceptions of social reality and personal beliefs are more important in shaping behaviour than material reality (Holstein and Miller, 2006; Sev'er and Trost, 2011).

Ideas, Global Culture, and Public Discourse Influence Family Life

Other social theorists and researchers believe that focusing on changes in the political economy, social structure, early psychological experiences, or social interaction cannot adequately explain current trends in sexuality, relationships, and family life. Instead, they emphasize the importance of prevalent ideas and, more recently, of global culture, such as advertising, media representations, and the Internet, when explaining choices about relationships and lifestyles.

Max Weber (1864–1920), one of the founders of modern sociology, argued that the proper subject matter of social science was social action or action directed towards others to whom we attach a subjective meaning (Scott and Marshall, 2009: 800). He also saw the development of modern societies as a process of increasing reliance on rational action and choices, rather than religious or mystical beliefs (ibid.). Weber wrote about how prevalent Protestant (especially Calvinist) ideas regarding individualism, hard work, rational conduct, and self-reliance led to the transformation of society and the entrenchment of capitalism in the nineteenth century (Abercrombie et al., 1994: 452). Since then, many theorists have focused on the influence of ideas and new technologies in shaping personal life, including the decline in religious authority; the growth of individualism; new ideas about gender equity or body rights; and the desirability of being rich, famous, or changing one's physical appearance through hair dye, piercing, tattoos, or cosmetic surgery.

Much has been written about the rise of individualism, including the widespread and growing belief that people have the right to choose their own cohabiting or marriage partners, to openly express their sexual preference, to be happy in their intimate relationships, to choose whether or not to have children, and to separate and look for new partners if their relationships turn out to be unsatisfactory. Particularly the generation growing up after the 1960s was called the "me generation" because this cohort placed unprecedented emphasis on their own self-development, education, and personal fulfillment, shunning some of the earlier concerns and obligations voiced by their parents. Before World War II, women who wanted to further their education and establish careers had been admonished for being selfish and contributing to the decline of the nuclear family. However, the post-war generation was more likely to downplay or disregard these ideas and values.

Post-structuralists have argued that as Western societies grow more consumer-oriented, old expectations and divisions—including the authority of the church and **state**, obligations to family and community, and social class divisions—become less important. In other words, in this view social structure is now less important than what people want to do or aspire to. Sociologists such as Anthony Giddens (1992), Elisabeth Beck-Gernsheim (2002), and Zygmunt Bauman (2003) have argued that intimacy has been transformed in postmodern society partly by the separation of sex from reproduction but also by the insecurity of relationships and new ideas about "creating one's own biography." Freedom from religious and family constraints has encouraged more people to live in ways that differ from their parents, including creating families of choice or groups of close associates with whom they want to spend time rather than spending time with biological relatives who oppose their values and lifestyle.

More people feel that they have the right to create households and lifestyles according to their own beliefs and desires. However, social scientists argue that beliefs and desires are not entirely invented by each individual but rather are shaped by images in the media, advertising, the Internet, films, and global culture (May, 2011). For example, by watching "extreme makeover" programs on television, we are encouraged to view our wardrobe as "uncool," out of fashion, and in need of replacement, and to see our aging bodies as undesirable and in need of expensive repair. We are continually told that our confidence and self-esteem are derived from our personal appearance and sexiness, which could encourage us to de-emphasize our education, personality development, intellect, occupational accomplishments, and caring responsibilities.

Post-structuralism also "deconstructs" or questions the origins and intended meanings of certain ideas and popular beliefs about "the family," arguing that prevalent images have been socially constructed. As such, they are a product of a certain historical period or organization, and may be used to advance particular political agendas or commercial goals. In the recent past, the family was often conceptualized by structural functionalists as a monolithic institution instead of a varying range of living patterns that have been transformed over the centuries, that change throughout the life cycle, and that represent gendered and cultural experiences. Except among some social conservatives, this **monolithic bias** with its assumptions about the nuclear family, the male breadwinner, and the stay-at-home mother is no longer considered valid. In addition, the state uses particular discourse or images of family to further its interests. For example, the French social theorist Michel Foucault (1979) argues that ideas about gender and sexuality are socially and politically created. In present-day North America, public discourses surrounding the role of non-custodial parents ("dead-beat dads") appeal to moral principles that do not appear to be contentious—that all parents should support their children even after separation or divorce. Yet much of the policy impetus has been driven by more pragmatic economic concerns, such as enforcing paternal child support, as governments committed to dismantling their welfare states redirect responsibility back to families (Mitchell and Goody, 1997; Dalley, 1998; Baker, 2006).

Post-structuralists also argue that public discourse, or the ways that people express certain ideas and the language they use, influences how people see themselves. For example, policy-makers and journalists often talk about "workless households" or "welfare moms" when they are discussing mother-led households with incomes assisted by state income support. This discourse encourages the general public to see these mothers in an unflattering light and perhaps to vote for cuts in income support that force beneficiaries into paid work (Mink, 2002). However, it also encourages these mothers to see themselves as social failures who are making no contribution to society even though they may be doing a considerable amount of housework and raising children into healthy and productive adults. Alternatively, they may actively resist their portrayal through social activism.

Recent social theorizing acknowledges and elaborates differences in family formation and structure, and refutes the "norm" of the nuclear family with father as earner and mother as care provider. Researchers note that socio-demographic trends in family life in most Western countries are moving in the same direction, as sexuality is becoming separated from marriage, and marriage is being reconstructed as a terminable arrangement with the greater acceptance of serial monogamy (Cherlin, 2010; McDaniel and Tepperman, 2010; Luxton, 2011; May, 2011). Child-bearing and child-rearing are also becoming separated from marriage, many couples are renegotiating their division of labour, and more same-sex couples are expecting family and state recognition of their living arrangements (Baker and Elizabeth, 2012b). At the same time, more immigrants with different family patterns are migrating to industrialized countries and indigenous family patterns are being re-acknowledged by governments, social workers, and academics. These social and demographic trends have led to a contestation of the nuclear family as a core concept in both kinship and policy and to a theoretical reworking of the meaning of family in the twenty-first century.

Theoretical Framework Used in This Book

I draw on several of the above theoretical frameworks in this book. Most importantly, I rely on feminist political economy theories, which suggest that people's personal and family lives are shaped by their access to social, economic, and institutional resources that are unequally distributed between men and women (Bakker and Silvey, 2008; Luxton, 2006; Vosko, 2002). The book particularly draws on research and theories about the impact of domestic divisions of labour on paid work in the current competitive environment. I also maintain that typical patterns of partnering, where women live with older men who have higher earnings, tend to augment the social expectations that women will shoulder the domestic and care work, creating a "second shift" of after-hours household work, especially for employed mothers (Hochschild, 1989, 1997; Johnson and Johnson, 2008). More often than men, women accept the day-to-day responsibility for child-rearing and housework, which gives them less time and motivation than men to pursue full-time careers or to gain promotion, but provides them with closer ties with their children (England, 2010; Kitterød and Pettersen, 2006; McMahon, 1999; Ranson, 2009). When men and women become parents, they often make differing choices and negotiate space for different activities, based on their gender and social/material resources (Fox, 2010).

The "motherhood penalty" research discussed in Chapter 6 shows that the careers of mothers tend to lag behind those of childless women and fathers (Baker, 2012c; Budig and England, 2001; Correll et al., 2007; Crittenden, 2001; Portanti and Whitworth, 2009). This research also demonstrates that employed mothers are typically viewed by employers and co-workers as less committed and ambitious than fathers or childless women. The careers of mothers tend to progress at a slower pace because having and raising children sometimes requires them to take time off work or reduce their employment hours, especially if they live in families where care and household management are viewed as women's work. Women themselves sometimes choose to give priority to their children when they are preschoolers, hoping to return to full-time work at a later date. However, taking leave or reducing working hours is often consequential, especially for those in professional or managerial careers (Baker, 2012a).

Second, the book draws on interpretive perspectives that acknowledge the differing subjectivities and identities of people depending on their physical bodies and socio-cultural experiences. Interpretive theories generally suggest that the meanings associated with particular actions or behaviours are socially constructed and that our subjectivities (including self-image, gender identity, attitudes, and decisions) are shaped by the ways in which we present ourselves to others and how they interpret, ignore, resist, or reinforce our actions (Butler, 1990; Goffman, 1959). In addition, I draw on performance theories of gender, which suggest that masculinity and femininity are not what people *are* but what they *do* (West and Zimmerman, 1987; Kimmel, 2008). The interpretive approach acknowledges that women and men sometimes develop differing priorities and make varying life choices, but even when women behave like men their actions can be viewed, evaluated, and legitimated differently (Kelan, 2009; Probert, 2005).

This book focuses on the social construction of gender and family life but I also acknowledge the relevance of **intersectionality**, a concept suggesting that the impact of sex and gender in social networks and employment situations could be compounded or alleviated by other factors, such as age, rank, marital status, sexual preference, ethnicity, culture, race, and institutional setting. Furthermore, I realize that not all women or men experience the same ambitions and domestic circumstances, even when they share the same age group, employment rank, or cultural background. Clearly, individuals differ but people also modify their attitudes and ambitions over time, with maturity but also with changes in their living arrangements, parental status, and circumstances in the workplace (Baker, 2012a).

Methods of Family Research

In this chapter, we have seen that scholars studying family and personal life use different theoretical perspectives when they approach their chosen topics, but they also rely on a variety of research methods. Family-related studies might be based on an examination or reanalysis of relevant statistics from official sources, such as government departments and international agencies such as the United Nations or the OECD (Organisation of Economic Co-operation and Development). In addition, researchers can develop their own questionnaires, reanalyze previously used questionnaires, interview participants, or hold focus groups. They can also draw on personal observations to gain information about the social context of the topic, or analyze historical documents or policy reports to understand past practices or current family policies. Most large-scale studies actually involve several methods of investigation at the same time.

Whatever methods researchers use, new projects always begin with a thorough and extensive review of previous research on the topic. Normally, researchers will use a computer-based library search that can identify academic journal articles, scholarly books, and reports that deal with similar topics, published both within their country and internationally. Before beginning any empirical research, these articles and books are read and summarized to identify their theoretical frameworks, methodologies, and major findings. Academic researchers sometimes hire graduate students to help them survey the literature because this can be a time-consuming job.

Second, if researchers are planning to do empirical research or gather original data through interviews or surveys, they normally must gain approval from ethics committees located within university research offices or government departments. This is done to ensure the community that research projects have the informed consent of the participants, that they will do no harm, respect people's privacy, and keep their answers confidential and anonymous. Ethics committees, comprised of researchers and community members, are particularly vigilant when researchers plan to interview "vulnerable subjects," such as young children, welfare recipients, prisoners, or abused women. Projects do not require ethics approval if researchers are not directly talking to participants but instead are relying on the analysis of statistics, public policy documents, personal diaries, family law reforms, court records, or documents from government departments. However, researchers may require the approval of the social agencies or government departments involved in any project.

After reviewing the findings of previous studies, many social researchers also search for relevant statistics on the topic, examining recent government census figures, labour market statistics, or household surveys to uncover patterns and trends for the topic within the country or internationally. Governments regularly gather statistics on a variety of topics, including cohabitation and marriage, employment and unemployment, fertility, divorce, and expenditures on social programs. International organizations such as UNICEF (United Nations Children's Fund) and the OECD maintain comparative statistics on many issues such as rates of cohabitation, marriage, fertility, divorce, maternal employment, child poverty, and the relative generosity of government programs for children and families. Some researchers will also purchase raw data gathered by government departments in order to analyze it in a unique manner. However, official statistics are not available on all topics within family studies, and these statistics sometimes provide limited information in comparison with specialized studies that question participants about their motives, attitudes, or behaviour and involve interviewing people in their own homes where it is possible to observe their households.

Consequently, many researchers create their own questionnaires or interview schedules. Some develop surveys and send them through the mail or by e-mail, or have them administered personally to participants by paid interviewers. For example, over a decade ago my research team mailed out a questionnaire to lone mothers receiving state income support but still expected to find paid work, asking them to rate their own health and the health of their children, their use of health services, employment-related experiences, and family circumstances. This survey was then compared with a previous study of the self-reported health of the wider population. The question behind this **survey research** was whether beneficiaries on low income are more likely to experience poor health, as family health problems are not always considered by policy-makers when they develop welfare-to-work programs (Baker, 2002a). Some researchers shy away from surveys that ask respondents to choose among a selection of answers or tick appropriate boxes; they believe that these kinds of self-report questionnaires provide superficial data even though answers may come from hundreds or even thousands of participants. Also, the response rates for such surveys are often low (less than 30 per cent).

Family researchers also use personal interviews that include both background contextual questions and open-ended ones where participants can talk at length about their personal circumstances and experiences with a particular family issue. These interviews are often recorded and transcribed in full so they can be analyzed, sometimes with the assistance of computer programs that electronically search for prevalent comments or themes. The study mentioned above also involved additional personal interviews with lone mothers, which investigated the details of family health issues, the mothers' employment experiences, problems with children and former partners, and their views of case management services (Baker and Tippin, 2004). In the same study, we also visited the government office providing case management and income support, to observe office practices, analyze the government's advice to their case managers, and hold focus groups with the case managers who worked with lone mothers.

A more recent project of mine and a colleague involved personal qualitative interviews with marriage celebrants and long-term cohabitants who had decided to legalize their relationship, in order to investigate why couples bother to marry when the legal and social advantages now seem so minimal. In this project, the research team interviewed marriage celebrants as "key informants" about wedding trends, as well as same-sex and different-sex men and women, to explore the social meanings attributed to cohabitation compared to marriage

---

 Box 2.1   Interview Schedule for Cohabiting Participants Planning to Marry

Background Information

Male/female; Marital status; Opposite-sex/same-sex relationship; Highest level of education; Occupation; Ethnic/cultural background; Age; Religious affiliation

- Have you previously been married/"civil unioned"? How long did the relationship last?
- Have you previously cohabited? How long did the relationship last?
- Do you have any children? How old are they?

Main Questions

1. How did you meet your current partner and how did you come to live together?
2. How long have you been living with (or married to) your current partner? (could ask for some details about partner, such as age and occupation)
3. If already married, how long did you cohabit before marriage?
4. When you began living together, was marriage or legalization something you discussed? Did you face any obstacles to marry at that time?
5. What made you decide to legalize your current relationship? Whose idea was it and how did the topic arise? Did one or other of you propose? Has that person initiated important changes in your relationship before? What role

or **civil union,** the reaction of friends and family to their decision to legalize their relationship, and wedding plans or experiences. This project was based largely on an interpretive or social constructionist framework, to see how the meaning of relationship formalization compared for same-sex and different-sex couples, and to explore the impact of age, sex, length of relationship, previous marital experience, parental status, and sexual preference on perceptions, relationships, and wedding experiences. The interviews were recorded and transcribed, and prevalent themes were discussed with the support of the participants' verbatim comments (Baker and Elizabeth, 2012a, 2012b). Box 2.1 presents the interview schedule used in this study.

Researchers also use focus groups to investigate topics, especially those relating to controversial opinions or commercial products. Several small groups of participants who share some similarity in social characteristics (such as their age, sex, parental status, or status as beneficiaries) can be brought together to explore their opinions on certain issues and participants can bounce ideas off each other or provide a variety of perspectives. The ideas

---

did your family and friends play in your decision? How did they react to your news? (search for details of negotiated and gendered behaviour)

6. How long will you wait (or did you wait) between the decision to legalize your relationship and the actual ceremony? If a long time, what are (were) you waiting for?

7. What sort of ceremony/wedding are you planning to have (or did you have)? Where was/will the ceremony [be] performed? Who presided? What made you choose this celebrant? What did you wear? Were your children involved in the ceremony? What did you promise to your partner? How many guests attended? Were your family there? What roles did your parents play? Where was the venue for the celebration? Did you have a honeymoon or go on a trip afterwards? How much, approximately, did the entire event (wedding/party/trip) cost? Did you encounter any difficulties in the lead-up to the ceremony or during the ceremony itself?

8. Do you think that your friends see cohabiting relationships as the same as legal marriage? What about your parents or other relatives?

9. What do you think are the advantages of legal marriage (or civil union)? What do you think are the advantages of cohabitation?

10. Why do you think so many people delay or postpone legal marriage these days?

Source: Interview schedule used by Maureen Baker and Vivienne Elizabeth in 2010 for their research project called "Negotiating the Transition from Cohabitation to Marriage."

and opinions of the various focus groups or members within the groups can then be compared. This method is prevalent in market research but can also be used for research on family-related issues such as whether or not to reproduce and how many children are feasible and desirable. Group discussions can be less expensive than individual interviews but they are difficult to record and transcribe if the researcher wants to compare opinions by the age, sex, and social background of participants.

Decades ago, sociological studies used **participant observation** to try to understand forms of social behaviour that were considered deviant or had been previously unstudied. This sometimes involved pretending to be a group member rather than openly admitting to be a researcher, which now violates most ethics rules. However, researchers still use participant observation when they already belong to the group under study or admit that they are a researcher who also wants to become a group member. Researchers also observe particular research sites (such as households, community centres, or clubs) as an outsider, in order to understand organizational practices or group values. Anthropologists, especially, may spend months or years studying family and cultural practices in other countries or cultural communities. In addition, social historians may rely on personal diaries or historical records from churches, social agencies, or governments to understand personal values and behaviour in the past. Sociologists and political scientists also review government or agency reports to analyze political discourse and social policies relating to issues such as child support, violence against women and children, income support for sole mothers, or the legalization of same-sex marriage.

Meeting ethics requirements, identifying willing participants for interviews or focus groups, arranging cultural visits, finding documents, or mailing out surveys can be challenging and costly in terms of both time and money. Furthermore, researchers often have quite different opinions about which method of research is the best for their particular project, but this also depends on the particular topic, the time available for the project, and the needs of the research sponsors who initiate or fund the project. Researchers are sometimes asked to investigate a topic in a certain way by a government department, a family agency, or another research sponsor. Therefore, the method of research used in family studies, as in other subject areas, might be decided by a number of factors, including feasibility and personal preferences, ideas about the validity and wisdom of certain methods of research, the time and resources available for the project, the requirements of the sponsors, or the availability of existing data. In fact, practical constraints sometimes outweigh academic ones when researchers decide which method to use in their search for new knowledge about family life.

Conclusion

Research on family and personal life has always varied in terms of theoretical perspectives and research methodologies, but academics have reconceptualized this field of study over the past three decades. They now place more emphasis on identity formation, gendered and cultural experiences, the influence of global culture, work/life balance, the analysis of power relations between partners, political discourse about families, people who live outside family units, and same-sex couples. The growth of post-structural and feminist theorizing in the social sciences and humanities has particularly influenced research and theory on family and sexuality, as more academics now acknowledge the considerable diversity in household formation, lifestyles, and identities that vary by gender and sexual preference, in different social settings, throughout the life course and throughout history. Although some researchers adhere to one theoretical or methodological approach and view all others as mutually exclusive, most combine several research methods and borrow ideas from more than one theoretical perspective in their research projects.

This book gives priority to a **feminist political economy perspective** but also draws on interpretive or post-structural research. By this I mean that the analysis of gender relations is central to this book, but I also focus on the ways that social class background, access to resources, changing labour markets and policies, and cultural practices shape people's intimate relationships and personal desires. At the same time, I note the areas where personal choices can be made (and are actually made) to create people's own biographies.

In the next chapter, I discuss the social research relating to relationship formation, which includes how people find suitable intimate or sexual partners, who they select as "dates" and "mates," and at what stage in their lives they tend to seek permanent intimate relationships. The two basic questions we ask are which patterns are new and how do we explain the changes?

Questions for Critical Thought

1. Was Talcott Parsons correct when he argued that families need a task-oriented and socio-emotional leader?

2. Can we understand anything useful about relationships and family life by studying public discourse or popular culture, including portrayals of family life in television serials or women's magazines?

3. If you were studying why and how same-sex cohabiting couples decide to legalize their relationship, which research method would you use?

Questions for Debate

1.   More useful information about family life can be garnered from a large e-mail survey that is representative of the larger population rather than relying on a smaller number of in-depth face-to-face interviews. Discuss.

2.   The "best" theoretical framework for understanding recent dating practices is social exchange theory. Discuss.

3.   It is no longer worthwhile to study the history of family and personal life in the nineteenth century, as it was so different from lives and relationships today. Discuss.

Suggested Readings

Bryman, Alan. 2012. *Social Research Methods*, 4th edn. Oxford: Oxford University Press. This comprehensive book provides students with an explanation and demonstration of the main approaches and techniques of social research.

Cheal, David. 2005. *Dimensions of Sociological Theory*. Basingstoke, UK: Palgrave Macmillan. This book discusses a range of sociological theories from the last 200 years.

Giddens, Anthony. 2009. *Sociology*, 6th edn. Cambridge: Polity Press. Chapter 3 of this British textbook contains a good summary of general sociological theories, and Chapter 9 discusses family theories.

Luxton, Meg. 2009. "Conceptualizing 'Families': Theoretical Frameworks," in M. Baker, ed., *Families: Changing Trends in Canada*, 6th edn. Toronto: McGraw-Hill Ryerson, 29–51. This chapter discusses three major sociological theories about the nature of family life.

Suggested Websites

Sociology Online
www.sociologyonline.co.uk
This UK resource contains information about sociological ideas, theories, and news.

Sociology Online Dictionary
sociology.socialsciencedictionary.com
This is a useful reference for basic sociological terms and theories.

Feminist Theory Website
www.cddc.vt.edu/feminism/
This website, from Virginia Tech University, provides information on different feminist theories, ethnic and national feminisms, and numerous feminist scholars.

3 Forming Intimate Relationships

Learning Objectives

◎ To understand how dating and sexual behaviour were regulated in the past.

◎ To explore research on current dating practices.

◎ To discuss reasons for remaining single or living alone.

◎ To investigate why cohabitation rates have increased.

◎ To explore the social/political implications of widespread cohabitation.

Introduction

Do men and women still search for similar kinds of intimate partners or do they locate partners and develop relationships differently from a **generation** or two ago? Family researchers continue to look for new trends in partnering and family formation because these can provide insights into wider social change. In this chapter we note that ways of locating new partners and establishing relationships have changed somewhat over the years in most Western countries. Essentially, developing intimate partnerships has become easier, less formalized, less gendered, and more a matter of personal choice. Furthermore, most couples in the liberal states live together before they marry.

Nevertheless, traditional attitudes and practices remain, and some of the same socio-economic patterns underpin personal preferences for intimate partners. Current research suggests that the timing of first sexual experiences and partner choices continues to be shaped by family circumstances, social class background, gender, social pressures, and cultural expectations. The state of the economy and opportunities for education and work can also alter the timing of family formation, whether or not couples buy a home together or become parents, and the number of children they actually have compared to the number they desire.

In Western industrialized countries, most people choose their own intimate partners, although elders in some cultural communities try to assist their young people to form viable partnerships and to prevent unsuitable liaisons. Among cultural groups that encourage arranged marriages, dating is seldom tolerated because parents expect to control their children's intimate relationships and the timing of marriage. In free-choice relationships, individuals may spend several years attending social functions or enjoying leisure activities with several different intimate partners before making any concrete plans to cohabit or share the future with any of them. Eventually, however, most individuals develop an exclusive relationship that they would like to be ongoing or permanent. Nowadays, most people cohabit in a marriage-like relationship before making a long-term commitment, a pattern that was socially unacceptable only a few generations ago, especially in middle- and upper-class society.

In Western countries, choosing a partner is usually based on such factors as physical attraction, similar outlooks and interests, compatible personalities, desire for emotional stability and parenthood, and love. However, these characteristics may depend on the type of relationship wanted at the time. Distinctions normally are made among the attributes expected from a "one-night stand," a suitable dating partner, a compatible cohabitation partner, and one who is potentially "marriageable" for life. What patterns are apparent in the way these decisions are made, and how have they changed over the decades?

The Social Regulation of Sexuality and Courtship

Dating and Sexuality in the Past

In nineteenth-century North America, as well as in the other liberal states, courtship, love, and marriage used to be constrained by an intricate network of social, institutional, and familial influences (Shorter, 1975; Ward, 1990). According to public norms, sexuality was restricted to marriage or at least to heterosexual couples who were formally engaged, although, clearly, a **double standard** existed for men and women. Premarital chastity was deemed more important for women, and those who proceeded to sexual intercourse were expected to marry quickly. If they did not, they could be perceived by other men as fair game for sexual advances or harassment. These women would be seen by other parents as "damaged goods" or "having a past," a reputation that would reduce their future chances of finding a suitable partner. However, men could use expressions of love and commitment to gain sexual favours from their girlfriends, and women could use the expectation of premarital chastity to pressure their boyfriends into a marriage proposal. If pregnancy occurred before marriage, their families and friends would pressure them to cement their relationship in legal marriage and to stay together for life.

Social history and comparative family studies reveal that current dating practices are relatively recent in westernized countries and are not as widespread as we might think in other parts of the world. Before the twentieth century, most young people did not develop relationships with a variety of partners before marriage because once a man and woman were seen together several times they became viewed by friends and relatives as a "couple." Furthermore, many young people voluntarily committed themselves to their teenage sweetheart through lengthy formal engagements, which then meant that no other dating partners could be accepted without violating the unspoken agreement of exclusivity.

Rules of **endogamy** were also quite strict until the 1950s. For example, dating and engagements between Protestants and Catholics were frowned upon in many liberal states, but public opinion especially opposed interracial, intercultural, and interfaith liaisons. Most people attended regular religious services and their church leaders encouraged high moral values and family-related behaviour that was gendered, endogamous, and favoured reproduction. In addition, parents and schoolteachers attempted to maintain strict authority over the behaviour of children and young people, who were typically given fewer choices about any aspect of their lives.

Before the 1920s, middle-class parents seldom permitted their daughters to participate in leisure activities with young men without the presence of chaperones, who might have been other relatives, servants, reliable neighbours, school teachers, or clergy. This was particularly the case for wealthier families, who valued female premarital chastity more than poorer families did. Rich families had more to lose in terms of lost reputation or family wealth if their daughters were forced into hasty ("shotgun") weddings with "inappropriate" partners. Some wealthy parents engaged companions to travel with their unmarried daughters in order to protect their reputations, but many middle-class parents simply restricted their daughters' activities outside the household to prevent any suspicion of sexual misconduct.

By the 1940s, more people began to differentiate between "dating" and "courtship." Dating was defined as a short period of getting acquainted with the available partners, while courtship involved developing a serious relationship with one partner leading to lifelong marriage. Men were given the freedom to date more widely than women and were generally accorded a wider social range. Dating activities were usually relatively public and were not supposed to include solitary or intimate activities other than hand-holding or chaste good-night kisses. As late as the 1930s, middle-class men might have dressed in a hat, jacket, and tie, and women in a dress, high-heeled shoes, hat, and gloves simply in order to go for a walk together in a public park and then return to one of their family homes for dinner. Couple activities particularly excluded any expectation of sexual intercourse, although we know that many unmarried couples did engage in sexual activities from records of illegal abortions, illegitimate births, adoptions, hasty marriages, and "premature" babies.

World War II became a turning point for many social attitudes and behavioural patterns, including dating and sexual practices. Dating, premarital sex, and abortion rates increased sharply during the war when young people were away from parents and chaperones (Kedgley, 1996: 148; Baker, 2001b). When soldiers were on leave at home or in foreign countries, they tended to take more risks with their sexual partners, as life seemed so dangerous and short and pleasures were few. Many couples married hastily before or during the war, which enabled them to live together when the man was on leave and to have sex without social disapproval (Montgomerie, 1999).

Post-war affluence gave middle-class individuals more choice in clothing, food, and entertainments; couples continued to "dress up" for dating, which involved attending social events such as dances or films, or going for a walk in a public park or down the main street of town. By the late 1940s, dating without chaperones had become widespread, but this was replaced by strictly gendered etiquette rules. For example, men were permitted to invite women to attend social functions with them but women were not allowed to ask men, at least not directly. Men were expected to provide the transportation and pay for all the expenses, while women were urged to behave as congenial, attractive, and accommodating companions. Many of these rules of behaviour have diminished but gendered patterns are still prevalent in dating, as we will see later in this chapter.

Early Patterns of Courtship and Engagement

Marriage was important to the social and economic well-being of both men and women in the past. However, marital choices were often limited to neighbours, school or work acquaintances, and family friends because most young people attended local schools, entered the workforce at a young age, or cared for their elderly parents at home, but did not travel outside their community unless they were financially well off. It was especially important for young women to secure a partner before they became older than their marrying peers ("left on the shelf" without a partner) or found their cohort of suitable partners shrinking so that they felt forced to marry someone less desirable. Women were expected to encourage only one or two such courtships before marriage.

From the eighteenth century, young men increasingly took the initiative to find their own brides but were expected to ask the father's permission to "court" her, or gradually develop a relationship leading to marriage. This sometimes involved a formal meeting, at which the young man addressed the woman's father formally and presented his credentials, somewhat like a job interview. The father, as well as other relatives, wanted to ensure that the suitor's intentions were "honourable," which meant that he sincerely intended to marry the daughter rather than just have a "good time." The father also expected some assurance that the intended fiancé would become a kind, thoughtful, and faithful husband who could adequately support his daughter. The father's permission might be acquired either before the "courtship" began or before any formal marriage proposal was accepted by the woman (Ward, 1990).

When the man's marriage proposal was accepted, the engagement (or betrothal) was publicly announced and thus became a binding agreement. However, the wedding might be delayed until he more firmly established his work life or career, until he saved money, or until he was able to persuade his father to share farm earnings or even to hand over the farm. When the exact date was decided, the "banns"—the couple's intentions to marry—were then read in church for three consecutive Sundays to ensure that anyone who knew of a reason why the marriage should not take place would have the opportunity to speak out. This was largely to ensure against "bigamy" or marriage to more than one partner at a time. Later, when the state became more involved in legalizing marriage, a licence was also required to ensure that marriage partners were acceptable and appropriate from the viewpoint of community leaders and the government.

Men often bought their fiancée an engagement ring made of gold or silver with a precious stone such as a diamond to represent high value and durability. This engagement ring symbolized their lifelong commitment and became a public contractual agreement to marry that could not be easily broken without mutual consent. If an engaged woman broke off the engagement, she was expected to return the ring. If he backed out after she or her family had made costly wedding preparations, she could sue him for "breach of promise" under English common law and possibly receive a payment for "damages" at the jury's discretion (Ward, 1990: 32). However, few jilted fiancées had the money to engage a lawyer and many knew that their former fiancé could not afford to pay even if they were successful in a civil lawsuit.

The Great Depression of the 1930s forced many couples to prolong their engagements and delay marriage, and also made people conscious of material security in a number of ways, encouraging them to focus on thrift, hard work, and self-sufficiency. In those days, few state income support programs or subsidized health-care services were available in the liberal welfare states, and families needed to save money for accommodation, food, clothing, transportation, and future health-care costs, which included doctor's fees for normal childbirths but also for childbirth complications or accidents. Credit cards were not widely used until the 1970s and any credit given was at the personal discretion of the shopkeeper or the doctor.

Young men often hesitated to propose or to finalize marriage arrangements until they could afford to support a wife and children because men were automatically designated as the family earner when they married. Birth control devices were unreliable and socially unacceptable before the 1960s, with babies expected shortly after marriage. Reticence, sublimation of sexuality through work, and sexual self-control were widely practised as means of limiting the number of pregnancies for a married couple, but unmarried couples could not afford to risk premarital pregnancy.

Before the 1950s, women were expected to leave their employment as their wedding date approached, regardless of how interesting or lucrative their positions were. They were expected to prepare for their wedding day and their marriage, when they would be responsible for ensuring that the home was a pleasant place and that the domestic chores were done. For middle-class women, a good marriage meant one to a kind, considerate man from the same religious and ethnic group who worked hard and earned a steady income that was high enough to support a wife and several children. He was also expected to come from a similar social class, preferably from a reputable family known by the woman's parents, relatives, or neighbours. A "good" marriage was also a gendered one, with **complementary roles** for husband and wife, who were said to be separate but equal.

For middle-class men, a suitable marriage meant one to an attractive, respectable woman with social skills, a pleasant personality, good health and child-bearing potential, and valuable skills in homemaking and money management. Education was desirable but middle-class women were expected to become homemakers and mothers after marriage rather than wage earners. A good wife also behaved in a respectable and socially appropriate manner. If she did not, she could damage her husband's career prospects, his personal reputation, and their shared social life, so he had to choose carefully.

Couples had to save sufficient resources and the man had to acquire a steady income before they could afford to marry and establish a household separate from their parents. Without social security programs or credit cards, men often had to ask their employers for higher wages or ask their parents for a loan in order to manage their new commitments. If the boss or parents agreed, the couple could marry, but many had to postpone their marriage plans for financial reasons. In some cases, parents or other relatives objected to the match or pressed the couple to postpone the wedding until the man completed his education or the couple saved more money.

When men and women became engaged, their friends and family would allow them more privacy and intimate relations. However, if she became pregnant, parents and friends in many instances would pressure the couple to marry quickly before the pregnancy was noticed by others. Ideas about social propriety were almost more important than the couple's feelings for each other or their future chances of marital happiness. As a result, many couples were pressured into marriage prematurely by unintended pregnancy. If an unmarried pregnant woman was unable or unwilling to marry or to have an illegal abortion, she might leave her community to give birth, surrender the infant for adoption, and return quietly to the community pretending that she had been visiting a relative. Private or church-run maternity homes assisted many unmarried mothers through childbirth and arranged for their children to be adopted into two-parent families. Otherwise, these women would have been subjected to disapproval or ostracism, and would have brought disrepute to themselves and their families. Early in the twentieth century, "closed adoption" practices were widespread, which sometimes meant that birth certificates were altered and no further contact was permitted between birth mothers and their infants.

If conception occurred before the wedding date, engaged couples might simply bring forward the marriage ceremony rather than permit the child to be adopted or to be (illegally) aborted. Their earlier wedding date would ensure that the child was "legitimate." A legitimate child was born with a legal father and was permitted to take his surname and inherit from him, whereas an illegitimate child took the mother's surname, had no legal rights from the father, and was stigmatized socially as a "bastard."

This brief overview of past dating and courting practices suggests that people had limited choices about sexuality and relationships because strict rules of behaviour were enforced within families, communities, and workplaces, and were also internalized by individuals. Even when individuals or couples disagreed with the rules or with their parents' wishes, few could afford, either financially or socially, to contravene them.

Current Dating and Sexual Practices

Since the 1960s, young people have gradually moved away from rigid and gendered expectations of dating and "courting" (Crouter and Booth, 2006; Sweeney, 2006). More people now attend social activities as individuals or groups rather than as couples, and others arrange to meet potential partners at social events. Improvements in contraception since the 1960s have enabled premarital sex without pregnancy, which has liberalized both attitudes and behaviours. In addition, sexuality increasingly has become a marketable commodity that is mythologized in the media and sold in the consumer-oriented economy as fantasies and pleasures (McDaniel and Tepperman, 2010).

British sociologist Anthony Giddens (1992) described the new sexuality as "plastic" because it was something to be discovered, moulded, and altered. However, other researchers have argued that the double standard of sexuality (with men having more freedom) has been eroded but has not entirely disappeared (Eaton and Rose, 2011). Women have become more assertive in dating practices, but Mongeau and Carey (1996) found that American men are more likely than women to interpret a first date initiated by a woman as a sexual overture. Coltrane (1998) found that men see "sexually aggressive women" as off-putting, although flirting with sexual overtones is still an integral part of dating for both men and women. Research has also confirmed that parents monitor their daughter's dating activities more closely than their son's, such as establishing stricter behavioural expectations, prescriptions, and rules (Madsen, 2008).

Bogle (2008) found that many college-aged young adults in the United States arrive at social events alone or in groups but "hook up" with partners for casual sex or the potential development of longer-term relationships. After a relationship has been established, an urban couple might attend a film or concert together or go to a bar or café, where they might share the expenses or the better-off of the two might pay, and then they might end up at one or the other's apartment or flat to listen to music, watch a video, talk, and/or make love. However, the unclear rules of the "hook-up script" leave young women "to learn the hard way," to have low expectations of forming a relationship, and to think that the double standard of sexual behaviour still applies (ibid.). Bogle notes that American students generally believe that others "went further" or hooked up more often than they did. Furthermore, peer pressure and female competition for scarce relationships favour men's desire for multiple partners and casual encounters. Women felt pressured to "dress up" for men and to try to impress them, but were labelled as "easy" or "dirty" if they had "too many" partners. She also found that exclusive couple relationships can develop from hooking up but it is men who typically decide to evolve the relationship. Once these students graduate from university, Bogle discovered that their dating expectations become more traditional, with more women expecting men to ask them out, pick them up for dates, and pay the expenses (Walsh, 2008).

Other research has also emphasized that heterosexual women spend a considerable amount of time and money making themselves attractive to men and that gendered patterns still exist in ideal partners (Abu-Laban and McDaniel, 1998; Crouter and Booth, 2006). Introduction services and dating agencies rely on some of the same characteristics found to be important when people seek their own partners, including similar cultural, religious, and educational backgrounds—but with the man older, more educated, and taller. Introduction services also show videos to their clients of potential partners, acknowledging that many choices are based on physical appearance, first impressions, or "chemistry." In an experimental study of speed dating in the United States, women's decisions emphasized men's intelligence, race, and affluence while men responded more to women's physical attractiveness, devaluing women's intelligence and ambition if it seemed greater than theirs (Fisman et al., 2006).

Desired characteristics in a dating partner still emphasize women's youthful appearance and men's height, strength, and occupational success (Bogle, 2008; McDaniel and Tepperman, 2010). According to social exchange theory, the closer the body approximates idealized images of youth and beauty, the higher its "exchange value," especially for women's bodies (Featherstone, 1991). Structural theorists argue that men's preferences for younger, attractive women and women's preference for taller, successful, older men can lead to a "marriage squeeze." This means that people edged out of the **marriage market** are older and less conventionally attractive women, and younger and shorter men with low education and incomes. Although men continue to search for younger women who are slim and attractive, research also suggests that women's earning capacity is becoming more important for "assortative mating," at least to white American men (Sweeney, 2004).

A study by Chilla Bulbeck (cited in Connolly, 2004) revealed that Australian teenagers have retained gendered expectations about future partners. The researchers asked secondary school students from South Australia and Western Australia to imagine their future at age 70 and 80 and to reflect on the successes and failures in their lives. Despite three decades of discussion about gender equity, teenage boys wrote about a future of wealth, sex with many beautiful women, fast cars, and sport. Although 65 per cent of the girls said that they wanted a career, their stories focused on romance, meeting Mr Right, shared parenting, and relationships involving mutual understanding. A man's earning capacity is still relevant to some girls, and being rich and famous was highlighted by many of the boys. The author noted that the expectations of future fame and wealth are quite unrealistic, but also that discrepancies between the stories of men and women encouraged her to predict more divorce in the future (ibid.).

Sociologists now talk about "commodity feminism" or "post-feminism" in which young women claim to gain "girl power" by taking on traditionally male jobs or becoming celebrities, while dressing in an openly sexual way with all of the trappings of traditional femininity (such as lacy undergarments, dark lipstick, dyed hair, sequins, and high-heeled shoes) (Hopkins, 2002; Bulbeck, 2005). Post-structural feminists argue that these women "choose to do femininity" in their own innovative way rather than rejecting it as liberal feminists seemed to do in the 1970s. However, this "choice" is so often focused on consumerism and overt sexuality, which could encourage other people to perceive and treat these women as sexual "objects" rather than as competent and intelligent human beings.

Imagined partners are sexually/physically attractive and successful, but we also expect them to be considerate of our feelings and to share similar values and interests. Although some people dismiss or flaunt prevalent expectations, researchers continue to find that most people still internalize the importance of choosing a partner from a similar social background or from the gendered hierarchy in social and physical characteristics. Furthermore, parents still worry that their children will short-change themselves by choosing a partner who is "not good enough" for them.

Despite general insistence on the importance of personal choice in locating intimate partners, high rates of separation among dating and cohabiting couples suggest that decisions may not be based on qualities that lead to lasting relationships. Personal judgements based on physical appearance and sexuality are widespread in the popular media. Relationship instability is actually being encouraged by focusing so much on sexuality, fashionable appearance, and material success rather than shared values, companionship, or knowledge of the person's personality or social background. Heavy reliance on appearance contributes to short-term relationships in cultures that already focus on individualism, self-development, and personal choice.

Dating Abuse

Much of the research on dating violence and **abuse** has been done in North America and focuses on men abusing women. One of the first studies was conducted among American university students by Makepeace (1981), who reported that one in five dating relationships contained some elements of physical **violence**. During the 1990s, the Canadian government invested research money on this topic and Barnes, Greenwood, and Sommers (1991) found that 42 per cent of Canadian dating relationships among students in tertiary institutions included some form of force or violence. DeKeseredy and Schwartz (1994) also found that Canadian girls who experience violence in elementary school are more likely to become victims of dating violence in college and university.

More recent American and Canadian studies link childhood experiences of maltreatment, parental conflict, and domestic violence with more involvement with adolescent dating violence, both as perpetrators and victims (Tschann et al., 2009; Wolfe et al., 2009). This research clearly indicates that abuse and violence are not confined to marital relationships. Research has also found that some young women who are abused remain with their abusive boyfriends, even misperceiving the abuse as an indication of love. In addition, women also abuse men but men are often better able to fight back or deal with the consequences.

External factors such as economic dependency and presence of children contribute to wives' decisions to remain with abusive partners but these factors are rarely present in dating relationships. Some researchers explain the willingness to remain in an abusive dating relationship by the pervasiveness of abuse in heterosexual relationships but also by arguing that some young people are socialized to view gender relations as a "battle of the sexes." Women who stay in an abusive dating relationship or agree to become a cohabiting partner may also have lower self-esteem, feelings of obligation to the abuser, or fear of reprisal, or have experienced an upbringing that normalized physical, sexual, or verbal abuse. However, some individuals avoid live-in relationships altogether and remain single.

Remaining Single

Living alone has become easier in the twenty-first century, with urban facilities, household labour-saving devices, greater autonomy and freedom given to those living outside marriage, and more women earning their own living. Single individuals typically experience different lifestyles than long-term cohabiters or married people. They are more likely to rent than to own their home, to eat out in restaurants, to travel abroad, and to seek entertainment outside the home. At the same time, unpartnered men and women tend to maintain closer relationships with their parents and siblings than married people, who are often preoccupied with their spouse and children (Connidis, 2009).

Single women who have never married also experience more stable career patterns and higher earnings than married women (Beaujot, 2000; Baker, 2010c). This reflects the fact that single women tend to acquire more formal education and less often take employment leave, as married women more often do in order to move with a husband's job or to raise children. Nevertheless, unmarried women seldom achieve such high-status or well-paid positions as men, who tend to receive their education in different fields, to achieve more prestigious positions, and to receive higher pay than women. Even when women remain single, they are less likely to be encouraged by their bosses, friends, and relatives to excel in paid work, and employment practices often assume that men are more committed or qualified (OECD, 2007a).

Although singleness and childlessness among women have been associated with higher levels of education and occupational success, singleness among men has been related to lower education and lower employment rates than for married men (Koropeckyj-Cox and Call, 2007). This suggests that remaining unmarried provides more opportunities for both men and women to follow atypical gender paths. For women, this may mean uninterrupted careers, but for men, opting out of marriage reduces their obligations to earn money to support a family. This offers men more opportunities for leisure pursuits or alternative lifestyles, part-time work or self-employment, career changes, retraining, and continuing education.

At all periods in time some single men and women have remained celibate, such as those who join certain religious orders or live in remote areas, but we can no longer assume that never-married people refrain from intimacy and sexual activity. Some single people engage in covert relationships, attempting to protect themselves from the risk of public disapproval because their partner is gay or lesbian, or married to someone else. However, most single people introduce their sexual partners to family as well as friends, even though these people might mistakenly see these relationships as a prelude to marriage.

Some unmarried people have a series of intimate same-sex or different-sex relationships throughout their lives but never settle into long-term cohabitation or marriage. This might represent an attempt to create a life free from domestic responsibilities or it could indicate problems with maintaining intimate relationships. Others live in marriage-like relationships but never legally marry. Official statistics tend to blur these distinctions when they label people as "never married," but some governments are now gathering separate statistics for cohabiting couples. This permits researchers to discern differences between singles who cohabit and those who do not, as well as between cohabiters and married people. However, it will still be difficult to distinguish between those living alone who are celibate and those with active sex lives.

Remaining single or childless is often said to bring loneliness in later life, but single people often remain socially active, retain close contact with siblings and parents, travel widely, and belong to more clubs and organizations than partnered people (Connidis, 2009). Furthermore, single lifestyles are more socially acceptable now than they used to be, because the age of marriage has increased, marriage rates have declined, separation and divorce rates remain high, and cohabitation has become more prevalent (Sarantakos, 1996: 64–5). In addition, same-sex networks and singles organizations offer social support for those living outside family households. These factors contribute to raising the quality of life for singles and create more public acceptance of non-family lifestyles.

Single people tend to report lower levels of life satisfaction than married people, although this seems to be changing as the attitude towards singleness becomes more positive among younger people. Several studies indicate that unmarried men report more health problems and lower levels of well-being, and show that, statistically, these unmarried men experience higher premature death rates than married men and than all women (De Vaus, 2002; Waite, 2005). These data suggest either that some unhealthy, unhappy, and anti-social men never marry or that the institution of marriage is particularly beneficial to men. Kaufman and Goldsheider (2007) found that both men and women in the United States believe that men need to be married more than women do. However, younger, more educated, and less religious people are less likely to link marriage with life satisfaction.

Friends and relatives usually give up trying to "marry off" their single friends as they grow older, and never-married people learn how to reply to questioning remarks about their single status. Many have developed networks of friends in similar circumstances, who normalize living alone and emphasize the lifestyle advantages, such as higher disposable incomes (for men), more opportunities to travel, time to devote to career (for women), and spontaneity in leisure pursuits. Pressure to marry and bear children tends to lessen after people pass the age when their cohort has married, and especially after women reach menopause.

High levels of life satisfaction are related to perceptions of social support and the maintenance of intimate relationships, which contribute to satisfaction regardless of sexual preference or marital status. Married people can be lonely, lack trust in their partner, have few friends, and experience little social support (Dykstra and Fokkema, 2007). Generally, single people are forced to become more gregarious than partnered people and many have developed a wider network of acquaintances and friends. Nevertheless, considerable social pressure is still placed on them to marry, even in later life, unless they are openly gay or lesbian. Well-meaning married friends and relatives sometimes treat heterosexual singles as less fortunate, lonely, or in need of matchmaking, and these attitudes and pressures reduce their life satisfaction.

Finding Partners: Advertising versus Tradition

In Western countries, most people find their intimate partners at school or work, in clubs or bars, at other social functions, or are introduced through friends and relatives. However, for decades people have also advertised for intimate partners. In 1982, I analyzed personal advertisements in a Canadian daily newspaper, including the ways that heterosexual men and women described themselves and what they asked for in potential partners (Baker, 1982). At that time, men and women tended to present themselves in traditional gendered ways despite this relatively unconventional way of seeking a partner. Men more often described themselves as "tall" and "successful" business or professional men, gave their age, and asked for "attractive" younger women for a lasting relationship or "recreational sex." In contrast, women tended to describe themselves as petite, slim, and attractive and asked for business or professional men who were the same age or older. Just as in previous decades, women focused on lasting relationships or marriage. Similar gendered advertisements were found in Canadian newspapers from 1975 to 1988 by Sev'er (1990).

In a content analysis of 1,094 personal advertisements from four British newspapers, Jagger (2005) found that 61 per cent of advertisers were men but more of the advertisers over 45 years old were women. Men were more likely to mention their age but more women qualified their age in some way that suggested it was problematic. For example, they described themselves as "a very young 39-year-old female," "55 years young," or "young 60-year-old widow"; or they described themselves in the language of "positive aging," providing an optimistic, upbeat, physically active version of self. Jagger also noted the relative youthfulness of the advertisers using qualifying statements about age, with both males and females in their thirties revealing age-conscious identities ("male 37 but feels much younger"). The devaluation of age and aging has implications for advertisers when marketing the self, and advertisers seem to feel the need to reconcile the way they look with the way they feel (Turner, 1995; Jagger, 2005).

In Jagger's study, most people who stated an age preference wanted someone of a comparable age to themselves but men were more likely than women to ask for a younger partner. Among the older advertisers, men were most likely to say that they wanted a younger or much younger woman, although nearly one-fifth of older women also requested a younger man. Jagger (2005) showed that the ability to negotiate lifestyle choices from a diversity of options is shaped in complex ways by gender and age, but argued that individuals are still negotiating their identities around socially proscribed expectations that focus on the value of youth.

When people advertised for "companions" in the newspaper, they often spoke on the telephone before meeting in person, and then first met in a public place for their personal safety. Now, more people search for partners on the Internet where they can screen candidates and then communicate by e-mail with preliminary questions about their habits and interests and detailed self-descriptions before agreeing to talk on the telephone, use Skype to interact in real-time audio and video through the Internet, or meet in person. However, creating a false identity either in newspaper advertising or on the Internet is easy and it can also be dangerous to assume that you know someone through e-mail correspondence if you actually have never met the person or even spoken to them. Nevertheless, the Internet is increasingly used to form relationships and arrange to meet for sex, especially among gay men (Couch and Liamputtong, 2008; Rosenfield and Thomas, 2012).

Sociologists have become more interested in Internet relationships because they transcend geographical distance and are forged on the basis of common interests rather than common locality. They are disembodied, which provides more scope for fantasy, deception, and experimentation, making it possible to explore identities and sexualities. Men can pretend to be women and women can pretend to be men. Finally, these relationships tend to be uninhibited, which means that people can engage in more self-disclosure and riskier or harmful behaviour (Gilding, 2002). Relationships formed through cyberspace have been called "hyperpersonal" because some people can reveal more of themselves, feel more attraction, and express more emotions on a keyboard than in a face-to-face meeting. Instead of worrying about their appearance, they can concentrate on the message (Wallace, 1999).

Research on Internet dating has demonstrated that people can be rather strategic in the way they present themselves in cyberspace (Whitty, 2007). One of the differences between initiating a relationship online and in a face-to-face situation may be the depth and breadth of self-disclosure. People are able to tell an online partner many details about their past and present before they agree to meet, although the accuracy of this information may prove to be a stumbling block for continuing the relationship once they have actually met (McKenna et al., 2002). The American study by Hall et al. (2010) found that men using online dating services were more likely than women to misrepresent their relationship goals, their personal interests and attributes, and their assets, while women were more likely to misrepresent their weight. Box 3.1 shows that online dating has become prevalent in Canada in recent years.

Despite these new forms of dating and obtaining sexual pleasure, a substantial minority of young people do not engage in dating and premarital sex. In cultural communities that prefer arranged marriages, social activities continue to occur within a mixed-age community, which enables parents and other relatives to monitor young people's behaviour and to prevent them from forming inappropriate couple relationships. Other cultural groups permit dating but believe that sex before marriage is risky, culturally unacceptable,

Box 3.1   Online Dating in Canada

A recent cross-Canada survey conducted by Leger Marketing came to the following conclusions:

- 25 per cent of Canadians have tried online dating. The percentage rises to 36 per cent if you look at people between the ages of 18 and 34 (much higher than in 2009).
- Still, the majority of people do not plan to try online dating as 69 per cent of them said that it is not likely they could find love online.
- 64 per cent of singles using online dating say that common interests are most important when looking for a match.
- 49 per cent of singles using online dating say that physical characteristics from photos and videos are most important when choosing a match.
- 39 per cent of all the Canadians surveyed said that they actually read over all of the information provided in a dating profile.
- Online dating has seen a huge increase in popularity in the last few years in Canada and the rest of the world.

The Canadian-owned dating site Plenty Of Fish, for example, reports a 40 per cent increase in memberships over the last two years. Plenty Of Fish currently has 33 million registered users from around the world.

Source: Dating Site Reviews, at: www.datingsitereviews.com, 18 Oct. 2011.

or violates religious doctrine. A number of Christian groups, especially in the United States, have successfully encouraged substantial numbers of young people to take public vows of "purity" and "chastity" and to delay sexual intercourse (but not necessarily other forms of sexuality) until after marriage. These examples show that considerable diversity remains in patterns of partnering.

What has social research concluded about attractiveness and desirability in intimate partnerships? Generally, researchers have found patterns in partner choices for dating, cohabitation, and marriage but these vary substantially by gender, sexual preference, and culture, and the patterns are changing over time. Characteristics considered desirable and practices felt to be necessary by our grandparents and parents may now appear old-fashioned or overly rigid and gendered. In addition, global youth culture seems to be blurring some of the international variations but accentuating generational differences. Nevertheless, partner choice is clearly shaped by socio-economic circumstances, family experiences, and psychological factors. Furthermore, new trends are apparent in living arrangements before marriage.

The Transition from Dating to Cohabitation

Research suggests that dating couples begin to live together for a number of different reasons. For different-sex couples, cohabitation typically becomes a form of trial marriage, providing an opportunity to see if they are suitably matched and can "justify the next step" (Carmichael and Whittaker, 2007b; Coast, 2009). Cohabitation has become part of the "courtship" process and is now considered to be a normal "pathway" to marriage, at least in the liberal states (Dempsey and de Vaus, 2004; Manning et al., 2007; Qu et al., 2009). For same-sex couples, however, circumstances are different. Given their exclusion from legal marriage in the past, it is unlikely that many same-sex couples would view their live-in relationships as trial marriages. However, as same-sex marriage, civil union, or civil partnership becomes legally possible and more customary, same-sex couples may also begin to view their cohabiting experiences as trial marriage.

The second form of cohabitation is co-residential dating, in which roommates become intimate or dating couples decide to share accommodation largely for practical reasons, such as saving rent money or travel time to see each other. This practice is becoming more prevalent among young people, who can live together without facing serious or immediate pressure from family members or others (Baker and Elizabeth, 2012a). For different-sex couples, social pressure may urge them to legalize their relationship, but the pressure for same-sex couples might include opposing their choice of partner.

Among a minority of couples, cohabitation is actively chosen as a permanent alternative to marriage. Different-sex couples may reject the patriarchal or religious overtones associated with marriage or want to avoid its legal ramifications, but same-sex couples may have no way of legalizing their relationship. Finally, there are long-term, different-sex cohabitants, typically with children, for whom cohabitation is largely indistinguishable from marriage. Heuveline and Timberlake (2004) suggest that this group of cohabiting couples may simply be indifferent to legalizing their relationship. However, formalization becomes less relevant with the widespread acceptance of cohabitation and the decreased salience of marriage as a cultural ideal, and when governments or social agencies make less differentiation between married and cohabiting couples. This is especially the case in places such as Sweden or the Canadian province of Quebec. Box 3.2 provides some of the justifications for initially cohabiting from our New Zealand research (Baker and Elizabeth, 2012a, 2012b), in which cohabiting participants eventually legalized their relationships.

Many couples now begin to cohabit without any intention of marrying or formalizing their relationship but simply to enjoy being together and to see

Box 3.2   Interview Participants Discussing Their Decisions to Cohabit

- "The relationship reached a point where we were essentially living at one of our houses anyway. . . . We were essentially spending every night together and it just seemed to make good common sense. . . . And the timing was right then just because her friends were sort of going overseas and so she was going to move into the room upstairs which has got a bit more room and stuff like that. So it just seemed like the right time and I moved over when she moved upstairs." (Male, about 30, now in civil union with female)

- "I wasn't really going to be able to afford to live by myself or find a flat that would take a [large dog] in so I ended up living with [male partner]. . . . It kind of made sense at the time in terms of our relationship as well but it was quite affected by those factors." (Female, about 30 years old, now married)

- "That was just early on in our relationship so marriage wasn't necessarily something you think about so early in a relationship. I don't see living together and marriage as being linked. So there's no sort of thought that if we move in together we will have to get married or anything like that." (Male, mid-30s, now married)

- "It's cost beneficial to live together but also I mean at the end of the day it just means you get to spend more time together when you're both working. You only get a few hours left in the day either side that you can see each other. So if you are compatible, there's no real reason why you should live separately." (Male, about 40, "engaged" to another male)

- (First meeting) "We kissed and kissed until the sun came up. Then I drove home. . . . We were both quite traditional, I suppose, in our values around certain things and so we didn't leap into the sack straight away even though it crossed my mind, trust me. I certainly wanted to but we courted before we jumped in the sack." (Male, mid-40s, in same-sex civil union)

Source: M. Baker and V. Elizabeth. 2011. Interviews with long-term cohabitants who decided to legalize their relationships.

how their relationship develops over time. Even couples who are committed to each other often postpone their weddings until they can see some valid reason to formalize the relationship and until they are certain that they have made the right choice of partner. While many partners separate before making a long-term commitment, different-sex couples who stay together typically decide to marry after three to five years of cohabitation, although some take much longer and others never do officially formalize the relationship.

Rising Rates of Cohabitation

In many Western countries, cohabiting relationships (also called consensual unions or **common-law relationships**) have become more prevalent and socially acceptable in the past 40 years. Because most governments did not report them in their official statistics until the 1980s, it is difficult to measure longer-term trends. However, we know that the percentage of cohabiting couples in Canada has increased from 6.3 per cent of all couples in the early 1980s to 15.5 per cent in 2006, although the figure is much higher in Quebec (Wu, 2000: 50; Statistics Canada, 2007d). In 2011, common-law couples accounted for 16.7 per cent of all census families, which represents an increase of 13.9 per cent since 2006 (Statistics Canada, 2012a). Le Bourdais and Lapierre-Adamcyk (2004) argue that cohabitation in Quebec, as in Sweden, is nearly indistinguishable from marriage while in the rest of Canada it is still accepted predominantly as a childless phase in conjugal life, as in the United States.

The other liberal states share similar increases in cohabitation. For example, the government of the United Kingdom reported that cohabitation rates increased from 9 per cent of all couple families in 1996 to 15.3 per cent in 2010, with most cohabiting couples under the age of 45 years (Fairbairn, 2011; UK Office of National Statistics, 2010). Australian figures indicate that cohabiting couples increased from 4 per cent of all couples in 1982 (Dempsey and De Vaus, 2004) to 14.9 per cent in 2006, with 78 per cent of marriages registered in 2008 involving couples who had previously cohabited (AIFS, 2008).

Cohabitation increases as legal marriage rates decline, but this living arrangement remains more prevalent among younger couples and lower-income groups. Table 3.1 shows the percentage of the Canadian population aged 15 and over who are cohabiting, revealing the decline after the age of 30 (VIF, 2010: 35). Although most long-term cohabiters eventually marry (around the age of 28 to 30), demographers predict that this will be less likely in the future.

The increase in cohabitation rates is linked to several changes in the larger society. Improvements in birth control have enabled heterosexual couples to have regular sexual intercourse without risking pregnancy, which has encouraged sex outside marriage, although many people are still concerned about sexually transmitted diseases (STDs). More employment opportunities for women have reduced the importance of legal marriage for their income security. The declining influence of organized religion and the growth of individualism have encouraged couples to follow their own relationship choices rather than social conventions or parental wishes. Cross-national variations in the prevalence of consensual unions also suggest that these rates are shaped by laws, policies, and cultural values.

Table 3.1 Percentage of Canadian Population 15 and Over Who Are Currently in a Common-Law Relationship, by Age, 2006

Age	Percentage of Canadians Living Common-Law
15–19	1.5
20–4	12.3
25–9	21.8
30–4	18.7
35–9	15.5
40–4	13.9
45–9	12.1
50–4	10.0
55–9	7.9
60–4	6.2
65 and over	2.5
All age groups	10.5

Source: VIF (2010: 35). Derived from Vanier Institute of the Family. 2010. *Families Count*. Ottawa: VIF, p. 35.

Cohabiting relationships used to be viewed as temporary arrangements, but as they become more prevalent, long-term cohabitation looks more like marriage and is often treated as "marriage-like" by governments when they are considering access to income support and social services. It is not always evident which couples are legally married and which are cohabiting unless you gain personal knowledge about them. They may refer to their "partner" even when that person is a legal spouse. Some cohabiting women wear a wedding-like ring, while some married women wear no wedding ring and retain their maiden name. If we knew more about these people we might discover that some cohabiting couples share bank accounts while some married couples keep their money separate. Yet despite the similarities, researchers have found important statistical differences between the two types of relationships, although these are diminishing as more couples cohabit.

The first difference relates to the relative instability of consensual unions compared to marriage, especially among young people (Bradbury and Norris, 2005; Lichter and Qian, 2008; Liefbroer and Dourleijn, 2006; Qu and Weston, 2008). Statistics Canada reports that first common-law relationships are twice as likely to end in separation as first marriages, but also notes that first unions of younger couples are more likely to end in separation than those of older couples regardless of their marital status (Statistics Canada, 2002b). More recent Australian data indicate that cohabiting relationships are three times more likely than legal marriage to end in separation (Qu and Weston, 2008). One reason for the relative instability of cohabitation clearly relates to the youthfulness of people who typically live in these arrangements.

Cohabiters tend to differ in some other ways from those who never cohabit. For example, cohabiters are more likely to report no religious affiliation and to have been previously divorced. Dempsey and De Vaus (2004) found that Australian cohabiters who were recorded in the 1996 and 2001 censuses included more men than women, more people with Anglo backgrounds, fewer Asian immigrants, and fewer people reporting a religious affiliation. Baxter (2002) notes that Australian women in cohabiting relationships are more likely than married women to be employed full-time, to have fewer or no children, and to expect an egalitarian division of labour. Several other studies, such as Baxter et al. (2005) and Davis et al. (2007), show that cohabiting men do more housework than married men, while cohabiting women do less housework than their married counterparts. American research has found that only a minority of women (15–20 per cent) are involved in multiple cohabitations but that "serial cohabiters" are over-represented among disadvantaged groups, especially those with low income and education (Lichter and Qian, 2008).

Researchers have also identified a relatively new kind of relationship they call "living apart together" (LAT). Couples in these relationships may be married but most would be cohabiting, spending allocated days together at regular intervals, such as weekends or holidays, but living apart the rest of the time, sometimes studying or working in different locations. In the United States, Strohm et al. (2009) estimate that about one-third of adults not married or cohabiting are living in these kinds of arrangements, which are especially prevalent among young people and gay men. Although some males have always worked far away from their homes—especially forestry workers, sailors, and soldiers—more middle-class professional women are now commuting and more students are completing university degrees in other cities or countries. In addition, some previously married parents and older partners live apart from their current intimate partners in order to maintain their independence and separate homes, although this arrangement tends to raise living costs (Funk, 2012). The pattern for more couples to live apart is another indication of the rise of individualism and the variety of living arrangements, but it also suggests that educational and employment opportunities, as well as concerns about independence and the practicalities of blending families, continue to shape family formation.

The Social and Policy Implications of Increased Cohabitation

The rise in consensual unions has given policy-makers cause for considerable debate. First, they have had to decide whether these relationships should be considered similar to or different from legal marriage in terms of spousal entitlements and obligations (Wu, 2000). One entitlement we mentioned is to have relationships rights such as gaining the right to make health-related decisions if the partner is in an accident or in hospital. Another is the right to become a beneficiary to the partner's health insurance plan or retirement benefits. Second, if couples separate acrimoniously and ask the courts to divide their shared assets, should the state proceed in the same manner as for legal marriages? In many countries, legal reforms already require the equal division of family assets when marriage partners separate, unless doing so would create inequity or unfairness, but this legislation does not always cover cohabiting couples.

Although some cohabiting couples want more legal rights, others choose to keep their personal arrangements outside any legal requirements. They may see cohabitation as a private choice that involves less commitment, fewer obligations to their partner or his/her kin group, fewer religious or conventional connotations, a less gendered division of labour, and the option to leave without complications when the relationship is no longer mutually beneficial (Barber and Axinn, 1998; Elizabeth, 2000; Rolfe and Peele, 2011). Alternatively, they may see no practical advantage to legalizing their relationship or they may believe that the church and state have no right to intervene in their personal lives. The lack of legal protection, however, has sometimes left female heterosexual partners with fewer assets and less income after separation. This is especially relevant for a cohabiting couple with children, where one partner has supported the family financially while the other (usually the woman) has provided unpaid domestic services and child care. If the relationship ends, these mothers and children could become impoverished unless the fathers continue to support them, the mothers are able to find decent-paying work and affordable child care, or the state supplements their incomes.

Some governments have resolved these issues by deeming heterosexual couples to be "married" in terms of their rights, responsibilities, and the division of their joint assets after living together for a specified time (usually between one and three years, depending on the jurisdiction). If partners do not wish to divide their property equally upon future separation, they must sign a legal contract to specify alternative arrangements. However, all states agree that parents must support any children they produce, whether or not the parents are legally married or living with the children.

The rise in cohabitation is perceived by social conservatives as a negative trend, but having children outside legal marriage is considered a potential problem of greater proportions. In most Western industrialized countries, more babies are born outside legal marriage now than in earlier decades, although most are born to cohabiting couples. This dramatic increase in births outside marriage worries some policy-makers because the lower stability rates of these relationships could have negative implications for children's well-being. In Australia, 34 per cent of births in 2010 were to parents who were not in a registered marriage (ABS, 2011). Canadian figures show that 38 per cent of live births in 2006 were to women who were not married or living with their legal spouse (Statistics Canada, 2008b), compared to 9 per cent in 1975 and 4 per cent in 1960 (VIF, 2000, 1994). Notable provincial differences are apparent in the Canadian statistics, with a high of 61.5 per cent of births outside marriage in Quebec and a low of 26 per cent in Ontario in 2006 (Statistics Canada, 2008b). The vast majority of these children are born to couples in their twenties and thirties who are cohabiting, but these couples tend to have more stable relationships than younger childless cohabiters (Wu, 1996).

When more couples enter consensual unions, relationships typically become less stable at the national level (Beck-Gernsheim, 2002). If these relationships are unprotected legally, separations could lead to disputes about how assets should be divided, whether financial support should be paid, and where any children born to the couple should live. Cohabiting fathers have a higher probability of separating from their partners than married fathers and, subsequently, of losing contact with their children. Goldscheider and Kaufman (1996) argued that although cohabitation in the United States usually represents a lower level of commitment to partners, it also means that men are more likely than women to reduce their commitment to children. A father who is not living with his children can have a positive influence on them if he is involved, but a substantial minority of fathers are not involved, as we will see in Chapter 7. Furthermore, his tenuous relationship with the mother on issues of parenting can also bring conflict into the children's lives. Goldscheider and Kaufman argued that more research is needed on the impact on children of parents' commitment to each other.

In a qualitative study in the United Kingdom, Lewis (1999) found that cohabiting and married parents both said that they made commitments to each other and to their children. However, the commitments of cohabiting couples tended to be private, while the married ones were public. The younger generation of parents talked about commitments as personal issues that were internally driven, whereas their own parents talked more about obligations that were externally imposed. Jamieson et al. (2002) found that legal marriage was seen as irrelevant to commitment by many Scottish young people (ages 20–29 years), although some saw legal marriage as important for children.

Cohabitation is viewed by many young people as a good way to test their relationship but cohabitation is less stable than marriage. Furthermore, American researchers have also found lower levels of interpersonal commitment by men but not women in cohabiting relationships (Stanley et al., 2006). They also found that the quality of cohabiting relationships and levels of satisfaction tend to be lower than marriage, but couples who plan to marry tend to have higher relationship quality. Nevertheless, many couples "slide" from dating to cohabitation in a non-deliberative and incremental way, without fully considering the implications. Stanley et al. (2006) describe this as "sliding versus deciding," which they argue contributes to lower commitment and increases vulnerability in times of stress. Compared to dating, cohabitation encourages couples to remain in relationships that are not fully satisfying but are more complex to end, and these couples could also slide into unsatisfactory marriages.

Cohabiting women in Australia are more likely than legally married women to be employed full-time (Baxter, 2002; Baxter et al., 2010), which suggests they are more likely to have the financial resources to leave unhappy relationships. Although some cohabiting relationships last a lifetime, most end in separation or legal marriage. One interesting question about these trends relates to why so many of the couples who decide to stay together eventually marry when there appear to be diminishing differences between cohabitation and marriage? Also, why do some cohabiting couples who subsequently marry arrange wedding ceremonies that retain many of the conventional symbols of traditional (patriarchal and heterosexual) marriage? These questions are addressed in the next chapter.

Conclusion

In today's urban society, living outside marriage is increasingly feasible and desirable, although two incomes can certainly purchase a better living standard, especially when one is earned by a man. Nevertheless, remaining single has become easier with urban apartment living and household labour-saving devices. Full-time employees can now save time with "fast food," same-day dry cleaning and laundry services, housecleaning services, handyman services, dishwashers, vacuum cleaners, microwave ovens, and automatic banking machines. In addition, liberal social and sexual attitudes and more effective birth control have enabled more people to enjoy a satisfying sexual life outside cohabitation or marriage. However, less than 10 per cent of people avoid marriage altogether.

Most young people in the liberal states are delaying marriage but not sexual activity. Those who prolong their education usually remain at home with their parents longer than early school-leavers, but young people who find steady work earlier tend to leave home, cohabit, marry, and reproduce at younger ages. However, more young people from low-income families now attend university with scholarships and loans, and more women graduate from university and move into professional or business positions. Clearly, choices about education, paid work, and family formation continue to be shaped by gender, culture, and social class but also by the economic conditions in the larger society.

The distinction between being "married" and "never married" has been blurred in recent years by more liberal sexual behaviour and the practice of cohabiting without a legal ceremony. This suggests that the social and legal importance of marriage will probably continue to subside as living arrangements are seen more as personal choices than as sacraments or unions regulated by religion or government. In the next chapter, we will examine more closely the transition from cohabitation to legal marriage.

Questions for Critical Thought

1. Do any aspects of the double standard of sexual behaviour and attitudes still exist? Can women have as many sexual partners as men without social repercussions?

2. Social exchange theorists have argued that potential partners value different attributes for men and women on the "marriage market." Is there any evidence that this has changed?

3. Has the single life become more socially desirable in recent years or do most young people still want a permanent partner before midlife?

Questions for Debate

1. Internet dating is far superior to any other form of finding partners. Discuss.

2. Can you break up a cohabiting relationship as easily as a dating relationship? What constraints might exist to separation after long-term cohabitation?

3. Fifty years from now, most couples will cohabit without marriage. Discuss.

Suggested Readings

Bogle, Kathleen. 2008. *Hooking Up: Sex, Dating, and Relationships on Campus*. New York: New York University Press. This book is based on qualitative interviews with American middle-class white college students about their sexual practices and dating relationships.

Ward, Peter. 1990. *Courtship, Love, and Marriage in Nineteenth-Century English Canada*. Montreal and Kingston: McGill-Queen's University Press. Through analysis of letters, diaries, and public records, Ward shows that courtship and marriage in nineteenth-century English Canada were influenced by social, institutional, and family constraints.

Wilson, Sue J. 2009. "Partnering, Cohabitation and Marriage," in M. Baker, ed., *Families: Changing Trends in Canada*, 6th edn. Toronto: McGraw-Hill Ryerson, pp. 68–90. This chapter describes the way that people develop intimate relationships, noting changes in sexual behaviour, dating patterns, and cohabitation as well as practices within legal marriage.

Suggested Websites

Centre for Research on Families and Relationships
www.crfr.ac.uk
This consortium of researchers in the United Kingdom is based at the University of Edinburgh. Their website contains information about current research projects.

Plentyoffish.com
www.plentyoffish.com
This is an example of a free online dating service, which can also be used by researchers to analyze how people present themselves to others and what kind of partners they want.

4 Formalizing Relationships

Learning Objectives

◎ To understand how the meaning of marriage has changed.

◎ To investigate the differences between consensual unions and legal relationships.

◎ To search for patterns in personal choices in regard to marital or long-term relationships.

◎ To investigate the similarities and differences between same-sex and different-sex marriage.

◎ To discuss research findings on marital satisfaction, conflict and violence, and the durability of marriage.

Introduction

In this chapter, I investigate several theoretical arguments and numerous research findings about the changing nature of marriage. We need to understand if patterns of commitment, domestic work, child-bearing, and relationship stability really differ between cohabitation and marriage, and why cohabiting couples decide to formalize their relationships when in some jurisdictions it seems to make little social or legal difference. We also want to know how much social change has actually occurred over past decades in both different-sex and same-sex marriages.

The British sociologist Anthony Giddens (1992) argues that intimacy in postmodern society has been transformed, partly by the separation of sexual activity from reproduction, and this transformation holds the potential for the radical democratization of heterosexual relationships. In response to this claim, numerous scholars, such as Bittman and Pixley (1997), Jamieson (1998), and Rhoades et al. (2009), point out that more people may want intimate and egalitarian marriages but there is little empirical evidence that heterosexual relationships substantially differ in this respect from a few decades ago. The gap may actually be growing between our expectations of equality, intimacy, and self-fulfillment and the reality of current patterns of work and everyday family life. Let us examine some of these arguments further by investigating how and why committed couples decide to make the transition from cohabitation to marriage.

Negotiating the Transition from Cohabitation to Marriage

Despite the increasing similarities between cohabitation and legal marriage, they are still perceived as different by many people, especially lawyers, government officials, people with strong religious values, and older parents and relatives. For many young people, marriage is still viewed as a "rite of passage" or a public event that symbolizes maturity, legitimacy, and adult status (Cherlin, 2010; Gross, 2005). Legal marriage is also seen as a long-term commitment to an already intimate partner, with accompanying legal rights and obligations. In contrast, cohabitation is often viewed as a transitional living arrangement or even a form of residential dating that involves a lower level of commitment.

Although many couples make private commitments to each other, decisions to marry after a period of cohabitation might signal a higher level of commitment or at least a desire to make a public commitment and to celebrate their relationship with family and friends. For many people, marriage has retained its symbolic value as a cultural ideal and even become a marker of prestige in an era of declining heterosexual marriage rates and increasing public acceptance of same-sex relationships (Baker and Elizabeth, 2012a; Cherlin, 2010). After years of cohabitation and even after buying a home and raising children, most different-sex couples and many same-sex couples choose to formalize and celebrate their relationships (Manning et al., 2007). However, many couples delay the wedding until they have saved enough money for the type of wedding they desire (Boden, 2003) or until one partner proposes marriage to the other, usually the man in a heterosexual relationship (Sassler and Miller, 2011).

A decision to legally marry might also be based on more practical concerns. It could represent a desire to produce children together with assurance that they will be considered "legitimate" by older family members as well as by the state (Steele et al., 2005). Marriage after cohabitation could also represent an attempt to prevent guardianship concerns with children from a previous relationship or to alleviate immigration problems when crossing international borders. In addition, formalization can represent an attempt to gain kinship rights in the event of serious illness and hospitalization, to draw on the partner's insurance policy in the case of disability, or to inherit if one partner dies prematurely (Duncan et al., 2005; Schechter et al., 2008). Some of these issues seem more relevant for older people and this partly explains the higher marriage rates as people age.

Baker and Elizabeth (2012a, 2012b, 2012c) investigated how people negotiate the transition from cohabitation to marriage, drawing on 50 qualitative interviews in New Zealand with marriage celebrants and long-term cohabitants who had decided to formalize their relationships. Same-sex marriage was legalized in New Zealand in April 2013, but when we completed our interviews in 2011 the government had already established a second category of formalization in 2005 called "civil union," which enabled both same-sex and different-sex couples to formalize their relationships. Although civil unions offered similar rights and privileges to heterosexual marriage, civil union partners could not legally adopt children and marriage remained the preserve of heterosexual couples. Furthermore, the legal rights acquired through the Civil Union Act did not necessarily apply if same-sex couples live in countries opposing such union (Baker and Elizabeth, 2012c).

Both the celebrants and the cohabitants in our study reported that cohabitants typically formalized their relationships to make a public commitment and to celebrate their successful relationship with family and friends. This was the same for couples who married or had civil unions and for same-sex and different-sex couples, although same-sex participants placed a greater emphasis on the importance of gaining legal rights and kin acceptance through formalization. In our study, cohabitants and their partners did not always agree about whether to marry or the timing and nature of their wedding. Furthermore, some of the same-sex participants decided to formalize their relationship despite family opposition, as well as disapproval from some of their gay and lesbian friends, who were antagonistic to the idea of same-sex marriage. These friends saw it as unnecessary, heterosexist, and patriarchal, or in the case of the civil union legislation in New Zealand—as "second-class" marriage (Baker and Elizabeth, 2012c).

Our interviews revealed four pathways in their decision-making about formalization, although some of these are overlapping. They include proposals by one partner, mutual decisions, negotiated decisions with partners, and the gradual relenting to social pressures from family and friends. The couples where proposals occurred tended to be younger and more conventional than those who made mutual decisions, but the proposal sometimes followed an initial suggestion by the woman or younger partner; some proposals followed a mutual discussion. In different-sex relationships, the marriage proposal typically came from the man, and when it came from the woman, the man sometimes re-proposed before the "engagement" was fully accepted and made public. Among the same-sex participants in our study, the proposal more often came from the older partner even though the initial idea typically came from the younger partner, who felt more vulnerable without legal rights or a public commitment.

The participants in our study who eventually gave in to the social pressure to marry were varied in their backgrounds, age, and social circumstances, and this pressure came from their parents, other relatives, their own children, and their friends. Those involved in prolonged negotiations with partners were usually older, at least one was divorced or had been previously involved in another long-term cohabitation, and one partner typically opposed marriage as patriarchal, heterosexist, or simply unnecessary. The opposing partner eventually relented and agreed to marry in order to preserve the relationship or to solidify their legal rights as they grew older. In several cases, the verbal agreement to marry or have a civil union had not been acted upon at the time of the interview, suggesting that becoming engaged can serve as another delaying tactic to actually getting married (Baker and Elizabeth, 2012b).

Our research and other studies suggest that more couples are living together without formalizing their relationships but many eventually decide to "take the next step" to marriage, which is widely seen as a higher level of commitment. However, the decision to marry sometimes involves considerable negotiation between partners about why to formalize, who will benefit, when it should happen, and in what kind of ceremony. Some individuals remain in a cohabiting relationship longer than they choose because the partner is not convinced of the merits of marriage or they have insufficient funds to celebrate the event in the way they choose.

Box 4.1   Marriage versus Civil Unions/Civil Partnerships

Social reformers and progressive activists have led the fight to legalize same-sex unions, arguing that human rights are violated when these relationships are not acknowledged or respected by the state or employers. However, legalizing same-sex unions has been strongly opposed by certain religious groups and social/political conservatives, who view these unions as contrary to religious doctrine, to stable patterns of heterosexuality, and to reproduction, and believe that they represent the decline of the traditional family, the institution of marriage, and public morality. In Canada, same-sex marriage was formally legalized in July 2005, while New Zealand initially created a new category of formalization called "civil union" in 2005 before legalizing same-sex marriage in April 2013. A number of other jurisdictions created new legal categories called "civil union" (Hawaii and Illinois) or "civil partnership" (United Kingdom and Ireland), instead of opening marriage to same-sex couples. In some jurisdictions, these new forms of legalization were also available to different-sex couples, while in others they are reserved for same-sex couples. Civil unions/partnerships typically provide some but not necessarily all of the recognitions and rights afforded married different-sex couples. However, the creation of these alternative forms of formalization usually represents a political compromise between progressives and conservatives that offers some rights and protection, while respecting the traditional idea that marriage is a partnership between a man and a woman with a primary purpose of child-bearing.

Source: Baker and Elizabeth, 2014. *Marriage in the Age of Cohabitation: How and When People Are Tying the Knot in the Twenty-First Century.* Toronto: Oxford University Press.

Who Marries Whom?

Many young people in Western countries insist that they marry for "love" but sociologists always argue that "love" is socially constructed, shaped by interaction and negotiation, gendered practices, past relationships, socio-economic circumstances, and cultural beliefs. The origins of romantic love in Europe date back to feudal times when marriages were arranged to suit family alliances, to provide heirs, and to improve or maintain family wealth, and "love" was not considered essential to the participants in the contract (Schultz, 2006). Husbands and wives were not expected to have their emotional needs gratified within marriage, although that sometimes did happen. Instead, they sought satisfaction in their children, their home and work, in same-sex friendships, or in other relationships. Wealthier people were more likely to develop love relationships but these were often outside marriage and did not always involve sexual activity. Instead, they involved idealized or romanticized love, public acts of gallantry, and deferential attention.

In the past century we have come to associate love and marriage in the West. However, we "fall in love" according to implicit gendered and class-based ideals of attractiveness and appropriate partners, as well as considering our personal values and needs. In addition, this tends to happen at a similar stage in the life cycle as our peers, such as when we complete our education and find regular employment. Nevertheless, the ways that we locate our partners and our ideas about acceptable behaviour before marriage have certainly changed in recent decades. In the last few decades, efforts to locate different-sex and same-sex partners are now more explicit, "recreational sex" is more open, and the search for new partners now operates in public places, newspapers, and the Internet. More individuals now have intimate relationships at an early age and experience several sexual relationships before marriage, while a minority remain chaste until marriage or for life. Most couples cohabit before legal marriage in the liberal states and many delay marriage until they reach 28 to 30 years of age. In addition, more couples avoid legal marriage altogether compared to the 1960s and 1970s.

Sociologists have relied on several theoretical approaches to explain how people choose their marital partners or long-term relationships in free-choice systems. Based on a structural approach, the theory of social **homogamy** suggests that people tend to date and marry those from similar socio-economic, religious, and cultural backgrounds and those from similar age groups. These people usually live in the same neighbourhoods, attend the same schools, join the same clubs, and therefore have more opportunity to meet and socialize together. They also feel comfortable with each other because they share similar social backgrounds, lifestyles, and world views. For example, Canadian statistics show that religion still matters in the choice of marriage partner, as over 90 per cent of respondents who were Muslim, Hindu, or Sikh, and over 80 per cent of Catholics and Jews, married partners of the same religion, as Table 4.1 indicates (Clark, 2006). This explanation, however, cannot say why specific individuals choose each other rather than anyone else from their community of social equals.

Table 4.1 Religion of Partners in Conjugal Unions in Canada, 2006

Religion of Respondent	% of Partners Reporting Same Religion
Sikh	96.9
Muslim	91.4
Hindu	91.2
Catholic	84.0
Jewish	82.6
Christian	82.3
Buddhist	80.8
Protestant	78.7
No religion	74.7
Orthodox Christian	74.3
Eastern religions	72.6
Other religions	54.5

Source: Adapted from Clark 2006. Statistics Canada, Table A.1 at: www.statcan.ca/english/freepub/11-008 XIE/2006003/tables/interreligious_table A1...11/20/2008.

A variation of the structural theory argues that the ideal heterosexual partnership in a patriarchal and capitalist society requires the male to be older, taller, and more successful occupationally because he is expected to be the breadwinner, main decision-maker, and family representative in the community. The woman is expected to be smaller, attractive, and congenial, but not necessarily well-educated or a high earner because her main role is to raise children and maintain the home even if she also earns some household money. Although the laws in Western societies usually give men and women equal rights, vestiges of patriarchy continue in domestic relations. Many individuals are unaware that they are choosing partners based on these ideals because they have internalized patriarchal gender relations.

Based on the psychoanalytic approach, the theory of complementary needs (Winch, 1955) argues that psychological variables are more important than structural or socio-economic ones in determining attraction and mate selection. Rather than choosing a partner like themselves, people select someone with a different personality, who they think will complement their emotional needs, including the need for attention, care, love, deference, or social status. If two people have equally powerful personalities and are very successful occupationally, their "egos" might clash. If one is eager to get ahead in the world while the other is more concerned about being supportive and kind, then these two people may find each other attractive and compatible marriage partners. Another psychological theory suggests that choosing a life partner involves searching for one's ideal mate, who sometimes resembles our opposite-sex parent. Even though young people often vow that they will never marry anyone like their mother or father, they sometimes subconsciously pair up with someone remarkably similar.

A more sociological variation of the ideal mate theory suggests that images of desirable partners are socially constructed, including both positive and negative characteristics of opposite-sex parents, older siblings, and experiences with previous partners. In addition, media representations, including fashion magazines, videos, and advertising, increasingly focus on sexuality, youth, and beauty, especially for women. Many people internalize these idealized images even though they are designed to increase consumption. In a gendered and competitive "marriage market," both men and women attempt to attract the best possible partner they can, considering the attributes they have to exchange. This explanation is derived from social exchange theory.

Developmental theories of mate selection, based on the idea that relationships are negotiated as well as socially constructed, argue that the development of "courtship" is predetermined by neither social nor psychological variables. Instead, who one marries is the end product of chance encounters and a series of interpersonal interactions characterized by disclosing more personal information but also advances and retreats, changing definitions of the situation, negotiations, and resolution of tensions. People may meet unexpectedly and find each other good company, but the path to greater commitment and finally to marriage or a more committed relationship has been portrayed as similar to riding an escalator. Once you step on, it is difficult not to ride to the top because interpersonal and social pressure to enhance commitment comes in various forms. One partner might persuade the other that living together rather than separately would be easier and cheaper, as well as desirable. Alternatively, one partner may receive a job offer in another city and request the other to follow, leading to long-term cohabitation or legal marriage. Relatives and friends might pressure a cohabiting couple to legalize their relationship and once wedding plans are made, they are difficult to cancel even if one partner has second thoughts.

Table 4.2 portrays the various theories of mate selection or marital choice discussed above. Many researchers would combine various theories in their attempt to explain who marries whom, but the fact that sociologists identify patterns in the choice of heterosexual partners suggests that gender, age, social class, religion, and culture still shape people's opportunities and decisions about marriage. Yet, the very existence of cultural and lifestyle diversity in urban areas makes it easier for individuals to follow their own preferences.

Table 4.2 Theories of Mate Selection or Marital Choice

Structural Theories and Social Homogamy	Psychological Theories	Social Construction and Social Exchange Theories	Developmental Theories
• People marry those who are similar in age, socio-economic background, religion, and culture, who also happen to live nearby (social homogamy).	• People marry those they think will complement their psychological needs (complementary needs).	• Initial attraction is based on socio-cultural ideals about desirable mates, including those gained from popular culture and media representations.	• Decisions about commitment and marriage are influenced by emotional advances and retreats, negotiation between partners, conflict resolution skills, and chance factors, as well as social pressure from parents and friends.
• Patriarchal social structures expect the man to be older and taller, to have more education and income, and to be the dominant decision-maker.	• People marry partners who subconsciously remind them of parents, siblings, or "significant others" from the past.	• People compete for partners in a gendered and competitive "marriage market," choosing those with socially desirable attributes.	

The Rise in Same-Sex Marriage

In the past 20 years, same-sex couples have been openly living together and more governments have permitted them to formalize their relationships. However, the numbers remain very small: only about 0.6 per cent of all couples living together in Canada and Australia in 2006 were same-sex partners, compared to 0.7 per cent in New Zealand (Statistics Canada, 2007b). More recent figures show an increase in same-sex couples in Canada, at 0.8 percent of all couples living together in 2011 (Statistics Canada, 2012a). The United States government estimated that 1.0 per cent of couple households consisted of same-sex partners in 2010 (US Census, 2011b).

These figures include only those living in stable relationships who report their status to the census-takers. Some individuals who regularly have same-sex relationships live alone while others may identify as bisexuals and live in heterosexual marriages. Studies suggest that about 3 per cent of American men and less than 2 per cent of American women report that their sexual partners are exclusively of the same sex (Ambert, 2005). In addition, Black et al. (2000) estimated that 30 per cent of gay men and 46 per cent of lesbian women had previously been married to heterosexual partners.

Some same-sex couples are happy to share a home without any legal recognition, but this means that if one partner is rushed to the hospital, the other might not have any visiting privileges or decision-making authority if he or she is not legally defined as a "partner," "spouse," or "family member." If the couple has children, the other partner may not be seen as a "parent" by school officials, doctors, or immigration officers. In many countries, same-sex couples have fought for certain forms of legal recognition, including acknowledgement as legal partners, permission to marry, and equal access to assisted reproduction services, child-fostering, and adoption (McNair et al., 2002; Weeks, 2002; Schulman et al., 2012). These issues remain controversial and have generated strong opposition from some individuals and groups.

The fight to legalize same-sex relationships has been led mainly by social reformers who argue that human rights are violated when these long-term relationships are not acknowledged or respected by the state or employers. While a number of jurisdictions have created a new category of relationship called a civil union or civil partnership, this category, as discussed above, may not share all of the same rights as legal marriage. Its creation represents a political compromise that offers some legal protection while respecting the traditional idea that marriage is a legal partnership between a man and a woman (Moore, 2003). Other jurisdictions (such as Canada) have simply allowed same-sex couples the same marriage rights as heterosexual couples enjoy, although considerable controversy occurred over this political decision.

Legalizing same-sex unions has been strongly opposed by a number of religious groups, including the Catholic Church and fundamentalist Protestants as well as other social conservatives. Opponents tend to view civil unions and same-sex relationships as threatening to the institution of marriage, to public morality, to Biblical teachings, to stable patterns of reproduction and socialization, and to the norm of heterosexuality. Ironically, opposition is also apparent among some sectors of gay and lesbian communities, who see civil unions or civil partnerships as a "consolation prize" for denying them access to "real" marriage, or who generally view the legalization of same-sex relationships as mimicking heterosexual marriage, thereby making it "heterosexist" and "patriarchal" (Baker and Elizabeth, 2012c; Rolfe and Peele, 2011).

Denmark was the first country to legalize same-sex unions in 1989, while Belgium and the Netherlands followed in 2001 (Einarsdottir, 2011). Since then, many other countries have either legalized same-sex relationships or seriously debated the issue. In 2003, the Canadian government drafted legislation to permit **same-sex marriage** but the legality of this bill was immediately challenged and sent to the Supreme Court of Canada. In December 2004 the Supreme Court unanimously determined that the federal government has the right to redefine marriage to include same-sex couples. This meant that federal and provincial laws and regulations had to be amended, and the federal Civil Marriages Act of July 2005 formally legalized same-sex marriage. By the 2006 census, only 16.5 per cent of same-sex couples in Canada were legally married, but this increased to 32.5 per cent by 2011 (Statistics Canada, 2012a).

Are heterosexual and same-sex couples who share a home different in significant ways? Many studies find that gay and lesbian cohabiting couples do not differ significantly from heterosexual couples in their reasons for sharing a home and in some aspects of their relationships. However, they do differ in certain respects. For example, a number of studies find that same-sex cohabitants tend to be older but they also display less allegiance to **monogamy** and permanent relationships and are less conventional in their sexual identity. However, gay men typically display less commitment to monogamy than either lesbians or heterosexual couples, and cohabiting opposite-sex partners show less commitment to monogamy than married opposite-sex partners (Ambert, 2005). Same-sex couples also tend to divide their household labour more equitably and enjoy more autonomy in their activities, friendships, and decision-making than heterosexual married couples. Same-sex couples also report less approval of their relationships from their birth families and lower levels of commitment between the couple, and consequently have higher rates of relationship dissolution than heterosexual couples (Kurdeck, 1998, 2000; Patterson, 2000; Sarantakos, 1998; Schechory and Ziv, 2007; Solomon et al., 2005).

Researchers have also found that same-sex cohabitants who legalize their relationships typically expect to gain three things through formalization: better links with kin, the respect and acknowledgement of their relationship and partner, and the legal benefits and protections that have long been available to married heterosexual couples (Shipman and Smart, 2007). Unlike most heterosexual weddings, the process of legalizing relationships for same-sex couples is simultaneously personal and political because it contains an implicit critique of the marginalization of same-sex intimacy (Schecter et al., 2008). Even the style chosen for the ceremony is sometimes laden with political ramifications. For example, same-sex weddings sometimes entail a second "coming out," complete with all the attendant emotions that accompanied the first one (Baker and Elizabeth, 2012; Smart, 2007b, 2008). By making a public commitment before family, friends, and the marriage celebrant, the couple's sexual preference suddenly becomes clearly evident to all. The rise of same-sex marriage indicates greater diversity within intimate relationships and marriage, at a time when legal marriage rates for heterosexual couples are falling.

Legal Marriage Rates

Since the 1970s, the crude marriage rates (defined as the number of new marriages each year per 1,000 in the total population) have steadily declined in many countries. The decline in legal marriage is often attributed to the rise in informal living arrangements and the fading relevance of marriage as a form of financial security, especially for women (OECD, 2005b: 33). Cross-national differences are apparent in marriage rates but declining rates have created noticeable differences between generations and income groups, with older and wealthier people much more likely to marry.

Marriage rates vary with the rise and fall in living costs, the availability and cost of residential housing, the pressures of war, employment opportunities, and the availability of contraception. The Canadian marriage rate reached a low point of 5.9 marriages per 1,000 people during the Great Depression of the 1930s because couples could not afford to marry and establish separate households. However, the rate rose sharply during World War II, to 10.9, when people had more money and wanted to cement their unions in order to gain emotional security, sexual freedom, and possibly state income support if the husband was killed or injured. After the war, the rate declined until 1961, then increased to over nine marriages per 1,000 people in 1971, and then fell again. The Canadian marriage rate continued to decline from 8.7 in 1975 to 4.4 in 2008 as more people cohabited without legalizing their relationship, and has stabilized at that rate (Statistics Canada, 2003; HRSDC, 2012). In the United States, however, the marriage rate is 7.1 per 1,000 people (HRSDC, 2012).

The average age of first marriage has also increased in many countries since the 1970s, influenced by rising educational requirements for employment and higher housing costs. In Canada, the median age of first marriage in the 1971 was 22.6 years for women and 25 years for men, but this increased to 29.1 for women and 31.1 for men by 2008 (ibid.). Because so many people now divorce and remarry, the average age of all heterosexual marriages in Canada is 31.7 years old for brides and 34.3 for grooms (Statistics Canada, 2003). An Australian study indicates that legal marriage remains popular among most people in that country but especially among people over 40 years old, fundamentalist Christians, non-Christian religious groups, and Asian immigrants (Dempsey and De Vaus, 2004). Table 4.3 shows some cohabitation and marriage statistics for Canada and several other countries, but it is complicated by different ways of calculating them.

Since the 1960s, marriage vows have also been modified. Few brides now promise to obey the groom, which was a part of traditional vows in the past, and more couples now marry outside a church or registry office. In many

Table 4.3 Cohabitation and Marriage Statistics

Country	Consensual Unions, 2006	Crude Marriage Rate, 2006–10	Median Age of First Marriage, 2008–10	
	% of population over 20 years	Marriages per 1,000 population	Brides	Grooms
Australia	8.9*	5.5	27.6	29.6
Canada	8.9	4.4	29.1	31.1
New Zealand	9.3*	12.5**	28.2	29.2
United Kingdom	8.7	4.4	28.5	30.7
United States	5.5	7.1	26.5	28.4
OECD average	6.8	7.2	–	–

*Age 15 plus.
**Per 1,000 not-married population, 2010.

Sources: OECD, *Family Data Base*, Table 3F3.3.A, at: www.oecd.org; VIF (2007); Australian Bureau of Statistics (2011); HRSDC (2012); Statistics New Zealand; UK Office of National Statistics; US Bureau of Census.

jurisdictions, the state has certified marriage commissioners or celebrants, judges, justices of the peace, and clerks of the court to carry out official marriage ceremonies, although where people marry and who marries them varies by jurisdiction. For example, ministers of religion presided over 75.2 per cent of marriages in Canada in 2003 (Statistics Canada, 2007c), but this was the case for only 37.1 per cent of marriages in Australia in 2007 (ABS, 2008d). First marriages are more likely than remarriages to be legalized by ministers of religion. Nevertheless, in some places, weddings can now take place almost anywhere at any time and a wedding industry has developed in which private companies attempt to profit from helping couples to plan elaborate, unique, exotic, romantic, and expensive weddings. The average cost of a traditional marriage, including a wedding trip, has increased significantly in the past 50 years (Ingraham, 2008).

Lower marriage rates, as well as declining fertility and rising divorce rates, are viewed by many social conservatives as trends that demonstrate the decline in the family as a social institution. However, others view these trends as indicators of greater choice and personal freedom in society, permitting more people to form satisfying relationships. Although legal marriage rates are declining and the age of marriage is rising, most people continue to live in couple relationships. For example, almost three-quarters of Canadian women aged 35–39 years live with a partner, either legally married or cohabiting (Statistics Canada, 2007c). This suggests that "marriage" remains very popular if we define it in broader terms. However, marriage systems and cultural practices relating to marriage vary considerably by culture, as we see in the next section.

Cultural Practices in Marriage

All societies create rules about who is permitted to marry, who are preferred marriage partners, when the wedding should take place, what gifts are exchanged, who organizes and finances the celebrations, and where the new bride and groom should live. These rules may be cultural customs or traditions, but sometimes are written into law. For example, all societies develop rules against marrying close relatives (called **incest taboos**) in order to prevent inbreeding and congenital abnormalities in offspring and to limit conflict and jealousy within kin groups. In Western countries, parents, siblings, and (usually) first cousins are not permitted to marry, and incest taboos also include some relatives by marriage and adoption. In addition, people in Western or Christian countries are allowed to marry only one partner at a time although most states (but not all religious institutions) permit remarriage after legal divorce.

In many cultures, romantic love and sexual attraction are considered to be inadequate reasons for sharing a home. Elder family members in these cultures arrange marriages before young people have an opportunity to fall in love with an "inappropriate" partner. In the Muslim Middle Eastern and African countries and parts of Indonesia, India, and Pakistan, parents and older relatives feel that they are more qualified than young people to make these important family decisions that are expected to last a lifetime. Marriage is not about a personal or sexual attraction between the two individuals but instead is seen as an alliance between two families, designed to maintain and enhance their resources and reputation. It is a social institution for reproduction, child-rearing, and continuing the family line. Elder family members of either the bride or groom may make the initial inquiries and intermediaries sometimes help parents find suitable partners for their children. These intermediaries may be relatives, family friends, acquaintances with an extensive network of contacts, or professional marriage brokers who charge a fee for service (Madathil and Benshoff, 2008).

In **arranged marriage** systems, several potential partners might be identified, including the offspring of family friends. After some initial "short-listing" by the young person and her or his parents, the best possible choice would be invited to a family meeting accompanied by his or her parents and perhaps other relatives. The potential partners usually have a chance to meet, to talk with each other, and to see if they could feasibly develop a relationship leading to marriage. If the meeting does not progress well, another candidate might be interviewed with his or her family. When a match looks possible, the two families would meet again to discuss the future, to negotiate gifts and wedding expenses, and to make concrete plans for the wedding.

Immigrants living in westernized countries might encourage their young people to return home to their place of origin to marry a partner already selected by family members still living there. Increasingly, young people expect to exercise some personal choice over their marriage partner or at least to acquire veto rights, especially if they live abroad, have obtained a Western education, or have travelled in Western countries. However, young people may also be pressured to abide by the marriage decisions of their elders, especially if they live in remote rural areas, have little formal education, or have little means of support outside their family's assets.

In South Asian and African countries with arranged marriage systems, parents sometimes make pre-marriage agreements or even child betrothals with other parents before their children reach puberty. These arrangements, which could be initiated when the children are under the age of 10, are sometimes seen as legal contracts that cannot easily be broken without some form of compensation between families. Making such promises early in their children's lives precludes less desirable marriage choices and prevents inappropriate love or sexual attachments from developing among young people (Baker, 2001b).

In arranged marriage systems, greater importance is placed on financial security, potential heirs, and extended family solidarity than on sexual attraction or love between the bride and groom. Potential marital partners are urged to respect each other and their family's wishes, and it is hoped that love will develop after partners marry and share a home. Both families maintain a stake in marital stability, so it is not surprising that arranged marriages less often end in divorce than is the case with free-choice unions. However, in these countries, divorce is often legally restricted, sometimes making it easier for men to divorce their wives than for women to divorce their husbands. In addition, women might be motivated to make the marriage work if they cannot support themselves outside marriage or must forfeit child guardianship rights to the husband or his relatives in a divorce. Increasingly, young people throughout the world are influenced to seek a more intensive and egalitarian relationship as a result of Western education, international travel, foreign films, popular music, the Internet, and global advertising.

In Western countries, the law requires the consent of both bride and groom before a wedding can take place. Young people usually meet their future spouse in school, at work, at community functions, or somewhere in their neighbourhood. Friends and relatives may offer assistance by introducing potential partners but individuals make their own marriage choices based on their perceptions of compatibility and feelings of physical attraction and love. Similar interests and cultural backgrounds are valued in partners, yet other social and gendered ideas also influence our decisions, as discussed earlier in this chapter.

Despite the apparent differences between arranged marriages and free-choice marriages, decisions are shaped by some of the same considerations. In Western marriages, couples expect to marry for "love" but at the same time people marry for a variety of reasons, including companionship, emotional stability, regular and safe sex, the desire for children, and additional financial support. Being acknowledged as an adult and establishing a separate residence from parents may also be motivations for marriage, as the wedding is still considered by many people to be an adult "rite of passage" or social acknowledgement of the attainment of adult status, even when the couple has been living together. Love can certainly develop and thrive outside legal marriage, which suggests that people in all cultures marry for more than love.

Preferred Marriage Partners and the Exchange of Gifts

Some Eastern and African cultures have established preferential marriage rules that stipulate certain categories of people as the most socially desirable partners. In southern India, the cross-cousin or the child of the mother's brother or father's sister is considered to be the most desirable marriage partner, which helps to cement together the two families (Nanda and Warms, 2007). As discussed in Chapter 1, some countries permit more than one spouse at a time (called polygamy), with the typical pattern being for men to marry more than one wife (polygyny) but not for women to take multiple husbands (polyandry). Most polygamous countries do not permit men with insufficient financial resources to marry a second wife, which means that polygamy remains a status symbol for wealthier men. In some polygamous cultures, a man is expected to marry the widow of his dead brother even if he already has a partner (ibid.). This practice, called the levirate, provides some means of support for widows in cultures that do not encourage women to earn their own living. Marriage to a wife's sister (sororate) is encouraged in other cultures, especially if the first wife is infertile or dies prematurely. These customs indicate that marriage is conceptualized as a union or alliance between kin groups rather than as an intimate relationship between individuals (ibid.).

One legal spouse at a time is the law and custom in all Western countries, where bigamy is a criminal offence. The state's requirement of a marriage licence represents an attempt to eliminate bigamy, as does the Christian tradition of "reading the banns" (see Chapter 3). The waiting period between obtaining the marriage licence and celebrating the wedding ceremony may be a few days to several weeks, which is designed to discourage hasty marriages. Now that legal divorce has been made easier to obtain in many places, an increasing percentage of the population marries more than once over a lifetime, referred to as **serial monogamy**.

In cultures with arranged marriage systems, dowries have sometimes been used to attract partners for daughters, to cement alliances between families, and to help establish new households. Dowries could involve payments of money or gifts of property that usually accompany brides into marriage and become part of marriage agreements. Although the types of payment vary considerably, they might include household furnishings, jewels, money, servants, farm or pack animals, or land. If a woman has a large dowry, she can find a "better" husband, which usually means one who is wealthier, healthier, better educated, and from a more respected family. In some cultures, the dowry money becomes the property of the groom's family and in others it is used to establish the bride and groom's new household. Dowries have also been used to provide brides with some measure of financial security or insurance in case of partner abuse, divorce, or widowhood, but how effective this practice is depends on how much control women have over the money or property (Barker, 2003).

In **patrilocal systems** where the bride and groom reside with his family, the dowry money can be an important contribution to the household of the groom's parents. Clearly, this system encourages families to prefer sons over daughters, because males can bring new resources into the household through marriage settlements, males can more easily support the family through employment, and males also perpetuate the family name. Consequently, female fetuses have been aborted and female children and adults have been neglected or mistreated because of the economic stresses perpetuated in the dowry system. This system penalizes families with few resources if they must provide money or property in order to secure a husband for their daughter(s) but have no or few sons to attract dowries. For these reasons, dowries have been outlawed in some countries, such as India, although even there they continue to operate clandestinely in rural areas (Nanda and Warms, 2007).

In other cultures, the groom's kin group has been expected to pay a "bride price" to gain permission to marry the family's daughter, to establish and secure alliances, and to compensate for the bride's lost labour or child-bearing potential in her birth community (Fleising, 2003). This pattern has been more prevalent in subsistent horticultural economies (such as sub-Saharan Africa), in patrilineal societies, and in places where the bride customarily moves to the groom's community. However, dowries and bride prices are disappearing as both men and women become educated and westernized, as more people live in urban areas, and as women gain opportunities to enter the labour force and become self-supporting.

Residence, Relations with Kin, and Surnames

Marriage systems sometimes require either the bride or the groom to relocate and live with one kin group, leaving her or his own family of origin behind. Rules of patrilocality and patrilineal descent require the woman to move to the community or home of her husband's family and give priority to his kin group. The important kinship ties are passed from father to son to grandson, which is the most prevalent pattern with a long history in both Eastern and Western civilizations (Leslie and Korman, 1989: 48). Within this system, a wife would marry into her husband's family, and their children would become members of his kin group. With matrilineal descent, relationships are traced through the female line, downplaying the importance of the father's relatives. Matrilineal descent and **matrilocality**—living with or near the bride's kin group—were practised by some indigenous people in North America, including the peoples of the Iroquois Confederacy at the time of European contact (Brown, 1988).

If newly married couples are considered to be equal members of both kin groups, called **bilateral descent**, they might participate in the family activities of both the bride and groom and could inherit from either side of the family. Both kin membership and inheritance are based on bilateral descent in most Western countries, but among the British upper classes, primogeniture was the rule for inheritance until well into the twentieth century. This meant that the first-born male child inherited the family home or estate and subsequent children received an annual income or smaller amounts of family resources. This system of inheritance maintained the integrity of large landholdings but encouraged younger sons to move away, take on business or professional jobs, become career military officers, or emigrate. Throughout the colonies, younger sons of wealthy British families emigrated and were known as remittance men, after the regular remittance of allowance sent to them. The system also assumed that daughters would marry and be supported by their husbands, although rich daughters often entered marriage with private incomes from their fathers' estates. The system of primogeniture perpetuated legal inequalities that were sometimes resented by sons and daughters.

Upon marriage, surnames have traditionally passed through the male side of the family in the English-speaking or common-law countries, although this was often done through custom rather than law. The bride and the couple's subsequent children took the groom's family name because he was the legal head of the household and his name symbolized their legal and social union. Most couples still maintain this pattern because it seems easier, they think it is a legal requirement, or they feel that one name acknowledges their legal union. However, a name change may mean that the bride loses her professional identity or acquaintances who did not know of her marriage or her new name. In Quebec, married women are legally required to keep their birth names, although they may add their husband's surname to it, but in Ontario brides may choose either their (father's) surname or their husband's at the time of marriage (Baker, 2001b). In addition, anyone may create a new name by going through a legal name change or simply by adopting a new name, as long as this is not done for fraudulent purposes.

Western Weddings and Marriage Practices

We tend to think that Western weddings and marriages vary significantly from the cultural variations discussed above, but symbolic remnants of dowries and bride prices remain in traditional free-choice marriages, even in Western countries. Trousseaus or "glory boxes" consisting of special household items and fancy clothing are still collected by some girls and/or their families for their new home, their weddings, and the "honeymoon." Grooms sometimes purchase expensive (most often diamond) engagement rings to assure their fiancées' consent to marry and give (usually gold) wedding bands during the ceremony (although sometimes both partners exchange rings). Traditionally, brides arranged their weddings with their sisters and mother (Tombaugh, 2009), and the bride's family sometimes paid for the reception meal, while grooms and their families paid for drinks at the reception and for the wedding trip.

In Western countries, traditional weddings are redolent with symbolism that harks back to traditional practices and values of previous eras. The white wedding dress represents the virginity that used to be expected of brides. The bride entering the church on the arm of her father who then "gives her away" to the groom symbolizes the patriarchal exchange of the woman from the authority of one man to another. The throwing of rice or confetti after the ceremony represents the community's wish that the marriage will be fertile and that the couple will be blessed with many children. The sharing of the reception activities and expenses represents the joining together of two families.

Many of these traditions are fading with the rising age of marriage, more remarriages, and opportunities to create individualized wedding ceremonies. The prevalence of remarriages among older partners means that many of the financial costs are now paid by the bride and groom themselves rather than their parents. Although many couples eliminate some traditions from their weddings, a considerable number of couples marry in church, brides wear white dresses and are "given away" by their fathers, and friends and relatives throw confetti. This may be done even when the couple doesn't attend church, the bride is no longer a virgin and rejects patriarchal practices, and they plan to remain child-free (Ingraham, 2008; Otnes and Pleck, 2003). These wedding practices often represent either a desire to maintain cultural traditions or social pressure to retain some practices, regardless of their original meanings.

Since the 1970s, more women have retained their birth name after marriage. This is sometimes a professional decision for those who want to maintain a profile with colleagues, customers, or (in the case of politicians or public performers) their followers or fans. It might also be a feminist statement about unwillingness to lose a former identity. A few women actually choose new surnames that do not relate to their father or husband. However, many women continue to take their husbands' name upon marriage, often to the surprise of professional colleagues and kin. This may involve a conscious effort to discard a difficult or unpopular name, or a public statement about being married as opposed to cohabiting, or a statement about their unity in marriage. Furthermore, some people feel that life would be too complicated with a different name for husband, wife, and children, while some women assume their husband's name because they want to emphasize their new status or rite of passage.

Newly married couples in Western countries usually try to establish a residence apart from both kin groups after marriage, which is called a **neolocal residence**. Most couples prefer this arrangement even if it means accepting a lower living standard and later forgoing live-in child-care services. Although many couples with European backgrounds reside with parents at some point in their marriage, especially when they are in financial difficulty, most would define this living arrangement as a temporary and undesirable hardship. However, certain cultural groups are far more likely to live in extended families, seeing this arrangement as cost-effective, a solution to child-care problems, socially desirable, and culturally appropriate.

These cultural variations indicate that all social groups create customary expectations relating to marriage and weddings, although many of them are unwritten or even unspoken. Such customs evolve over time but individuals sometimes experience family opposition when they try to ignore cultural traditions or attempt to create their own. Both social pressures and the law ensure that couples intending to marry abide by at least some of these rules or practices. Although people have more choice about weddings and marriage partners than they did in the past, they still cannot marry more than one person at a time if they live in a Judeo-Christian country. The law also requires people to reach a certain age in order to marry (the age of majority) and stipulates that some potential partners are unsuitable (close relatives). Declining legal marriage rates suggest that more people are choosing to create their own consensual unions outside of matrimony, but if they legally marry, they often embrace at least some of the traditional practices.

Marriage Quality

Researchers have tried to understand why so many people see marriage as a desirable living arrangement. In one popular motif, "scheming" women are said to push reluctant bachelors into marriage; however, several studies have suggested that men see marriage as desirable and may even benefit more from marriage than women do. Bernard (1972) first popularized the research finding that married men in the United States experience fewer psychiatric problems and less physical illness, and also tend to live longer than single men, but found that this trend was less apparent for women. Bernard argued that men do well in marriage because they have someone to care for them physically and emotionally, to keep their households functioning, and to look after their children. In contrast, women marry at some cost to their own physical and emotional health because they are expected to continually cater to other people's needs as well as to their own.

De Vaus (2002) used this earlier American research as a starting point to see how marriage affected the well-being of men and women in Australia. When a range of mental disorders were considered (including mood swings, anxiety, and drug and alcohol abuse), he found that married people were less likely to experience these problems than single people. De Vaus concluded that regardless of whether they are married or not, women are more at risk of mood and anxiety disorders than men, but men are more at risk of drug and alcohol disorders. Marriage and child-rearing do not increase the risk for either men or women. However, married people are less likely to report these problems than never-married or separated/divorced people. Although people with these disorders may be less likely to marry in the first place or to stay married, De Vaus concluded that having a close relationship seems to act as a buffer to health-related problems.

Using American data, Waite (2005) demonstrated statistically that on a wide range of indicators of health and well-being, legally married people are healthier, happier, and live longer than never-married people, but only if they rate their relationship as "moderately good" or "excellent." Although acknowledging that unhealthy or unhappy people are less likely to marry and stay married, she also argued that a close intimate relationship assists people to fight against stress and poor health. However, a poor and unsatisfying relationship can damage people's health and well-being.

Marriage satisfaction research is usually based on a cross-sectional design done at one point in time, with few studies following the same couples over periods of more than 10 years. This is because longitudinal studies are expensive and difficult when people move away or withdraw from the research project. However, Karney and Bradbury (1995) surveyed 100 longitudinal studies of marriage from which they created a model to explain why some survive and others dissolve. They called it the "vulnerability-stress-adaptation" model. These researchers noted that marriage satisfaction and stability are influenced by a combination of individual factors, family variables, and life events. The "enduring vulnerabilities" are the strengths and weaknesses that each spouse brings to the marriage, influenced by their upbringing, social background, and their attitudes. Stressful life events are incidents, transitions, or circumstances that can impinge on their relationship and create tension or stress. Adaptive processes refer to the ways that people cope with stress and conflict, and how couples communicate and support each other. The authors concluded that the strategies for dealing with life events and resolving conflicts vary by these factors, which then influence marital satisfaction.

Some research suggests that couples married for a long time can impart their wisdom to the younger generation whose marriages are far less likely to last (Parker, 2002). However, the current cohort of young married couples is experiencing very different social, economic, political, and cultural circumstances than those married for many years. Nevertheless, marriage preparation courses and marriage counselling are becoming more prevalent, as therapists, policy-makers, and older couples express increasing concern about high rates of relationship breakdown, especially in the United States. Most of these courses, however, are targeted to those who are planning to marry and those whose marriages have already broken up. Few formal supports exist for ongoing relationships despite the fact that the research suggests that rewarding and lasting marriages require regular and intentional maintenance (ibid.).

Much of the sociological, social work, and policy research about couples deals with conflict rather than marriage durability. These studies find that male violence against female partners is surprisingly prevalent within intimate relationships, although female violence against males also occurs but is less often reported to authorities because of cultural ideas about masculinity and less physical harm caused by the violence. However, both are very consequential for individuals, families, communities, and the state.

Male Violence against Female Partners

If we look to the media, violence seems to be increasing but it may just be reported more often. Even in official statistics, the topic of violence within intimate relationships is researched, defined, and presented in different ways. While some researchers depend on police reports, others talk to people in the general population and rely on self-reported data. A 2009 study on family violence in Canada found that self-reported spousal violence remained at the same level as in a previous 2004 study, with 6 per cent of respondents with a current or former spouse reporting being physically or sexually victimized by that spouse in the five years preceding the survey (Statistics Canada, 2011: 5).

In this study, men were just as likely to report incidents of family violence as women, but women were three times more likely to report more serious incidents, such as being sexually assaulted, beaten, choked, or threatened with a gun or knife (ibid., 10). In addition, people under 35 years of age were more likely to be victimized than older people. Although the victims were less likely to report these incidents to the police in 2009 than in the earlier study, the seriousness of the incidents remained stable between 2004 and 2009. Furthermore, about 17 per cent of Canadians said that they had experienced some form of emotional or financial abuse from a partner, with put-downs and name-calling being the most prevalent form of abuse. Between 2000 and 2009, 16 per cent of all solved homicides in Canada were spousal homicides, with women being killed three times more often than men (ibid., 6).

An earlier Canadian telephone survey found that 29 per cent of women reported physical or sexual abuse by an intimate partner over their lifetime and one-third of these said they feared for their lives at some point in the relationship (Jaffe et al., 2003: 5). Physical abuse is not usually an isolated event, as some women have been assaulted and have sought help many times from friends, neighbours, social workers, and the police (Johnson, 1990; Leibrich et al., 1995). Adults who abuse their spouses (and children) have a higher probability of coming from families where their parents engaged in similar behaviour, and women who were abused during "courtship" have a much higher probability of being abused during marriage (O'Leary et al., 1989; Barnes et al., 1991). Furthermore, cohabiting women are more likely than married women to experience partner violence and also severe violence, including homicide (Brownridge, 2008). Separated women are more likely than those who are married or divorced to be assaulted and killed by former partners (Wilson and Daly, 1994; Krug et al., 2002: 96; DeKeseredy, 2009). This suggests that remaining in a violent relationship is dangerous for women, but that taking action to escape the violence can also have lethal consequences.

Comparative research suggests that physical abuse within intimate relationships becomes more prevalent when a society condones violence, when violence has become a form of entertainment in films and sports events, and when a country is engaged in war (Krug et al., 2002). Women become more vulnerable to physical, sexual, and emotional abuse if they see their male partner as the "head of the household" or if they are financially dependent on him and cannot support their children alone (Baker, 2001b: 110). Women are also more vulnerable to abuse if they are cohabiting or are separated from their partner and living in low-income housing developments with other single parents (DeKeseredy, 2005, 2009; Brownridge, 2008). Certain cultural groups, such as indigenous women in Canada, Australia, and New Zealand, report exceptionally high rates of abuse by male partners (McGillvray and Comaskey, 1998; Brownridge, 2003).

Domestic violence programs, operated by both government and private agencies, typically offer crisis intervention, first helping a woman to develop protection plans that could involve laying charges against her partner or former partner. The woman is also helped to find transitional housing for herself and her children, to engage a lawyer, and, if necessary, to apply for income support to cover living expenses. In both individual counselling and group therapy, battered wives are encouraged to view partner abuse as unacceptable regardless of the circumstances or their own behaviour, although most abused women find it difficult to erase lingering feelings that the abuse was somehow their own fault. Male abusers are more often charged with an offence and encouraged (or required) to accept counselling, which includes taking responsibility for their acts of violence rather than blaming their partners. They are also helped to control their emotions, develop better communication skills, learn non-violent behaviour from male role models, and redefine what it means to be a man.

Community agencies and school boards sometimes collaborate to develop violence-prevention strategies focusing on staff development and awareness, community involvement, and student programs (Wolfe and Jaffe, 2001: 290; Mullender et al., 2003: 147). One of the early American programs to promote violence awareness and safety skill development with school-age children was implemented by the Minnesota Coalition for Battered Women. The program targeted elementary and secondary students throughout the state to ensure that all children knew about alternatives to domestic violence (Wolfe and Jaffe, 2001: 290). Action against family violence also includes sensitization workshops for professionals, such as teachers and judges, to increase their knowledge of program options and the personal and social implications of this form of violence (DeKeseredy, 2009). In addition, support services for **at-risk families** have been provided when violence seems to be a possibility because of their stressful circumstances.

Despite these initiatives, Sev'er (2002) concluded that little has changed in the past two decades for urban Canadian women who do not turn to women's shelters. Many women remain in abusive relationships because they do not know where to turn for assistance, because they cannot find temporary and low-income housing, or because they cannot support their children on their own. Tolerance of abuse continues because some women feel that it may somehow be their own fault, while others fear reprisal from partners who threaten to kill them if they go to the police or tell anyone about the incident.

Over the past few decades, international concern and action have grown in regard to intimate partner violence against women, and various conferences have been held and resolutions and manifestos drafted in an effort to reduce its incidence (Baker, 2006). The first convention to declare discrimination against women as an international issue was the 1979 United Nations Convention on the Elimination of All Forms of Discrimination against Women. In 1994, the UN designated domestic violence as a human rights issue (Rodney, 1995). Conventions, however, do not have the same binding force as domestic law, although they place an externally monitored international standard of accountability upon signatory countries. United Nations conventions are also designed to raise awareness and have widened the terms of reference associated with domestic violence.

Most governments continue to express concern about all forms of domestic violence and abuse but the absence of public money remains the major impediment to establishing effective programs and services. Private donations as well as public funds support transition houses for battered women, and these safe houses are often staffed by volunteers and operate on the verge of closing due to lack of ongoing funds. Follow-up therapy and counselling may also be necessary for the entire family, but these services cost money to establish and maintain. Many women manage to leave abusive relationships to care for themselves and their children alone, or are able to find more satisfying relationships.

Despite acknowledging the serious nature of violence in intimate relationships, states have not always delivered sufficient program funding to deal with the rising number of reported cases, and some governments have encouraged cohabiting couples to marry regardless of the nature of their relationship. However, researchers have found "barriers" to legal marriage, as we will see in the next section.

Barriers to Legal Marriage

Policy discussion, especially in the United States, has often suggested that the plight of lone mothers living on low earnings or social benefits would be resolved if they simply married their male partners. Public campaigns have tried to convince low-income Americans of the value of marriage, and state income-support programs have been made less generous to encourage unmarried couples receiving social benefits to legalize their relationships. American research suggests that those with higher educational qualifications and incomes have much higher marriage rates than poorer and less-educated people. In contrast, the "disadvantaged" are only half as likely to marry but more often cohabit. When disadvantaged people do marry, their divorce rates tend to be higher, and these rates have been rising in recent years (McLaughlin and Lichter, 1997).

Qualitative and quantitative studies have uncovered a number of barriers to legal marriage among disadvantaged Americans. Edin and Reed (2005) reviewed the recent research and found that disadvantaged men and women highly value marriage but are unable to meet the high standards of relationship quality and financial stability they believe are necessary to sustain a marriage and avoid divorce. Many see marriage as "sacred," more committed than cohabitation, and something they want to have for themselves "some day." Many cohabiting partners with low income and low education are already parents and have had a child by another partner, although this child was not usually planned. Nearly one-third of poor American women aged 25 and older have had a child outside marriage compared to 5 per cent who were not poor (Hoffman and Foster, 1997).

American research suggests that low-income men and women do not view marriage as a prerequisite for child-bearing but they often say that children are better off when raised within marriage (Edin and Reed, 2005). However, the ideal of marriage remains unrealized because of the complexities of their lives. Their relationships are often conflict-ridden and involve partner violence and frequent separations. Furthermore, the stigma of divorce is deemed greater than the stigma of having a child outside marriage. Both men and women struggle to find employment that can pay the bills, and many couples experience bouts of unemployment and low-paid jobs. Before they can marry, many feel that they need a secure income, enough money for a mortgage on a modest home, some furniture, a car, some savings in the bank, and some money for a "decent" wedding (Edin and Kefalas, 2005).

Over the past few decades, legal marriage seems to have lost some of its instrumental value as more women become self-supporting, contraception and abortion are widely available, premarital sex and cohabitation have become more socially acceptable, and marriage is no longer necessary for women's social or legal status (Edin and Reed, 2005). In fact, legal marriage would make little difference to the daily lives of many mothers and fathers who are already cohabiting. Yet American research has found that the symbolic value of marriage remains. Edin and Kefalas (2005) argued that marriage has become a symbol of status and luxury rather than of necessity. It has become a relationship that carries much higher expectations of relationship quality and financial stability, and many of the poor cannot meet this higher marital standard.

Conclusion

Most young people, especially those living in smaller communities and rural areas, expect to find a partner, establish a household together, and produce children; but the timing of these events still depends on their gender, educational attainment, financial resources, social class background, and culture. Women still marry at younger ages than men, to men slightly older than themselves, and this age gap grows larger with remarriages after divorce. In some cultural communities, women are encouraged to marry well before the median national marriage age, especially if they are immigrants from countries that limit dating, expect premarital virginity for women, and prefer arranged marriages.

Although more people now cohabit without formalizing their relationship, the majority of people eventually marry and stay together for life. In both Western and Eastern countries, people marry for a variety of reasons, and many remain married even when their relationship is not particularly satisfying, either emotionally or sexually. Two can live cheaper than one, few parents want to forfeit the daily companionship of their children, marriage partners derive satisfaction and esteem from other aspects of their lives, and most married people want to grow old with their families intact.

Nevertheless, satisfaction seldom remains the same over the years of marriage, as children come and go and personal circumstances change. Levels of satisfaction tend to be the highest at the beginning of marriage as well as after many years of life together, but the middle years seem more prone to disappointments. Some of the problems in middle age are related to difficulties dealing with adolescent children, but even child-free couples report lower levels of satisfaction at this time. However, marital roles are changing as more mid-life women are employed full-time, while more men are able (or forced) to change jobs, return to school, or create their own businesses. Some of these transitions may strengthen levels of satisfaction but they may also push marriage partners towards separation.

Some couples who stay together into old age have always been satisfied with their marriages while others manage either to adapt to their disillusionment or to reinvigorate their relationship. Over time, most relationships are cemented with shared understandings, memories, children and grandchildren, and mutual love, caring, and companionship. Although social scientists tend to focus on conflict and marriage breakdown, most couples in reality remain together for life. Yet this is seldom reiterated in the media or in academic research.

Questions for Critical Thought

1. Is mate selection still socially regulated in any way? What patterns are evident in current choices of marital partners?

2. Why do cohabiting couples who eventually marry so often include the symbols of traditional weddings (such as virginal white dresses, gold wedding rings, and fathers "giving away" their daughters to their husbands)?

3. Why do women continue to live with men who abuse them? Why don't they leave when abusive incidents first occur?

4. Do young people still aspire to lifelong marriages or do these relationships now seem boring?

Questions for Debate

1. Are there any real reasons left to legally marry or is cohabitation the same thing?

2. Men need marriage more than women. Discuss.

3. If gender equity is a widespread value, why do men still propose to women?

Suggested Readings

Ambert, Anne-Marie. 2005. "Same-Sex Couples and Same-Sex-Parent Families: Relationships, Parenting and Issues of Marriage." Vanier Institute of the Family, at: <www.vifamily.ca>. Ambert surveys the literature on same-sex relationships and discusses the relationship between sexual preference, commitment, and family practices.

Edin, Kathryn, and Joanna M. Reed. 2005. "Why Don't They Just Get Married? Barriers to Marriage among the Disadvantaged," *Marriage and Child Wellbeing* 15, 2: 117–36.

Ingraham, C. 2008. *White Weddings*, 2nd edn. New York: Routledge. This book is one of the few academic studies of weddings, examining the institution of marriage and the "wedding industry" in America, and how both perpetuate romantic and sacred notions of heterosexuality.

Stanley, S.S., G.K. Rhoades, and H.J. Markham. 2006. "Sliding versus Deciding: Inertia and the Premarital Cohabitation Effect," *Family Relations* 55 (Oct.): 499–509. This American study suggests that many couples slide from dating to cohabitation, and from cohabitation to marriage with little actual decision-making.

Suggested Websites

Australian Bureau of Statistics
www.abs.gov.au
> This website contains a wealth of statistics and studies on families in Australia.

National Council on Family Relations
www.ncfr.org
> This American association provides an educational forum for family researchers, educators, and practitioners to share in the development and dissemination of knowledge about families and relationships.

5 Child-bearing, Child-rearing, and Childhood

Learning Objectives

◎ To understand how parenting, childhood, and adolescence have been influenced by changing patterns of family formation, education, and work; greater use of technology; professional practices; and new ideas about childbirth, parenthood, and children's rights.

◎ To acknowledge that socio-economic circumstances influence fertility choices and outcomes.

◎ To learn how social policies and professional practices have shaped the lives of parents and children, especially those who are poor, abused, neglected, or live with disabilities.

Introduction

In this chapter, I explore the ways that decisions and experiences relating to pregnancy and childbirth have changed over the decades and whether childhood in the twenty-first century is much different from how it was in the past. These questions can be approached by examining official statistics and by researching popular practices, beliefs, and theories, as well as public controversies and media representations about having and raising children. Generally, the research suggests that having children has become more of a choice but that social patterns exist in who chooses to reproduce, and in the timing and experience of childbirth. Second, childbirth has become dominated by medical and technological interventions. Third, perceptions of childhood, parenting styles, and the experiences of children and youth have varied over the decades with changes in the economic value of children to families, new ideas about child development, different forms of supervision, more influence from the media and technology, and broader changes in the larger society (Synnott, 1983; Wall, 2004, 2009; Albanese, 2009b).

Children's upbringing continues to be influenced by family members but it is increasingly shaped by factors outside the family, including computer games, advertising, the Internet, other children, and non-family care providers. In addition, educational expectations and opportunities have increased for all children but especially for those from lower-income families. Nevertheless, the research indicates that children's **socialization** and life chances continue to be influenced by their family situations, and these vary by gender, culture, and the political and economic circumstances of the community and country of residence.

To understand how societal changes have influenced child-bearing, child-rearing, and childhood, the central questions to be considered include how much change has actually occurred in recent decades and what factors continue to shape parenting practices and growing up in liberal states today? Let us begin by examining parenthood and childhood in the past.

Parenting and Childhood in the Past

In the nineteenth century, fertility and parenting practices differed considerably by gender, age, and social circumstances, just as they do today. However, they were particularly influenced by unreliable contraception, the assumption of heterosexuality, and gender roles. Marriage implied that the wife was sexually available to her husband on a regular basis, but unless couples used some form of contraception or abstained from sexual intercourse, many young wives spent a considerable amount of time pregnant and nursing, and some suffered numerous miscarriages. Contraception has been available for hundreds of years but in the past it was less reliable and socially unacceptable to purchase and use. The common view was that the purpose of marriage was reproduction, and using contraception or remaining childless was interpreted by some as a rejection of femininity/masculinity, religious values, and traditional marriage.

Both men and women were expected to marry and reproduce. Those who did not want children could avoid marriage, but single adults were continually pressured to find a partner and "start a family" unless they joined a religious order that promoted celibacy or were ill or disabled. Women's employment options were limited and single women were often expected to care for their aging parents or sibling's children. Instead of developing independent lives, many single women lived with relatives with little autonomy or status. In rural districts, some sons also remained on the family farm to assist their fathers and therefore found fewer opportunities to meet potential wives. When men did marry, they had to be prepared to support a wife and new baby within the first year of marriage.

Husbands were expected to continue the family line, represent the family to the community, earn the household income, and become the main disciplinarian of their children. While many wives became conscientious and nurturing mothers, others struggled with the lack of alternative occupations, the heavy domestic workload, and the social isolation of housework, especially in low-income rural families. Couples unable to reproduce were pitied, but childless married women were not always encouraged or even permitted to accept full-time jobs.

Households in the nineteenth century generally contained more children than today, as well as more relatives, servants, and paying boarders. In working-class families, pregnant women needed to carry on with their domestic chores right up until childbirth unless they could find relatives to help run the household. Infant and maternal death rates were higher than today and working-class mothers and babies were at greater risk because of their harsh living conditions and lack of health-care services (Bradbury, 2005, 2012). As soon as working-class children were old enough, they were expected to contribute to the family economy, first helping around the home, and later contributing their labour or wages to the household.

Nineteenth-century children sometimes worked in unskilled and danger-ous jobs until laws were enacted to abolish child labour and establish compul-sory education for children under 16 years of age. However, many low-income parents withdrew their children from school for periods of time when they needed their labour or permanently if they obtained permission from author-ities after the child turned 14 (Gaffield, 1990). In other words, childhood and especially adolescence were not much different from adult life in nineteenth-century low-income families.

Box 5.1   Child Labour in Canada

Canadian historian Bettina Bradbury here describes the issue of child labour in late nineteenth-century Canada.

> In the early phases of industrialization, between the 1860s and the 1890s, children as young as ten and eleven were employed in [Canadian] factories and workshops, though never in the proportion found in the early industrial revolution in Great Brit-ain or in the mill towns of the eastern United States. The dangers and exploitation that such young workers could face were revealed in several investigations and commissions during the 1880s [notably the Royal Commission on the Relations of Labour and Capital, which reported in 1889]. Commissioners uncovered horrible evi-dence in 1888 about the abuse of children. In Montreal, workers revealed that one cigar manufacturer disciplined young children by locking them up for hours in a small dark room. Other employers beat young children and imposed heavy fines as they attempted to control their youthful and unruly workforce and to teach them the discipline necessary for factory work. The revelations of the commission encour-aged the application of Factory Acts that had recently been passed but seldom enforced. By the mid-1880s most provinces had passed legislation to curtail the employment of girls under fourteen and boys under twelve in factories. These acts also placed restrictions on the kinds of work and times of day women could be employed. Early legislation was limited. It did not cover small workshops, such as the sweatshops where so many girls were employed sewing. Nor, initially, did it cover shops or even mines.

Source: Bradbury (2005: 85–6). Bettina Bradbury. 2005. "Social, Economic, and Cultural Origins of Contemporary Families" in M. Baker (ed). *Families: Changing Trends in Canada*, 5th ed. Toronto: McGrawa-Hill Ryerson, p. 85–6.

In contrast, middle-class families usually could afford to hire servants to help with domestic work, but the wife/mother remained responsible for managing the household. These parents sent their children to schools to learn to read and write but also to learn the value of hard work, discipline, religious values, and obedience. For the wealthy, early childhood was seen as a time of play and learning, and parents could afford to pamper their children and idealize them as symbols of innocence because they did not need their labour. Rarely were upper-class parents fully involved in daily child care, as babies were seldom breast-fed by wealthy mothers but rather by "wet nurses" hired for this purpose. The wealthy family home contained adult-only areas separate from the children's rooms where nannies and servants catered to their needs, and wealthy parents hired tutors to educate their children until they were sent to school. While boys sometimes boarded at distant private schools, girls were more often educated locally or at home. In the past, many privileged children were raised largely by servants and teachers but some nannies worked for the family for many years.

Prior to the late nineteenth century, neither church nor state protected children or granted them legal rights because they were considered the property of their parents. Adults learned to parent from their own parents and relatives, with some assistance from religious leaders, doctors, and teachers. British parents were discouraged from praising their children or allowing them to express themselves verbally because children were expected to be "seen but not heard," to obey their elders, and to abide by parental rules until they left home. Physical punishment was freely used to discipline children at home, but schools were also run with rigid and hierarchical rules attuned to the larger class-based society (Houston and Prentice, 1988).

By the 1920s and 1930s, governments and (male) professionals became concerned about high infant mortality rates and urged mothers to accept the new "scientific" child-rearing practices, including bottle-feeding with infant formula. They believed that mothers themselves were promoting child health problems through lack of knowledge about sanitation, nutrition, and care, and suggested that the worldly ambitions of the "new woman," who desired education and employment, would lead to the deterioration of family life (Strong-Boag, 1982: 161). Strict scheduling was recommended for infant care, which meant that if babies were hungry before the designated feeding time, they often were left alone to cry. Fathers were not expected to be involved in physical parenting, especially with infants, but they were urged to be understanding of the mother's responsibilities and to provide economic security for the family. Governments and voluntary organizations established special clinics for expectant mothers and babies as part of national campaigns to reduce infant mortality and improve baby care.

In 1946, Dr Benjamin Spock's *Baby and Child Care* first appeared, encouraging a more permissive approach to parenting and advising mothers to trust their "common sense" and enjoy their babies (Wall, 2009). In addition, developmental psychology, especially the research on "maternal deprivation" and attachment, began to influence child-rearing advice. The mother's absence during the early years, even temporarily, was thought to truncate children's development, which encouraged the celebration of "maternalism" and homemaking for married women.

By the 1960s and 1970s, ideas about child care became more flexible. Husbands were encouraged to take more interest in their wives' pregnancies and to support them at childbirth. Both parents were encouraged to cuddle children when they cried or wanted attention, to be verbally expressive in their affection, and to assist each child's self-development. At the same time, more mothers were drawn into paid work by rising living costs and labour market changes, which created child-care problems. Many mothers felt guilty about leaving their children with relatives or neighbours, but few public child-care services were available at the time. Feminists and other reformers who supported employment equity challenged the gendered division of labour both at home and at work. They lobbied for public child-care services with state regulation and subsidies, and also encouraged husbands to become more involved in childbirth, housework, and child-rearing (Benoit et al., 2002).

Over the past centuries, values about parenthood gradually shifted from emphasizing children's economic utility to the family to focusing on love, companionship, and enjoyment (Albanese, 2009b; Cameron, 1997). Children's economic contributions and their potential to support parents in old age became less important with compulsory education and old-age pensions. Redefinitions of motherhood later influenced how children were valued, particularly the new ideologies that focused on the mother's duty to support the well-being of the child and to raise "quality" children (Wall, 2009). The value of children was further enhanced by government programs focusing on children's welfare and rights rather than simply on their discipline and education. The economic utility of children has now been replaced with the ideology that children are a form of social capital and future investment for the nation (Jenson, 2004; Elizabeth and Larner, 2009).

Fertility Patterns

In recent decades, fertility rates have declined in most OECD countries. Demographers estimate that if each couple produced about 2.1 children, population stability would be maintained and countries could replace their deaths with new births. However, the total fertility rates (or the average number of children per woman who has completed child-bearing) are now below replacement levels, averaging 1.74 children per woman in 2009 across OECD countries (OECD, 2011a: 45). In Canada, the total fertility rate was even lower, at 1.66, but the fertility rate in South Korea has plummeted to 1.15 (OECD,

2011a). Even the Southern European countries now experience low fertility rates, obscuring previous correlations between high fertility, Catholicism, and traditional family values (Castles, 2002). Both Italy and Spain had total fertility rates of 2.4 in 1970 but 1.4 in recent years (ibid.). Table 5.1 shows the fertility decline in selected OECD countries from 1970 to 2009.

Table 5.1   Total Fertility Rates in Selected Countries, 1970 and 2009 (number of children per woman)

Country	1970	2009
Australia	2.9	1.90
Canada	2.0	1.66
Denmark	2.0	1.84
France	2.5	1.99
New Zealand	3.3	2.14
Sweden	1.9	1.94
United States	2.0	2.01

Sources: 1970 figures extracted from OECD (2005b: 29); Chart GE3.2. © OECD 2005; 2009 figures extracted from OECD 2011c. *Society at a Glance*, p. 45, GE2.1.

Policy-makers are concerned about declining fertility because it could lead to "population aging" or a higher percentage of seniors in the population, signalling future labour shortages, declining productivity, and fewer taxpayers to pay for social programs such as old-age pensions. Despite these concerns, fertility rates have been declining since the late 1800s, influenced by industrialization, urbanization, and the rising cost of raising children. Infant mortality rates began to decline in the 1920s with improved living standards and health care, permitting couples to produce fewer children because more were expected to reach maturity (Chesnais, 1992). Child-rearing costs also increased, while the benefits of large families declined when more people moved to urban areas, compulsory education laws prevented children from working, and governments developed old-age pensions. Declining fertility is also related to improvements in contraception, legalized abortion, preferences for smaller families, and the difficulty mothers experience combining earning and caring (Weston and Parker, 2002; Gray et al., 2007).

Women are now bearing their first child later in life, at an average age of about 28 years in OECD countries in 2009, compared to 24 in 1970 (OECD, 2011c: chart SF2.3A; OECD, 2007b: 45). The growing tendency to postpone pregnancy provides advantages for women, who can complete their education, find employment, and possibly become eligible for parental benefits prior to motherhood. However, postponing motherhood makes pregnancy riskier and contributes to lower fertility rates.

Most women cannot afford or no longer wish to refrain from paid work in order to raise large families (Castles, 2002). Yet governments can influence fertility rates: these rates remain relatively high in countries such as France and Sweden, which have formal care provisions for preschool children and flexible work arrangements for employed parents. Rates are also high in countries with large percentages of cultural minorities who value reproduction but where birth control is less accessible and unregulated child care is inexpensive, such as the United States. In contrast, women typically have fewer children when they must struggle to earn a living, and public discourse makes them feel guilty about "neglecting" their children.

Births outside marriage have also increased but most are to cohabiting women between 25 and 35 years old. In Nordic countries, over half of all births now occur outside marriage compared to about 10 per cent in 1960, while about 45 per cent of births in New Zealand, 32 per cent in Australia, and 28 per cent in Canada occurred outside marriage in 2004 (OECD, 2007a). Teenage birth rates have also declined, from an average of 34 births per 1,000 women aged 15–19 in 1980 to 16 in 2004 in OECD countries (OECD, 2005b: 86; OECD, 2007a). However, there are many country variations. The teen birth rate in Canada was 13.8 in 2004 but 50.3 in the United States and 3.5 in Korea (OECD, 2007a), suggesting that cultural, socio-economic, and social service factors influence these rates. The declining teenage pregnancy rate is usually applauded because early pregnancy is associated with disadvantage, including low education, poor earning capacity, and poor life chances for children and mothers (Battle, 2012; Hobcraft and Kiernan, 2001).

Cross-national variations in teenage birth rates are influenced by trends in sexuality, access to contraception, ideas about women's roles, and the percentage of disadvantaged groups in the population (OECD, 2005b: 86). Teen fertility rates remain relatively high in countries such as the United States with large percentages of visible minorities living on low incomes, few employment opportunities, and lack of access to contraception. These minorities tend to cohabit and marry at younger ages and place a higher value on parenthood as an indicator of adult status and love between partners (Mink, 1998; Edin and Reed, 2005).

National fertility rates also vary by parents' economic circumstances (OECD, 2008a: 63). The current stereotype is that poor people make more babies but this is not the case in many European countries that provide generous benefits for families. For example, in countries such as Austria, Denmark, France, Germany, and Sweden, the top income quintile (or one-fifth) of income earners have more children than the bottom quintile. However, in the liberal states, the poor are more likely to reproduce (ibid.). Furthermore, women with high levels of education and strong career commitment are less likely than other women to marry and have children (Weedon et al., 2006).

In the 1960s, the United Nations encouraged governments to support "zero population growth" and to develop reproductive services such as affordable contraception and legalized abortion. When fertility rates dropped farther than anticipated, some governments expressed concern about the national economic consequences of declining fertility. Researchers and policy-makers generally agree that lower teenage birth rates are socially beneficial but they do not always acknowledge the advantages of low birth rates for other women. Having fewer children enables women to pursue their educational goals and retain employment, which raises living standards and provides tax revenue for the state. Fewer children per family could also enable each child to receive more parental attention. Although developing countries attempt to counteract overpopulation and urban crowding by promoting family planning, the liberal states often fund these services only for low-income or "problem" families, urging wealthier couples to reproduce. This suggests that having children is not always seen as women's choice or the couple's decision but as something governments want to control.

Why Have Children?

Although most adults become parents, they are now more likely to question whether or not they really want to have children, how many they should have, and when they should start trying to conceive (VIF, 2008). In 2006, only 7 per cent of Canadian women aged 20 to 39 reported that they did not want any children; the average desired number of children for those women who wanted children was 2.2, while the average among men was 2.1 (ibid.). In Australia, only 5 per cent say their ideal is to remain childless (with more men than women saying this), and the ideal family size is slightly higher than in Canada (Weston et al., 2004). The actual fertility rates are also lower in Canada, where more mothers work full-time and the provinces provide lower levels of income support for mothers caring at home (Baker, 2006).

Raising children into socially responsible adults is a difficult task requiring vision, commitment, and years of hard work. Nevertheless, researchers have found that most parents see children as the natural outcome of marriage rather than a conscious choice. In attempting to explain why people continue to reproduce despite the well-publicized hardships of child-rearing, sociologists gloss over parental instincts or biological explanations and focus on two social reasons. One relates to social pressures while the other emphasizes perceived costs and benefits.

Since the 1970s, sociologists have argued that having children is viewed as a sign of maturity, normality, and sexual competence. These conclusions are reached after questioning parents and studying people's reactions to childless couples. When parents are asked why they had children, they usually portray the experience in positive terms, discussing opportunities to relive the joys of childhood, transmit their values and knowledge, and receive unconditional love. They also mention the desire to create their own social group and pass on their family name and genes (Cameron, 1990; May, 1995; Erfani and Beaujot, 2006). In contrast, individuals who choose *not* to reproduce tend to emphasize the negative aspects but are often stigmatized by others as selfish, irresponsible, immature, materialistic, overly career-oriented, lonely, and even psychologically unstable (Morell, 1994; Cameron, 1997; Baker, 2005b). Statistically, younger people view the childless choice more liberally, yet it is still widely accepted that married couples *should* produce children.

The social pressure to reproduce comes from many sources: religious leaders, conservative politicians, family, friends, and even strangers. Many churches have viewed the purpose of marriage as reproduction, and after the wedding ceremony friends and family often symbolize this expectation by throwing symbols of fertility (such as confetti or rice) on the couple. Governments and community leaders see children as necessary because they need future taxpayers, voters, workers, and consumers. Parents often want grandchildren to amuse them and later watch over them in old age, and siblings want nieces and nephews to expand their family networks. Parents expect to share their child-related experiences with friends, as well as stories about the joys and problems of child-rearing. Television advertisements, especially for cleaning products and fast food, show happy parents (usually mothers) interacting with attractive, healthy, and loving children, encouraging us to see child-rearing as desirable and rewarding. Consequently, many people romanticize child-rearing and downplay the disadvantages.

Another social theory about why people reproduce is that they believe children will enhance their lives in ways that compensate for the expense and hard work. Parents say they receive pleasure and a sense of achievement from watching their children develop, and that producing children enhances personal identity (Willen and Montgomery, 1996; Erfani and Beaujot, 2006). Reproduction is associated with maturity because it provides visible evidence of sexual and social competence, serves as a rite of passage from childhood to adulthood, and fulfills dominant conceptions of masculinity and femininity. The reported disadvantages include the time and cost involved and the loss of personal freedom. Nevertheless, most people highlight the social and psychological rewards, and believe that parenthood is superior to a childless marriage.

Statistical patterns are evident in who reproduces, with some people less likely to become parents. Differences are apparent by country, but men are more likely than women to reproduce because they have a longer period of fecundity and more men re-partner with younger women after separation or widowhood (Dykstra, 2006). Childlessness is also associated with "late starts" in independent living, education, and marriage, as well as high education and stable employment for women (Hagestad and Call, 2007). Women with postgraduate education and professional or managerial jobs are less likely than comparable men to marry and have children, partly because women perceive that child-rearing slows their careers (Baker, 2012a). However, the distinction between voluntary and involuntary childlessness tends to be blurred by circumstances and constraints (Rowland, 2007; Tough et al., 2007).

Circumstances leading to childlessness include war, male unemployment, financial insecurity, few opportunities to meet suitable partners, separation and divorce, and decisions made by partners. Individuals who make a conscious decision to remain childless tend to weigh the advantages and disadvantages and discuss the issues at length with significant others before finalizing their decision (Cameron, 1997; Gillespie, 2003). However, women who choose *not* to procreate are expected to account for their choices in ways that women who become mothers do not (Gillespie, 1999; Hird and Abshoff, 2000; Rich et al., 2011).

Infertility seems to be increasing in urbanized societies, with higher levels of pollution, stressful lifestyles, sexually transmitted diseases, higher rates of obesity, more substance abuse, and older marriages. Those experiencing fertility problems are encouraged to seek medical assistance, although the birth rates from reproductive procedures are often low and the price of treatment high. The fact that some couples are willing to spend large sums of money on assisted conception illustrates the continuing importance of parenthood (Baker, 2004c).

Assisted Conception and Surrogacy

Fertility problems seem to be increasing in Western societies but they might simply be reported more often now that couples can obtain medical assistance. Those experiencing problems can use the Internet to find information about the procedures offered by fertility clinics, the probability of success, potential risks, and personal costs. In countries with private clinics, patients with adequate resources can purchase the services they believe will help them, which could raise expectations about the effectiveness of medical intervention as well as the right to bear children.

Research suggests that fertility treatments tend to be stressful for marital relationships (Doyal, 1995; Malin et al., 2001; Baker, 2004c). For wives, treatments can involve injecting drugs that regulate ovulation but alter moods, as well as the painful extraction and implantation of eggs. For husbands, treatments may involve sex on demand, producing sperm specimens at inconvenient times, and dealing with a partner's mood changes. Both must maintain regular clinic visits and cope with the disappointment of negative results. The effectiveness rates of most procedures have recently improved but the probability of a single live birth remains higher for younger women even though older women are more likely to become patients. Fertility treatments can also be expensive, although those who end up with a healthy baby may find these costs acceptable.

A few decades ago, the success rates for fertility treatment were not as high as many couples anticipated and the chances of miscarriage and other complications were greater than for natural conception. Australian research showed that adverse infant outcomes, such as pre-term delivery, low birth weight, stillbirth, and neonatal death, were higher among assisted conception births compared to all births (Ford et al., 2003). In recent years, success rates appear to have improved. Nevertheless, Canadian figures from 2009 indicate that the chances of a woman having a single healthy baby through assisted reproduction still vary by age and were 21 per cent per (menstrual) cycle for women under 35 but only 7 per cent for those 40 years old and over (Canadian Fertility and Andrology Society, 2011).

The high profits gained from medically assisted conception and the increasing demand for treatment have led to state regulation of fertility research and services. Some governments require hospitals and medical practitioners to distinguish between medically necessary interventions and treatments requested for social reasons. Consequently, people with no medically diagnosed reason for infertility or who are at no risk of passing on a genetic disease may be unable to receive publicly funded services in some jurisdictions (Baker, 2005b). Also, some jurisdictions continue to offer treatment mainly to married couples or cohabiting heterosexual couples in long-term relationships. Most OECD countries also ban the sale of sperm and eggs, as well as payments for babies for women who become **surrogate mothers**, regulate access to information about the identity of sperm donors, and specify the rights of children conceived from donors. Some of these issues have been contested in the courts but changes in reproductive techniques have moved faster than the law.

Fertility treatments are still experimental although they have been "normalized" by fertility specialists, journalists, and some patients. However, the risk of multiple pregnancies and negative birth outcomes remains higher with medically assisted conception than from normal conception (OECD, 2005b). Critics argue that the success rates of reproductive technologies may be exaggerated by presenting pregnancy rates rather than live birth rates and by including multiple rather than single births. These interventions also tend to medicalize the natural act of child-bearing and reinforce the pressure for couples to reproduce (Baker, 2004c).

Laws do not permit embryos or babies to be sold but some countries have permitted couples to commission surrogate mothers and pay their medical, legal, accommodation, and travel expenses. Surrogate mothers tend to have lower household incomes than commissioning mothers because few women would agree to "make a baby" for a woman they had never met unless money was exchanged. Patriarchal societies can also use sex selection technologies to reinforce the cultural preference for sons, although this may involve a discreet violation of existing laws. Despite these concerns, reproductive technologies offer the experience of motherhood to more women and give them greater choice over how and when they reproduce. For example, lesbians can become mothers without the risk of unscreened sperm and can enjoy safer clinic or hospital conditions (Michaels, 1996; Letherby, 1999).

This discussion suggests that assisted conception can be fraught with legal and moral controversies. For example, if the state pays for fertility treatments, who should be covered, which treatments should be subsidized, and how many should be permitted to each patient? Should adult children born from donor insemination have the right to know the identity of the donor? Should egg or sperm donors be granted any "parental rights" after a child is born, which could give children three legal parents (Collins, 2005)? These are all issues that legal commissions and governments are currently struggling to resolve.

Pregnancy and Maternity Practices

Recent social research has focused on cultural representations of the body, and the pregnant body is of particular interest to family sociologists. Not so long ago, pregnant women went into "confinement," maternity clothing disguised the pregnant body, and few people openly discussed pregnancy and its physical symptoms. As birth rates have fallen and sexuality has become more explicit, pregnancy has become "normalized" and more publicly discussed, but it has also become sexualized (Dwyer, 2006). Like wedding dresses, maternity clothing has become scantier and more physically revealing, and pregnancy is now more often seen by middle-class women as a personal accomplishment rather than a normal life event.

Technological advances have enabled the fetus to be monitored and photographed, and fetal imagery and the discourse of fetal rights have encouraged people to view the pregnant woman as an "ecosystem" for a growing child rather than as an individual (Wall, 2009). Mothers are taught that their own behaviour (especially smoking or drinking alcohol) can negatively affect the development of their fetus, referred to as the "remoralization of pregnancy" (Weir, 1996). Canadian research by Knaak (2005) on the changing discourse about the importance of breast-feeding also supports this conclusion, arguing that public discourse shapes the choices of new mothers.

Most young women are employed when they become pregnant and governments typically offer paid leave at childbirth and adoption, which I discuss in greater detail in Chapter 6. Maternity benefits are gender-specific and focus on maternal and child health and women's employment equity, while parental benefits are gender-neutral and have been used to induce couples to reproduce and to encourage men to become more involved in infant care. Both have been seen as citizenship rights for employees. Comparative research suggests that the model chosen depends on political lobbying within the jurisdiction and the ideology of the party in power (Heitlinger, 1993; Gauthier, 1996; Hantrais, 2004). Political pressure may be national and come from women's groups or men's rights groups, or it can originate from supranational organizations (such as the International Labour Organization) that encourage member states to develop minimum standards (Hantrais, 2000). In any case, leave and benefit provisions coincide with existing social programs, political priorities, and current views of citizenship rights (Baker, 2006).

Childbirth experiences have always varied with socio-economic and cultural circumstances, including the woman's age, marital status, and physical and emotional health, the family's socio-economic situation, and the presence or absence of the father. In recent decades, a number of societal changes have influenced pregnancy and childbirth practices, including the rising age of women at first births and changing birth practices. Before the twentieth century, most births took place at home with the assistance of female midwives or neighbours. Gradually, (male) doctors persuaded the public that safer childbirths required medical interventions and sterile hospital conditions (Tew, 1998). In the liberal states, most babies are now born in hospitals. In the United States, for example, less than 1 per cent of births take place at home, a trend remaining essentially unchanged over several decades (MacDorman et al., 2010). Family physicians used to be in charge of most hospital births but specialist obstetricians have recently taken over; midwives are also involved in some jurisdictions.

Currently, childbirth involves a variety of medical interventions that may include electronic fetal monitoring, anaesthetics, episiotomies, induced labour, and routine procedures such as pelvic shaves and enemas. Caesarean deliveries have also become more prevalent but there is considerable cross-national variation. In 2010, the Caesarean section rate was 30.2 per cent in the United States, 30.8 per cent in Australia, 23.7 per cent in New Zealand, and 26.3 per cent in Canada, compared to 13.7 per cent in the Netherlands and 16.6 per cent in Norway (WHO, 2010: 87–94). Rates of Caesarean deliveries also vary by the age, social class, and ethnicity of the mother, with older, wealthier, and "white" women more likely to experience such deliveries (Baker, 2005c).

Considerable controversy exists over rising rates of Caesarean births. These rates are increasing partly because women are having their first baby over the age of 35, which medical practitioners define as high-risk births (Cherniak and Fisher, 2008; Lee and Kirkman, 2008). Doctors use Caesarean deliveries to limit childbirth risks (as well as their legal liability) and to regulate the timing of birth, but Caesareans are more expensive because they require more expertise and involve more recovery time (Tew, 1998). For these reasons, some critics wonder if these operations are being overused. Nonetheless, Caesarean delivery remains an option, especially, in some jurisdictions, for wealthier patients whose doctors are willing to accommodate them.

Wealthier women may ask their doctors for a Caesarean delivery because they can be scheduled in advance and because they believe they are safer.

Journalists have suggested that some women are even convinced that elective Caesareans provide aesthetic and sexual benefits over vaginal births, as an abdominal scar is seen as a lesser disadvantage than a "loose vagina" from vaginal birth that may impede sexual satisfaction. This has led to media articles about women who are "too posh to push" (Asthana, 2005).

The World Health Organization (WHO) has recommended that Caesareans be performed only when medically necessary, suggesting that the optimum rate is between 10 and 15 per cent of births (Gibbons et al., 2010). However, few countries have rates within these levels and in some jurisdictions the rates range from 25 to 46 per cent of all births. Doctors are also more likely than midwives to rely on technological interventions and drugs, suggesting that their patients require more postpartum care and recovery time, and their services are more costly (Tew, 1998; Monari et al., 2008). Higher-risk maternity cases are generally accepted by obstetricians rather than midwives and riskier births usually take place in hospitals, which raises the neonatal mortality rates of hospital births delivered by obstetricians compared to home births attended by midwives.

If doctors caution pregnant women that a vaginal birth could be risky, few patients could independently evaluate this advice. No one wants to take unnecessary risks, but the medical profession remains powerful enough in many countries to pressure governments to accept their practices and limit the powers of midwives. The fact that more Caesareans are performed on wealthier women suggests that doctors may have chosen to benefit financially from these operations without the necessary medical grounds for the procedures (Walker et al., 2002; Ford et al., 2003).

The **medicalization**, bureaucratization, and privatization of childbirth services have concerned many patients and their families, but have also forced health officials and hospital administrators to improve public birthing facilities. Private hospitals and birthing centres offer more luxuries to patients who can afford them; however, cost-cutting measures are widespread in both private and public institutions. In the 1940s and 1950s, women could expect a two-week "confinement," but now they are expected to give birth and leave the hospital within a few days or sooner. This short stay may be justified by health reasons but it has also served as a cost-cutting measure (Tew, 1998).

Health-care services are being regionalized in some jurisdictions and responsibility is being shifted from public institutions to informal networks and unpaid caregivers (Armstrong et al., 2002). Benoit et al. (2002) argued that non-urban women in British Columbia view the regionalization of maternity services in a largely negative light. They complain about the lack of choice in care providers, discontinuous care, and inadequate quality of care. However, many politicians believe that it is more important to reduce the cost of public health care, especially as more services will be needed in the future with an aging population.

Child-rearing Practices

Health organizations and governments have encouraged women to breast-feed their babies, which is associated with numerous health benefits, including providing optimum nutrition for infants, reducing infectious diseases, and lowering infant mortality (WHO and UNICEF, 1990). Middle-class women are more likely to breast-feed than low-income women but breast-feeding remains contentious when done in public places and has become problematic as more mothers remain in the workforce. Although most governments or employers offer parental leave, finding suitable opportunities to feed a baby has become challenging for employed mothers. The duration of breast-feeding is influenced by employment security, leave provisions, breast-feeding facilities when mothers return to work, and their job control.

When new mothers return home after giving birth, the couple's previous division of labour often changes. Although many mothers enjoy the time at home, household tasks that might have been shared before childbirth tend to become her responsibility. The longer a mother stays at home, the more traditional the division of labour becomes, although neither partner may notice the initial changes. Furthermore, isolation and depression are sometimes a problem for new mothers. Evenson and Simon (2005) confirmed that parenthood is *not* associated with enhanced mental health and noted that non-parents in the United States report lower levels of depression than parents. Their research and other studies conclude that depression levels are particularly high among lone parents, those with low incomes, and parents residing with minor children, which suggests that these factors serve as stressors. However, they conclude that the emotional disadvantages of parenthood are not greater for women than for men, although women typically report higher levels of depression.

Increasingly, young mothers are encouraged to contribute to household income but some choose to care for their children at home, seeing this as their vocation or a worthwhile but temporary job. This option is especially available for partnered mothers with higher household incomes. Other mothers might take unpaid or partially paid parental leave for an extended period because affordable infant care is expensive and difficult to find. Even if care is available, parents want to ensure that the number of staff is sufficient to keep the infants clean, fed, stimulated, and free from infectious diseases, and that care providers are well qualified. Finding a skilled care provider to come to the child's home or who will welcome an extra child in her home is also difficult. Licensed family homes are available in most cities but child minders or sitters usually operate outside these regulations. Informal care is seldom regulated by government yet remains the most prevalent type of child care for employed parents in the liberal states (Baker, 2006: 148).

Families remain important places for children to develop a sense of identity, to distinguish what is important in life, and to develop optimism about adulthood. Young people implicitly learn from their parents and siblings how to get along with others, or how to argue and fight. From observing their own parents and those of their friends, children develop impressions about what it is like to be married, to become parents, to negotiate and make compromises, and to resolve interpersonal differences. These may be negative, ambivalent, or positive lessons and they sometimes leave young people confused. In recent decades, educators and governments in the liberal states have placed more emphasis on parenting education and individual responsibility for child outcomes. Wall (2009) discussed the recent proliferation of educational material designed to convince parents of the importance of secure attachments and adequate stimulation in children's early years. She argued that the current approach to parenting is intensely child-focused, compared to the earlier idea that children should adapt to an adult-centred home.

Socialization and Gender Roles

Considerable research has focused on how children are socialized to become adults. For years, academics argued about the relative influence of "nature" over "nurture" (or biology versus culture) in human behaviour, and these debates continue today with increased interest in the genetic basis of behaviour and health. However, pre-1950 ideas about the biological basis of gendered behaviour in children were challenged in the 1960s and 1970s with **social learning theory** and the growing body of research about how children are socialized into "sex roles" (later called "gender roles"). Social researchers demonstrated that male and female infants may be born with different bodies but that differences are usually augmented by social practices that vary by culture.

Parents often treat girls more gently, dress them in pink, give them dolls to play with, and protect them from dirt and rough play. In contrast, male infants are often dressed in blue. Today, it might be argued that much of the blue–pink dichotomy is determined by clothing manufacturers and marketers, especially at the bottom end of the market, where it can be difficult for parents of low income to find much of anything other than pink for the girl and blue for the boy. In contrast to girls, as boys grow older they are given action toys, discouraged from showing vulnerabilities, and expected to engage in rough physical play with boys and men. Girls are encouraged to see their mothers as **role models** as they grow up, to help her around the house, and to develop an interest in appearances and relationships. In contrast, boys are expected to perform less housework but are encouraged to develop sports-related skills, help their father with outdoor chores, and focus on employment training. By the 1980s, researchers were investigating the impact on children of gendered practices in the home, schools, and the media. In Chapter 6, we see how parents "perform gender" through their unpaid household work and the potential this has to shape children's attitudes and behaviour.

Research on Fathering

Although parenting research has emphasized mothering, more research now focuses on fathering. The media often suggest that more fathers are "New Age males" who care for children at home while mothers earn the household income, but social pressure and financial constraints discourage this role reversal, except for temporary periods (Doucet, 2006; Wall and Arnold, 2007; Merla, 2008). Many fathers who care for their children on a full-time basis are unemployed or marginally employed, and have not really chosen housework and child care over paid work. Nevertheless, research suggests that these fathers often differ from mothers in terms of their parenting style, providing more verbal direction, independence, and rough physical play. Furthermore, full-time fathers experience more problems than stay-at-home mothers do because the fathers seldom integrate into existing support groups or children's play groups. Neighbours and relatives often criticize "house husbands" for not accepting the masculine role of earner and family head. Furthermore, unemployment often lowers men's decision-making power in the household and raises marital conflict (Cherlin, 1996; Beaujot, 2000).

Some separated or divorced fathers spend more time alone with their children than they did during cohabitation or marriage. In Chapter 7, we discuss recent research on fathering in the "post-divorce family," noting that most children live more of the time with their mother, spending weekends or holidays with the father, often with his new partner and step-siblings. Considerable research is now being done on the impact on children of living in more than one household. Generally, the research indicates that children are often quite resilient (Pryor and Rodgers, 2001; Smyth, 2004).

Same-Sex Parenting

In recent years, an increasing percentage of same-sex couples have been raising children. Statistics Canada reported that 9 per cent of same-sex couples had children under 25 years old living at home in 2006, with 17 per cent of same-sex women parenting compared to 3 per cent of same-sex men (VIF, 2010: 40). Most of these children come from previous heterosexual relationships although some lesbian women have undergone donor insemination (Patterson and Chan, 1997). One reason why same-sex couples have fought for relationship rights is so both are accepted by educational and health authorities as legal parents of the children. In 2006, only 16.5 per cent of same-sex couples in Canada were legally married, but this increased to 32.5 per cent by 2011, including slightly more women than men (Statistics Canada, 2012a). Same-sex couples who are parenting often create a network of "fictive kin" or friends, former partners, and willing relatives who provide social support and role models for their children (Ambert, 2005).

Researchers in several countries have investigated the impact of same-sex parenting on children's well-being. Meezan and Rauch (2005) reviewed

American research since 1970 and found that the children of same-sex couples studied are doing about as well as children normally do and that these parents are as likely as heterosexual ones to provide supportive environments for their children. Generally, the research suggests that the development and well-being of children do not differ much by the sexual orientation of their parents. However, methodological problems are inherent in studying small populations that are difficult to locate, and the research does not yet show whether the children studied are typical of the general population of children raised by gay and lesbian couples. Most of the studies are based on small convenience samples because these couples are relatively rare (Amato, 2012).

Research notes that same-sex parents tend to report *better* relationships with their children than different-sex parents, although children's perceptions of their family relationships are remarkably similar (Tasker, 2010). However, researchers note that lesbian and gay parents differ in several ways from heterosexual parents, as same-sex parents tend to be older and more affluent, more have actively chosen parenthood, and lesbian co-mothers normally become more involved in child care than heterosexual fathers (ibid.). In examining how parental marriage might influence children raised by same-sex couples, Meezan and Rauch (2005) note that it could help ensure their financial well-being and reinforce the stability of parental relationships, as well as increase their social acceptance. Same-sex marriage is relatively new in the United States, but the fact that different states offer varying legal arrangements provides a useful setting for research. Shapiro, Pearson, and Stewart (2009) found that Canadian same-sex parents reported fewer worries about discrimination and fewer depressive symptoms than those in American states where gay marriage is not legally accepted.

Parenting Challenges and Children's Well-Being

Young people and their parents often face considerable challenges from their household circumstances. For example, children of immigrant parents tend to experience a wider gap between peer expectations and the values of their families. Many are taught to respect their elders and cultural values, listen to parental advice, protect the family's privacy and reputation, and minimize family conflict. Those who come from cultures favouring arranged marriages may fear the prospect of dating, as their parents would disapprove, but at the same time may be unable to accept their parents' choices for them. Forced to act as family translators, some young people from immigrant families feel caught between two cultures.

The challenges of parenting alone without another adult in the household will be discussed in Chapter 7, but single parents as well as same-sex parents often report discrimination in both housing and employment. Lauster and Easterbrook (2011) found that Canadian anti-discrimination laws covering family status and sexual orientation still have an important role to play, as these families continue to experience discrimination in the Vancouver rental market. Especially single mothers continue to face problems as income support and social housing become more difficult to access and more single mothers are forced to search for private rental accommodation.

Raising children with physical, emotional, or intellectual disabilities remains challenging for many parents. In 2006, 4.4 million Canadians living in private households reported having a condition that limited their everyday activities. While most of these are seniors, 3.7 per cent of children are living with disabilities, with more boys than girls (VIF, 2010: 8). Most preschool children with disabilities have chronic conditions such as asthma or attention deficit disorder. However, the percentage reporting learning disabilities, speech impediments, and psychological disabilities has increased, although this could represent greater medicalization and diagnosis of childhood problems rather than an increase in disability. Among the Canadian children reported to be living with disabilities in 2006, 41.7 per cent had "severe" to "very severe" disabilities (ibid.).

In the past, most children with serious disabilities were institutionalized in residential schools supported by the state, but since the 1980s many of these children have been cared for at home and integrated into local schools, while group homes and sheltered workshops have been created for adolescents and adults. These trends have enabled children to become better integrated into their communities and possibly have created stronger bonds between children and parents. However, more of the care work and cost has been taken on by families, especially mothers, which diminishes their opportunities to develop stable employment. In most jurisdictions in the liberal states, governments now make only token contributions to the costs of raising children with serious disabilities, and the lack of sufficient institutional care is growing. This issue was emphasized in Ontario at the end of April 2013 when the Ottawa mother of a severely autistic 19-year-old left her son at a Developmental Services Ontario office because she and her husband could no longer cope with their son's many needs (CBC News, 2013).

Researchers have also attempted to measure the general well-being of children and young people living in different jurisdictions, and organizations such as the United Nations Children's Fund (UNICEF) regularly produce "league tables" showing how various countries compare to the OECD average and whether or not recent changes have occurred. A report from the New Zealand government (New Zealand Ministry of Social Development, 2008) indicates that school truancy is rising and immunization rates are relatively low in that country. Child poverty rates, youth suicide, road death rates for youth, and early child-bearing rates are higher than the OECD average. At the same time, literacy rates are above average, more children are participating in early childhood education, and fewer children now live with parents without any school certificates, or who have not even completed elementary or high school. In New Zealand, Internet access in the home is relatively high and youth unemployment rates are relatively low.

Some children manage to grow into healthy, happy, and productive adults, despite being raised in difficult circumstances such as poverty and war. Researchers such as Michael Ungar (2008) in Canada and his international colleagues have been trying to understand what makes children "resilient," including cultural, community, relationship, and individual factors. They have found that resilience is specific to country, community, and culture but is influenced by factors such as a strong sense of cultural or national identity, meaningful rites of passage, age-appropriate work opportunities, positive mentors, expressive and caring parenting, personal assertiveness, problem-solving abilities, and self-awareness. Studies such as these emphasize the importance of parenting under difficult circumstances.

The Extension of Adolescence

Parents usually grant more autonomy to adolescents than younger children, allowing teenagers more privileges and choices in their daily life, involving them in family decisions, and encouraging them to develop adult skills and ambitions. This involves encouragement to become educated and to develop job experience, interpersonal skills, and good judgement about relationships. Social historians and sociologists have investigated historical transitions in the life cycle and noted that adolescence has been prolonged in Western societies as young people remain in school longer and depend on their parents for accommodation, meals, and financial assistance. In Canada, 26 per cent of 25–29-year-olds lived in the parental home in 2006 compared to only 15.6 per cent in 1986 (Statistics Canada, 2007b). In 2011, 42.3 per cent of young people aged 20 to 29 lived with their parents (Statistics Canada, 2012a). Canadian young people who leave home earlier than their cohort tend to come from separated or divorced parents, larger families, to be less religious, and grow up in small towns (Beaupré et al., 2006).

Adolescents and young people must deal with physiological and emotional changes, educational choices, relations with friends, new dating experiences, and imminent occupational decisions. They tend to be caught between childhood and adulthood, and sometimes feel that social expectations are unrealistic. Many young people find it financially difficult to leave home even though they are physically mature. They may resent parental restrictions, feel that their parents are unreasonable and old-fashioned, and yearn for independence.

As children mature, they are confronted by media representations and advertisements for consumer goods that encourage them to aspire to material wealth, fashionable clothing, international travel, and personal fame, and many students feel compelled to work part-time to afford this kind of lifestyle. Gaining job experience and acquiring spending money may prove useful but many of the available jobs are low-paid service positions and could interfere with their studies. Although more adolescents and young adults now work part-time while they are students, fewer parents require them to pay "room and board." Young people may be expected to pay for some of their educational expenses, clothes, and leisure activities but many parents continue to pay for their daily living expenses.

Adolescence is often a time of questioning about family history and parents' earlier activities and relationships. More young people now live with only one parent or in stepfamilies, and they may want to know details of their parents' past, including reasons for their marriage breakdown. About 1 per cent of babies are born from assisted conception, including sperm donations or donated eggs (Ford et al., 2003), but this percentage is expected to rise in the future. Undoubtedly, these young people will want to know something about their backgrounds and may press their parents for answers. As children grow older, they tend to question parental authority and want to establish the superiority of their own ideas and knowledge. Despite these conflicts, most parents derive considerable satisfaction from seeing their children grow into thinking individuals and watching them blossom into physical maturity.

Older people often think of adolescence as a time of hope, anticipation, and preparation for the future, but some young people are depressed by their parents' relationship, their poor socio-economic circumstances, world events, and perceived constraints to their future employment and happiness. They may demand more autonomy than their parents are willing to give them, and when they are constrained they may engage in acts of rebellion to show that they are individuals capable of making their own choices. Many teenage children are critical of parents' values, lifestyles, and appearance, and friction may occur between parents over how to deal with their teenage children.

Some families with adolescents experience considerable conflict. Studies show that at this stage in the family life cycle, parents reach their low point in life satisfaction, marital satisfaction, and satisfaction with their children (Van Laningham et al., 2001; Blanchflower and Oswald, 2008; Qu and Weston, 2008: 20). If parents have been married for years, interactions between them may become less person-oriented and more associated with household tasks and obligations. Financial obligations also increase as teenage children grow and develop their interests, but some parents also acquire responsibilities for aging parents at this stage. Both husband and wife are likely to work in mid-life and their jobs may require additional time and commitment as they gain seniority.

More parents now experience marriage breakdown by the time their children reach their teen years. Some re-partner and live in stepfamily situations, but others (especially women) remain alone, struggling with financial constraints as well as with rearing children at this difficult life stage. Those who have re-partnered may feel that they are caught between their current partner and biological children who do not always get along with their step-parent (Pryor and Rodgers, 2001). Step-parents report lower levels of satisfaction with their stepchildren than parents do with their biological children, but adolescent children also report lower satisfaction with step-parents than biological parents (Qu and Weston, 2008: 21). Many children lose regular contact with their separated father, as we discuss in Chapter 7.

Parents with adolescent children typically find that raising them is a complex task requiring patience and understanding. Teenage mood swings may also coincide with mothers' menopausal symptoms or mid-life concerns of either parent. Some adolescents are confused and distressed, turning to alcohol, drugs, or promiscuous sex. Many refuse to talk to their parents about their feelings, partly because they are unsure of how to express their concerns but also because their peers may discourage them from confiding in parents or other adults. Peer pressures remain strong, and belonging to a peer group is often given precedence over family communication and co-operation.

A minority of parents despair at the way their young people have turned out, and may blame themselves, their spouse, or their former partner for the outcomes. An American study suggests that parents' marital histories, changing family structures, levels of parental control and authority, and household economic circumstances influence adolescents' emotional adjustment and behaviour (Cavanagh, 2008). Research on children's outcomes generally report that adolescents are most likely to thrive when they are raised by parents living in long-term marriages with adequate financial resources, who care deeply for each other as well as for their children, and who take an interest in their activities (Ambert, 1997; Amato, 2005). Compared to the 1970s, young people now continue to live with their parents and siblings for several more years, which could cement relationships or perpetuate conflict. Some children and young people, however, experience considerable turmoil and conflict within their homes, requiring intervention by the state.

Child Welfare Issues

Before the 1920s, children who were abused, neglected, or delinquent were sometimes removed from their homes and, along with orphans, were placed in institutions that provided basic care, education, and training. These children's institutions sometimes found foster homes or adoptive parents for children who could no longer live with their parents. Over the years, psychologists and social workers came to believe that institutional care facilities failed to provide children with adequate love and stimulation, were costly to run, and provided disciplinary challenges for care workers (Swift, 1995; Krane, 2003). After the 1960s, the liberal states began to provide more home support for at-risk families, including income support and home visits by professionals who provided counselling and advice about budgeting and disciplining children. The state also regulated existing children's institutions and foster homes, and screened potential foster and adoptive parents. New procedures were developed to deal with family casework and higher educational standards were required for social workers. State interventions were guided by new principles, such as the "principle of least intrusion" and **family preservation** (Krane, 2003). Some jurisdictions, such as Quebec, provided child protection programs run by the state, while others, including Ontario, mandated private agencies to offer these services.

By the 1970s, "problem" children were less often placed in institutions and more often supported at home. Foster parents were subsidized by the state to care for abused and neglected children, although the payments barely covered their costs. Foster care was seen as a temporary solution that permitted children to maintain contact with their birth families while receiving care by unrelated but loving couples who might eventually adopt children who could not return to their parents. The state attempted to ensure that the family environment for fostering and adoption was suitable for the child's well-being. Often, the father was the breadwinner and the mother was a full-time care provider, and they were expected to be young, healthy, caring, and have a stable income (Speirs and Baker, 1994).

As more mothers entered the workforce and child-rearing costs increased, foster parents became more difficult to find. Social workers also became worried about the implications of placing children with strangers, especially those outside their cultural group. Now, many jurisdictions encourage grandparents and other extended family members to care for children when parents can no longer manage. The trend to **kinship care** is often justified by "the best interests of the child" and, more specifically, by the concept of "family preservation," or providing a sense of family support and continuity in the children's lives. However, kinship carers tend to receive less state support than non-related caregivers, which means that this practice can be seen as a form of neo-liberal restructuring designed to save public funds (Connolly, 2003; Baker, 2006).

Researchers have demonstrated that standards of care are also less rigorously applied in kin care than foster or residential care (Hunt, 2003; Worral, 2008). Today, care providers who would have been considered unacceptable foster parents in the past because of their older age, single-parent status, low income, poor health, existing parenting problems, or substandard accommodation are now approved. Unrelated foster care usually moves the child into a home with a stable income, but children cared for by relatives are more likely to continue living in poverty. Considerable research indicates that remaining in impoverished households can be detrimental to children's well-being and life chances (UNICEF, 2005, 2008).

Over the past three decades children's rights have been expanded, and in some countries neither parents nor teachers have the right to physically punish children under their care (UNICEF, 2003). Child abuse registries are kept in some jurisdictions but they record only a fraction of cases. The number of reported cases has risen dramatically but it is not known whether this indicates an increase in abuse cases or results from new reporting requirements.

Public attention initially focused on physical abuse but began to focus on sexual abuse in the 1980s, when studies found that more adults had been victims as children than previously acknowledged. Research also noted that sexual abuse tends to occur during the daytime, in the home of the victim or friend, and by a male relative or family friend (Baker, 2006). While girls are more vulnerable than boys, many young boys also are sexually abused, usually by men. Community leaders continue to search for new ways to identify potential abusers before an incident occurs and to deal effectively with perpetrators. However, reports are difficult to verify because such abuse usually occurs without witnesses and allegations are sometimes made decades after incidents.

Child abuse includes sexual, physical, and verbal mistreatment as well as parents' failure to provide nourishment, emotional support, education, shelter, and health care. Measures to control abuse include the appointment of children's advocates, the establishment of children's help lines, the integration of home visiting services, and closer monitoring of children. The UNICEF report on child maltreatment argued that effective strategies include home visits to all families with young children by a variety of qualified health, education, and social service staff rather than targeting children assumed to be at risk (UNICEF, 2003). This report also argued that child abuse strategies must address the economic circumstances of parents because those living in impoverished and stressed conditions are more likely to abuse their children (ibid., 21).

Most adults who are abused as children do *not* become child abusers, although various factors accumulate to augment the risk. Parents who abuse alcohol and drugs, lack social support, and live in impoverished and violent homes are more likely to maltreat their children. Maltreatment contributes to children's depression, anxiety, and hostility, as well as to certain types of behaviour such as physical inactivity, smoking, alcoholism, drug abuse, risky sexual practices, and suicide (ibid., 19; VIF, 2011). Lack of affordable housing encourages women and children to stay in abusive homes and creates overcrowded conditions that heighten family tensions and promote contagious and chronic diseases.

Children are also negatively affected by witnessing violence in the home. Each year about 12 per cent of North American women experience intimate-partner violence and 10 million children witness this violence (Graham-Bermann and Edleson, 2001: 3). A more recent Texas study reported that 32 per cent of the children in the sample witnessed parental violence in the previous year, leading to above-average rates of childhood depression (Nguyen and Larsen, 2012). In New Zealand, 6 per cent of children witnessed "adults hurting other adults" in the home, while 16 per cent witnessed adults hurting children (New Zealand Ministry of Social Development, 2008). Many mothers who experience domestic violence fear for their children's safety, but this fear is sometimes viewed as minimal or is dismissed by complex and often hostile court systems (Jaffe et al., 2003: 17). A shift in awareness towards recognizing the effects of domestic violence on children has been precipitated by research and international conferences (Krug et al., 2002: 103). Consequently, many countries have amended child custody policies to take into account the parents' history of domestic violence. There is clear evidence of growing concern about the cost of violent behaviour to individuals, families, employers, and taxpayers.

Low-income, indigenous, and visible minority children have been overrepresented in the caseloads of child welfare systems in the liberal states (Baker, 2006). The former practices of keeping indigenous children in state-regulated residential schools or encouraging adoption by white families have fallen into disrepute. Many of these children suffered from cultural confusion and reported some form of abuse after living with white foster families or in residential schools. Kin care is now viewed as less contentious because it keeps children within their local community and cultural group. Consequently, considerable effort has gone into trying to apply foster care processes and standards to kinship care. Even though research comparing child well-being in kin care with foster care is underdeveloped and sometimes contradictory, governments continue to encourage these practices (Connolly, 2003).

Disadvantaged children are identified by a number of risk factors, including growing up with persistent poverty and parental unemployment, with parents who have low education, are involved in substance abuse, and/or are mentally ill or depressed. Risk factors also include living in families struggling to integrate into the prevailing language or culture. Child-care researchers and child welfare experts argue that these disadvantaged children can benefit most from early childhood services to counteract inequalities of opportunity (UNICEF, 2008: 9).

State Support for Child-rearing

Child advocates have argued that raising children is expensive and governments should provide more assistance with parenting costs. Some researchers measure the cost of children as a percentage of household income because the wealthy spend more than the poor on all aspects of living costs, including child-rearing. For example, Douthitt and Fedyk (1990: 29) showed that two-child families in Ontario, regardless of their income, typically spend at least 18 per cent of their gross income on their children. Parents meet these costs by working longer hours, increasing time spent on household work rather than hiring help or using labour-saving devices, reallocating income to child-related goods, or decreasing their savings (ibid.). Parents tend to spend less than child-free couples on restaurant meals, recreation, tobacco and alcohol, adult clothing, and gifts, and they save less money.

Child-rearing costs can also be measured in absolute terms. Canadian researchers in Manitoba estimated the cost of raising a child to age 18 in 2004 was about $167,000 Canadian (VIF, 2010: 130). Australian researchers found that the average cost of raising the first child from birth to age 18 in 2006 varied between $209,203 and $273,454 Australian, depending on the city of residence. This included paying modest prices for housing, energy, food, clothing, household goods and services, child care, health, transport, leisure, and personal care (Henman, 2006).

Researchers also measure the cost of children in terms of "opportunity costs" or lost earnings for mothers or how much the earnings of mothers fall below those of childless women. In Canadian research, Zhang (2009) controlled for the woman's age, education, work experience, and the number of children, finding that at age 30 mothers earned an average of 12 per cent less than childless women. This gap increased to 20 per cent for mothers with three children. The "child penalty" was even higher for educated women and those interrupting their employment for more than three years.

For over a century the state has been supporting families with children (Baker, 2006), including widows' benefits, mothers' allowances, child allowances, maternity and parental leave and benefits, subsidized child care, and the enforcement of child support after parental separation. Country variations are apparent in support provided for families with children, as Table 5.2 indicates, with some investing more in cash benefits but less in social services. In this table, Canada and the United States look particularly ungenerous compared to the others.

Many governments subsidize child-care costs, especially for employed parents with low incomes. Some governments focus on not-for-profit centres or licensed homes (Jenson and Sineau, 2001b) but since the 1990s the liberal

Table 5.2 Social Spending on Family Benefits* as a Percentage of Gross Domestic Product, 2007

Country	% of GDP
Australia	2.4
Canada	1.0
Denmark	3.3
France	3.0
New Zealand	3.0
Sweden	3.4
United Kingdom	3.2
United States	0.7

*Including child allowances and tax benefits.

Source: Figures extracted from statistics associated with OECD 2011a, chapter 2. www.oecd.org/social/family/doingbetter.

states have been funding for-profit care, including franchised services (Baker, 2011d; Brennan, 2007a, 2007b). This is particularly a problem if the main care provider closes after bankruptcy, as was the case with ABC Learning Centres in Australia in 2008 (Kruger et al., 2008).

Governments could subsidize child care generously for all parents (as in Sweden, France, and Quebec), or they could target meagre subsidies to low-income employed parents, as in many American states. In countries such as New Zealand, two-parent families requiring child care formerly paid the full cost if they had average incomes, but in 2007 the government introduced 20 hours a week of "free" child care for children attending early childhood education centres (although it does not always cover the full cost). The Australian government provides a tax rebate for low-income parents using child-care services but the cost has been relatively high for middle-income parents. The Canadian government provides relatively generous tax breaks to cover the child-care expenses of employed parents, but the required official receipts are sometimes difficult to obtain from informal carers. Provincial governments in Canada subsidize child care for low-income families but these subsidies cover only a fraction of the actual costs (Beach et al., 2009; Friendly and Beach, 2005; Friendly and Prentice, 2009). A recent study found that in 40 of the American states, the annual cost of centre-based infant care exceeded 10 per cent of the median income for a two-parent family living in that state (NACCRRA, 2011).

Even when governments subsidize child care, the subsidy can vary. If governments see preschool care mainly as early childhood education, they may subsidize only a few hours a week. If they want to encourage maternal employment, they may subsidize care that covers the entire work week. Usually, subsidized spaces are regulated by government but the regulations can be minimal, covering mainly physical facilities, or they can be extensive, also covering the educational program and carer qualifications.

Whatever arrangement is favoured by the state, the number of children requiring care usually outstrips the availability of spaces in highly recommended centres. The shortage of regulated spaces means that most employed parents with preschool children are forced to rely on unregulated care or sitters in the liberal states (Baker, 2006; Beach et al., 2009). Caring for children is a challenging job yet generally pays the minimum wage or less, which means that child-care centres often experience problems attracting and retaining trained staff.

Most governments want to ensure that children are cared for by qualified providers in safe and stimulating environments but they are not always prepared to fund it. The provision of high-quality care is expensive, especially for infants, and costs rise when governments require professional qualifications for providers, educational programs, nourishing food for children, and congenial facilities. When the entire costs are passed on to parents, most cannot afford this kind of care. Consequently, both government and employers sometimes subsidize child care but want to ensure that the costs are manageable. France, Sweden, and Belgium have chosen to provide high-quality, government-regulated child care, but few English-speaking countries offer the same level of services (Brennan, 1998, 2007a; Jenson and Sineau, 2001a). The liberal states tend to keep social spending low and rely on parents to pay most child-care costs.

Countries vary in the focus and level of child-care subsidies but most jurisdictions use subsidies to encourage low-income mothers to enter paid work. Paid childbirth leave and affordable child care are necessary for women's employment equity, but these programs alone will not resolve the gender-based inequalities in work. The structure of paid work needs to be altered to remove the assumption that it is separate from personal life. The design of leave programs must acknowledge that women's feelings of obligation to children and partners have encouraged them to accept part-time or temporary employment, limit overtime work, take unpaid leave, relocate with their partner's occupation, and accept lower wages. Therefore, social programs need to focus on providing affordable and accessible child care, improving pay equity, raising girls' interest in occupational achievement, and increasing the participation of both boys and men in child care and housework. However, reforms that cost public or employer dollars are less likely to occur under neo-liberal restructuring or in economic hard times.

Conclusion

Although parents may see children as their pride and joy (or the bane of their existence), policy-makers increasingly view them as a form of "social capital" or a future national resource (Jenson, 2004; OECD, 2011a). Some governments have increased the level of child benefits, extended parental benefits, and expanded subsidies for child-care services. However, fertility rates continue to decline in many places as society becomes more individualistic and parenting remains consequential for employment opportunities, living costs, personal freedom, and lifestyle. Mothers in particular are expected to juggle the timing of child-bearing with the demands of paid work.

Having children is becoming more of a choice for women and couples, but childbirth is also becoming less natural and influenced more by medical interventions. Pregnant women are expected to be mindful of fetal health and well-being, and to regulate their own behaviour to ensure that they bring no harm to their fetus. Through imaging technology potential parents can view the fetus before birth and these images may enable decisions to be made about whether or not to continue with pregnancy. Policy-makers and interest groups also use these images to consider whether fetuses should have legal rights.

All this suggests that having and raising children today is considerably different from how it was in previous decades. As infants and toddlers, children are thought to need more extensive adult attention and stimulation, and as they grow older we expect them to acquire more education and work experience. Children are now given more opportunity to develop their identities and to express their personal views. As more mothers accept full-time jobs, the daytime supervision of children becomes more complicated for parents. School authorities still expect them to take an interest in their children's education and participate in school activities, but many employed parents have limited time to do so. More parents now depend on organized after-school activities and paid care providers to supervise their children while they are at work. At the same time, communities are perceived as more dangerous in terms of vehicle traffic, sexual predators, illicit drugs, and negative influences from the Internet, television, and videos. This suggests that the expectations of parenting and typical parenting experiences have changed over the past few decades, causing additional stress for all parents but especially for those with low incomes who live in dangerous neighbourhoods. In the next chapter, issues of employment and family money are examined in more detail.

Questions for Critical Thought

1. How did the early research on maternal deprivation influence public attitudes towards maternal employment?

2. Why have birth rates declined in the liberal states over the past century? How would you explain cross-national differences?

3. Is there any research evidence that the child-free choice is becoming more socially acceptable?

Questions for Debate

1. Are women who have elective Caesarean births "too posh to push," as some journalists suggest?

2. Why would fertility clinics want to focus on pregnancy rates rather than live birth rates in advertising their services?

3. Should the state fund fertility services for lesbians who want to become mothers?

4. Should the grandparents or extended families become the carers of children who are abused or neglected by their parents, or does this just perpetuate the problems?

5. Are parents neglecting their preschoolers by placing them in daycare centres while they work?

Suggested Readings

Albanese, Patrizia. 2009. *Children in Canada Today*. Toronto: Oxford University Press. This comprehensive text discusses the history of childhood, social theories relating to childhood, and several issues affecting children.

Baker, Maureen. 2011. "The Political Economy of Child Care Policy: Contradictions in New Zealand and Canada," *Policy Quarterly* 7, 1: 39–47. This article compares child-care policies in New Zealand and Canada, noting contradictions between public discourse and the actual assistance provided.

Doucet, Andrea. 2006. *Do Men Mother?* Toronto: University of Toronto Press. Based on narratives of Canadian fathers who are primary caregivers of children, this book explores the interplay between fathering and public policy, gender ideologies, social networks, and work–family policies.

Fox, Bonnie. 2009. *When Couples Become Parents: The Creation of Gender in the Transition to Parenthood*. Toronto: University of Toronto Press. This book is based on the author's interviews with heterosexual couples as they make the transition to parenthood. It illustrates the way particular versions of mothering and fathering are negotiated.

Nash, M. 2012. *Making "Postmodern" Mothers: Pregnant Embodiment, Baby Bumps and Body Image*. Basingstoke, UK: Palgrave Macmillan. This book provides a multidisciplinary, empirical account of pregnant embodiment and how it fits into wider sociological and feminist discourses about gender, bodies, "fitness," "fat," feminism, celebrity, and motherhood.

Suggested Websites

Australian Institute of Family Studies
www.aifs.gov.au/
This Australian government agency includes on its website several recent studies on maternity care and information on various aspects of child-rearing and child abuse, among other topics.

Childcare Resource and Research Unit
www.childcarecanada.org
The Childcare Resource and Research Unit (CRRU) focuses on early childhood education and child care (ECEC) and family policy both in Canada and internationally.

Centre for Families, Work, and Well-Being
www.worklifecanada.ca
This University of Guelph centre provides information about child-care research projects.

6 Household Work and Money

Learning Objectives

◎ To understand how families divide their household labour.

◎ To acknowledge that opportunities to earn, borrow, spend, and save vary by age, gender, marital status, parental status, and earning capacity.

◎ To understand the interrelationships between "doing gender" and combining earning and caring.

◎ To investigate the government policies designed to help families integrate earning and caring and to reduce family poverty.

Introduction

In this chapter, I argue that patterns of paid and unpaid work tend to change for both men and women when they partner, marry, and become parents. Fathers usually increase their commitment to paid work, spending longer hours earning money to support their families, while mothers tend to reduce their hours of paid work in order to spend more time on child care and domestic work. These gendered patterns have begun to converge slightly as more mothers work full-time, reducing time spent on household tasks, child care, and leisure. Some fathers pursue further education, retrain, or become unemployed or self-employed, enabling them to share some of the domestic work. However, husbands and fathers are more likely than single men and all women to work full-time and overtime, while wives and mothers are far more likely than men or single women to work part-time and take responsibility for household work. Although parents might willingly accept these gendered patterns, they can impede mothers' opportunities to become self-supporting, distance fathers from home activities, and provide children with gendered role models. Furthermore, the more time parents spend on paid work, the less time they have to spend on household work, and consequently more employees pay others to care for their children, prepare their meals, and clean and repair their homes.

This chapter also discusses a number of government policies designed to bolster family incomes and help employed parents to combine earning and caring, but I argue that these policies have not always been sufficient to counteract women's lower wages, labour market transformations, or high rates of marital separation. When parents separate, the children often live with the mother, and the daily care of children substantially increases the household work of lone mothers and often interferes with employment. The changing patterns of paid work in the liberal states, including the "24-hour economy" and deregulated labour markets, impact many aspects of family life and reduce time spent with family (Barrette, 2009). New patterns of paid work alter the organization of housework and care work, the management of household money, and the scheduling of family activities, but they also shape personal ambitions. Although the work lives of husbands and wives are beginning to look more similar, large differences still remain in income and hours spent at work. This suggests that personal choices about earning and caring are constrained by wider socio-economic conditions; in addition, these choices vary by age, gender, marital status, household income, and culture.

Cohabitation, Marriage, and Housework

When couples share a home, a number of maintenance tasks are necessary to sustain the household, including cooking, cleaning, laundry, shopping, and household repairs, as well as personal care and emotional work to keep relationships strong. Some of these tasks can be creative or enjoyable but others might seem mundane or even tedious even though they are necessary. If a couple owns a car or buys a house with a garden, the level of maintenance work increases. When children arrive, the workload rises exponentially, with more food preparation, cleaning, laundry, and constant supervision of the children.

Most couples search for ways to reduce their domestic work, but this usually costs more money than doing it themselves. For example, some parents occasionally use takeout meals to reduce the cooking and washing up, but these meals are often lower in nutritional value and more costly. Families with higher incomes can afford to eat out more frequently as well as to hire outsiders to clean their homes, do household repairs, and help care for the children. However, most families cannot afford hired help and must do the housework and much of the child care themselves. As more mothers work longer hours for pay, most couples find that managing two full-time jobs as well as the household work remains challenging and time-consuming, stretching them to the limit and making them "time poor."

Individuals initially develop their standards of cleanliness and orderliness from observing or reacting to their parents, and they further develop or alter these habits over the years. When couples first move in together, how do they establish a division of labour? Studies from many countries indicate that who performs domestic tasks is not always based on joint decision-making but more often coincides with conventional ideas about "doing gender"

(West and Zimmerman, 1987; Kimmel, 2008), as well as being influenced by upbringing, culture, and the availability of household resources. Generally, researchers find that among heterosexual couples, indoor housework and child care remain women's responsibility throughout much of the world, although husbands will "lend a hand" if their wives are pressed for time. However, cohabiting couples normally develop a more egalitarian division of labour than married couples, possibly because they tend to be younger and less likely to have children (Davis et al., 2007). However, women who attempt to resist the gendered consequences of marriage by cohabiting without marriage often find that they gradually slip back into conventional arrangements (Baxter et al., 2010; Elizabeth, 2000).

Early Studies of Household Work

Before the 1970s social scientists seldom analyzed patterns of housework and child care, but when they did they saw these tasks as women's "role," suggesting that the division of household labour was determined mainly by biology but also by culture. For example, many of the early structural functionalists, such as British anthropologist Bronislaw Malinowski (1884–1942) and American sociologist Talcott Parsons (1902–79), argued that the nuclear family was universal and based on a biological division of labour that subsequently led to different social roles (Luxton, 2009).

"Maternal instincts" and women's ability to lactate were thought to make them more suited biologically and psychologically to perform other domestic tasks. Men in preliterate societies were considered to be more suited physically to warfare, hunting, and protecting their kin group because of their larger size and superior strength. Academics argued that men rather than women typically supported families in industrialized societies because men were stronger, more rational, and more "task-oriented" than women (Parsons and Bales, 1955). Furthermore, early social scientists argued that the father's physical presence within the family was no longer required after conception whereas the mother continued to breast-feed each child. In other words, biology shaped their destiny and women were destined to become housewives, even in industrialized societies.

In the 1960s, Friedan (1963) identified the isolation of the American suburban housewife and her lack of meaningful work as major causes of women's malaise and "oppression." Friedan's *The Feminine Mystique* both contributed to the rebirth of the North American feminist movement and encouraged social researchers to study household work more systematically. Until the 1970s, few sociologists had studied this work although they had investigated many other occupations. The first sociological studies of housework include Lopata's American study, *Occupation: Housewife* (1971) and Oakley's British research, *The Sociology of Housework* (1974). These sociologists redefined housework as "work" rather than a natural extension of women's role or an activity motivated by love, and noted its characteristics as gendered, unpaid, potentially isolating, low-status, and not always chosen by the incumbents (Baker, 2001b).

Throughout the 1970s and 1980s, sociologists in many countries investigated the household division of labour. For example, Fletcher (1978) and Phillips (1988) revealed a traditional gendered pattern of household work in New Zealand families, noting that wives rather than husbands accommodated their housework around their employment but sometimes resented doing so. Luxton (1980) examined family life in an isolated Canadian mining town, arguing that housework was "more than a labour of love," involving gendered and class expectations and power relations. Hochschild (1989) showed that American mothers working full-time often experience a "double day" or a "second shift" when they arrive home to unpaid housework, child care, and emotional work.

Current Studies on Household Work

In investigating patterns of household work, researchers have carried out both qualitative studies, which rely on face-to-face interviews, and quantitative time-use or time-budget analyses derived from government data and survey questionnaires. Time-budget research asks large numbers of participants to record their activities at regular intervals during particular days, usually on a specific day during the week and on the weekend. Analysts then make statistical comparisons between the responses of various categories of participants, such as men and women; mothers, fathers, and childless couples; cohabiting, married, and single people; the young and old; and those working full-time and part-time. This analysis can tell us whether or not men do more housework when their wives increase their paid work, and if younger couples create a different sort of division of labour than older couples.

All the governments of the liberal states produce official statistics on paid and unpaid work and have been carrying out this research long enough to draw conclusions about changes over time. These studies find that women do much more unpaid work than men, although men are often involved in community volunteering such as coaching sports teams and usually do most of the household repairs. The time spent in unpaid work varies cross-nationally, with the smallest male/female differences apparent in social democratic countries such as Denmark.

If we divide unpaid work into its component parts, we find that women and mothers do more routine or daily housework and child care than men and fathers. Table 6.1 provides combined data from all of the OECD countries indicating that men and women spend comparable amounts of time only in volunteering and gardening/pet care. In all other tasks, women spend

Table 6.1 Minutes per Day Devoted to Unpaid Activity for Men and Women, Ages 15–64, OECD Countries

Task	Men	Women
Cleaning	10	43
Construction and repair	13	3
Cooking and food clean-up	21	83
Gardening and pet care	15	14
Physical child care	7	24
Shopping	18	28
Teaching, playing with children	6	10
Total child care	12	35
Volunteering	4	4

Source: OECD. 2011. *Society at a Glance*, 2011. Figure 1.11E. www.oecd.org/social/indicators.

considerably more minutes per day than men. Using similar types of data, other studies find that parents do more housework than non-parents, married women more than cohabiting women, older women more than younger women, and women working part-time more than those working full-time (Baxter et al., 2010; Neysmith et al., 2012; Ranson, 2009). Cross-national studies also show that housework and gender inequality in European countries are influenced by the level of technological development, religious culture, and individual religious beliefs (Voicu et al., 2008).

Gendered household work is usually divided into indoor and outdoor tasks. In moderate-income and lower-income families, women continue to do most of the indoor household tasks and caring work, as well as the planning, arranging, and supervision. Much of the outside work, including maintenance and repairs, is done by men (Baxter et al., 2008; Johnson and Johnson, 2008; Ranson, 2009). This indoor/outdoor split even includes women cooking in the kitchen while men cook outside on the barbecue. In higher-income families, couples often contract outsiders for some of the domestic work and most household repairs, send their young children to high-quality preschools, or hire nannies or housekeepers to live in their home. However, the mother is more likely than the father to hire and supervise the help, and these couples often retain a gendered division of household labour for other household and caring tasks.

Parents usually encourage their children to share some of the housework to help them develop "responsibility," but research suggests that children's contributions are slim and that mothers expend more time and energy encouraging them to do this work than it takes mothers to do the work themselves. If a child fails to perform a designated task, the mother usually does it, rather than another child or the father. Furthermore, research in many countries has found that daughters perform more household work than sons

(Goodnow, 1989; Evertsson, 2006; Haley, 2008) but also that children are more likely to do gender atypical tasks if their same-sex parent also does them (Raley and Bianchi, 2006).

The division of labour among gay and lesbian couples appears to be more egalitarian than among heterosexual couples (Ranson, 2009). Although biological mothers in lesbian households might do more mothering tasks, co-mothers tend to do more child care compared to heterosexual fathers. Furthermore, the housecleaning and cooking in gay and lesbian households are more likely to be evenly shared on the basis of individual tastes and abilities (Nelson, 1996, 2001; Dunne, 2000; Schechory and Ziv, 2007; Solomon et al., 2005). For heterosexual couples, housework and child care often become sites for "doing gender," reinforcing the biological and social differences, but the domestic division of labour also represents differences in priorities and interpersonal power.

Household Work, Paid Work, and Stress

The fact that husbands and wives perform different household tasks is not necessarily a problem, but when paid work increases the household division of labour does not always change. Canadian studies have found that although women increased their paid work from 1986 to 2005, they still did more domestic work than men (Lindsay, 2005). Men's time on housework has increased slightly over past decades but this can be largely explained by the fact that more men are living outside nuclear families and that dual-earning households typically hire help with housework and child care.

In many countries, wives who work full-time do less housework than those who work part-time or are outside the **labour force**. Wives employed full-time either lower their housework standards, encourage other family members to share the work, or hire someone to clean their houses or care for their children. Having a larger number of children clearly represents more work for mothers. Yet, many women continue to retain all or most of the responsibility for indoor housework and child-rearing tasks, including the hiring and supervision of cleaners, care providers, and other family members (Ranson, 2009). Women with less than high school graduation and older women are more likely to accept sole responsibility for housework even when they engage in paid work (Marshall, 1993, 1994). More women than men report that they organize and supervise household work and that they engage in "multi-tasking," which is to say that they complete several tasks simultaneously (Eichler et al., 2010; Neysmith et al., 2012). Canadian research also suggests generational, social class, and ethnic differences in patterns of housework, as well as gender differences.

Gazso-Windle and McMullin (2003) used quantitative Canadian data to explore the relationships among time availability, relative income, gender ideology, and the time spent on housework. They concluded that there is some evidence that partners, but especially husbands, "trade off" the time they spend in housework by doing more paid work. In addition, those with higher incomes and education spend less time on housework but more time on child care. Ironically, wives spend *more* time on housework when their wages are higher or closer to their husband's, which suggests that being a successful earner could mean something different for men and women. Some women may feel that they have to compensate for their success in the (male) breadwinning role by performing extra domestic tasks. Alternatively, the husbands of high-earning women may resent their "intrusion" into breadwinning and consequently may resist sharing domestic work. These researchers concluded that egalitarian notions about gender behaviour are more likely to influence men's participation in child care than in housework.

Considerable research has shown that men and women disagree about how much housework they actually do, and that many wives (but fewer husbands) see the division of labour at home as unequal and unfair. Some women have grown increasingly resentful as they intensify their work by becoming more efficient and disciplined. In 2008, I interviewed 30 university-based academics to investigate the impact of gender, marital status, and parental status on academic careers (Baker, 2012a). One of the questions asked was who does the housework in their home and Box 6.1 shows some of their gendered answers. This study suggested that the domestic division of labour remains a source of conflict in many homes, even among highly educated and full-time workers (Baker, 2010b).

Researchers from numerous countries conclude that women tend to accept responsibility for more of the household work even when they work full-time (Bittman and Pixley, 1997; Potuchek, 1997; Craig, 2006; Kitterød and Pettersen, 2006; Edlund, 2007; Craig and Bittman, 2008; OECD, 2011a:14). Australian research found that women with university education tend to work longer hours for pay than other women but also that both men and women with university degrees spend more time with their children than less-educated people do (Craig, 2006). "Domestic outsourcing" or the purchase of market substitutes for domestic labour has helped women resolve the time pressure created by an increasing commitment to paid work (Bittman and Rice, 1999).

When mothers with several children accept a paying job, they often work weekends or part-time, or alternate shifts with their male partners in order to integrate paid work and family life (Drolet and Morissette, 1997). Yet family conflict is highest if couples work shifts over which they have no control because co-ordinating child care, leisure, and other family activities becomes more difficult (Marshall, 1998). Employment leave is sometimes the only way to deal with family emergencies, but mothers are far more likely than fathers to disrupt their work schedules to balance this conflict (Baker, 2010c; Craig, 2006).

Box 6.1 Household Division of Labour among University-based Academics, 2008

Men Academics

"We share the housework 50/50 but I don't do the washing because I'm incompetent at it [laughter]. I might wash the wrong colours together so she's quite happy to do all of that." (senior rank, no children, cohabiting with senior academic)

"We share it. Share it 50/50? I like to think so [very small laugh] but that might be disputed." (senior rank, no children, married to intermediate ranking woman)

"I do the things that I like doing and she does the rest (laughter). . . . I think she does something along the lines of 65 per cent and I do the rest. She would probably say that it's more like 75 per cent." (intermediate rank, no children, cohabiting with junior-ranking academic woman)

"Split pretty evenly. We've got kind of vague things we'll do. I do the dishes. Half the cooking." (junior rank, no children, married to employed woman)

"My wife I have to say does most of it but I mean I do the cooking and I try to clean up in the evenings". (junior rank, father, married to homemaker)

"She carries the lion's share of it." (junior rank, father, married to homemaker)

Women Academics

"Most weekends are filled with housework . . . I come back (to work) on Monday morning and some of my colleagues say, 'have a good weekend?' and I think, what did I do on the weekend? [laughter] Spent most of Saturday, anyway, cleaning the place, catching up on housework." (senior rank, mother, cohabiting with semi-retired man)

"That was one of things that led to our separation . . . I realized we'd both come home from work together and I went into the kitchen and started doing (the dinner) and he sat and read the paper." (intermediate rank, mother, remarried)

"I think it's really important that women don't just play the victim and say, 'Oh, my husband doesn't support me.' They have to make them." (intermediate rank, no children, remarried)

"I don't mind [doing 80 per cent of the housework]. . . . It really is a question of competency." (senior rank, mother, remarried to senior professional man)

"I should hire somebody to clean the house but somehow I don't ever get around to it. And I think it's the fact that I somehow feel that I should clean up my own mess." (intermediate rank, single mother)

Source: From M. Baker's qualitative interviews with academics working full-time in New Zealand.

Employees have found it more difficult in recent years to take time off work, as globalizing labour markets are becoming more competitive. Mothers are more likely than fathers to give priority to young children and to household tasks, but if new mothers quit their jobs they may not be able to find comparable work when they are ready to re-enter the workforce. Even if they take an extended **parental leave**, they may find themselves later in a different position with similar wages. Marriage and child-rearing usually encourage fathers to take their earning obligations more seriously, while new mothers often reduce their hours of paid work and increase their unpaid work. Unless housework is shared at home, women workers could be disadvantaged by having less energy and time to devote to employment.

People who live in the liberal states tend to work longer hours than those in other types of states but there is little variation in the gendered division of domestic labour or time spent in leisure activities (Gershuny and Sullivan, 2003). Furthermore, work/life stress has been found to be more prevalent among mothers than fathers and among parents with more children at home (Crompton, 2004). It is also more prevalent in some countries than others, depending on hours of work, holidays, family leave entitlements, and public child-care services. Crompton (2004) found lower levels of work/life stress among employees who reported that they shared housework and child care, and among those who worked shorter hours and lived in countries with institutional supports for employed parents (such as Finland and Norway). This suggests that the stress related to balancing employment and family responsibilities can be lessened by couples sharing their domestic work and by governments ensuring that employees are entitled to family leave, adequate vacations, and child-care services.

Household Money and Wealth Accumulation

Social scientists often argue that wealth is developed and passed on through families, who protect their resources through careful investments and strategic marriages. They also argue that knowledge of people's class background (or the income and wealth accumulation of the family of origin) is crucial to understanding their ambitions, desires, and lifestyle choices, because people's material existence shapes what they think is possible and desirable. For over a hundred years, sociologists such as Thorstein Veblen (1899) have argued that "new money" is different from "old money" and that the very notion of "nouveau riche" implies that those who recently acquired money often feel the need to show off their success through "conspicuous consumption" with expensive cars, homes, and furnishings. The concept of the "trophy wife" further suggests that rich men can afford to marry much younger and beautiful women who enhance their status through their appearance.

Gilding (2005) used the *Business Review Weekly*'s list of the 200 richest people in Australia to examine how families accumulate and transmit their wealth. He noted that family businesses that grow and survive often develop into larger corporations, but most small and medium enterprises remain as family businesses. Furthermore, family relationships are still pivotal in the transmission of wealth across generations. Wealthy families protect their assets through business partnerships with trusted relatives and pass on their assets to spouses and children. They also create holding and investment companies and "family trusts," which help to minimize the payment of taxes. Gilding argues that the Australian taxation system encourages the formation of "family entities," which limit the dispersal of family fortunes, but similar conclusions could be reached for the other liberal states.

Most families accumulate little wealth although most eventually buy a home and one or more cars. However, the value of household assets has generally increased among higher-income households in many OECD countries in the past two decades as household incomes have been maintained or increased through wives' employment and the resale of houses (Girouard et al., 2006). Nevertheless, levels of household debt have also increased since 1990, reaching nearly double the level of disposable household income in countries such as Australia and New Zealand (ibid.). In Canada, household debt increased by 75 per cent from 1990 to 2008, at a rate six times faster than household income (VIF, 2010: 136). The fastest-growing component of debt has been consumer credit, which includes personal loans, credit card loans, and lines of credit (ibid.). The accumulation of household debt is encouraged by rising material aspirations, lower inflation rates, financial deregulation, higher house prices, and easier access to credit (Legge and Heynes, 2008).

Families generally accumulate most of their assets through home ownership, but over the past 30 years rates of home ownership have declined slightly in Canada and New Zealand, to about 68 per cent of households in 2006 (NZHRC, n.d.; VIF, 2004: 117). In 2009, 65.1 per cent of Canadians owned their own dwelling but rates vary by jurisdiction, with the lowest rates in the Far North (Statistics Canada, 2012b). Home ownership rates have remained stable in Australia at about 70 per cent (ABS, 2010; Reserve Bank of Australia, 2003), but as in other countries the rates rise with age and relationship formation and are higher for married than cohabiting or separated people (Baxter and McDonald, 2004).

Canadian figures indicate that the highest rates of home ownership are among richer people and those aged 55–64. Among the richest fifth of households with members in the 55–64 age group, 93 per cent owned their home in 2006 compared to 55 per cent of the poorest households within this age group (Hou, 2010: Table 1). Home ownership rates also vary by family configuration; elderly couples have the highest rate of home ownership at 88 per cent, but rates are the lowest for the unattached elderly (mainly women) at 44 per cent and sole-mother families at 48 per cent (VIF, 2004: 117). This shows that women without male breadwinners and retired unattached females are disadvantaged in the housing market. Home ownership rates could decline in the future with more cohabitation, later marriage, more separations and re-partnering, and increased job insecurity.

Affordable housing is a growing problem for urban families, especially those with more than three children, new immigrants, seniors living alone, and mother-led families. About 13 per cent of Canadian homeowners spend more than 30 per cent of their income on shelter, including mortgage payments, property taxes, and/or condominium fees, a level that is considered financially stressful (VIF, 2010: 127). Low-income families are most likely to live in rental accommodation and most pay market rents in Canada. Welfare advocates have argued that reliance on the private housing market means that many low-income families are forced to live in unhealthy, overcrowded, and unsafe accommodation, which can encourage the development of respiratory ailments, the spread of infectious diseases, depression, and anti-social behaviour. Substandard housing can also have negative and permanent consequences on children's health, behaviour, and development (Jackson and Roberts, 2001; Singh and Ghandour, 2012).

Lack of affordable housing can create overcrowded conditions that heighten family tensions and keep women and children living in abusive households. Moving too many times because of an inability to pay the rent also has detrimental consequences for children's school performance and peer relationships. Transition housing provided by voluntary organizations and sharing accommodation with relatives and friends are temporary solutions to problems of affordability. In many countries, the state has helped to expand housing stocks and to improve the quality and affordability of housing because these governments equate home ownership with social stability and family well-being.

Access to income clearly shapes opportunities to own a home, enjoy comfortable accommodation, and accumulate wealth. In recent years, researchers have focused on national rates of **child poverty** as an indicator of the relative generosity of parental wages and family benefits. The United Nations Children's Fund and the OECD regularly publish comparative statistics on the percentage of children living in households with "low" incomes, usually defined as less than 50 per cent of the median income in that country, after taxes and government transfers and adjusted for family size. These figures show that poverty rates tend to be high in the liberal states, such as the United States, Canada, and New Zealand, and much lower in the social democratic states, such as Denmark, Finland, and Sweden (OECD, 2008a). However, poverty rates are much higher when children live only with their mother, especially if she is reliant on state income support.

Since the 1970s, social researchers have also explored the connection between who earns household money and decisions about how it is spent. They concluded that the social meaning of money is important because who brings it into the household and how it is distributed relate to ideologies of gender and marriage (Pahl, 1995). Since the beginning of wage labour, husbands have been the primary earners in most households with European origins. The ideal of the **family wage** spread until, by the early 1900s, unions negotiated higher wages for married men than single men or women on the grounds that married men were normally household earners. This wage was supposed to be sufficient to permit male breadwinners to support themselves, a wife, and two or three dependent children. As this employment practice was implemented, wives' earnings became viewed as supplementary income and less significant, regardless of how much they earned (Zelizer, 1994).

Although the husband earned most household money in the past, he did not always manage it alone. Often he kept some for himself but gave the rest to his wife, who was responsible for buying necessities for the entire household. Sometimes husbands and wives managed their money jointly, but when the husband managed the earnings alone he usually gave his wife a set amount of "housekeeping money." If wives earned their own money, they often used it to buy food or clothing for the children or to purchase household items; but some wives saw their personal earnings as their own money and kept it separate from household money. Current research suggests that the idea of the **male breadwinner family** continues today even though most wives are also earners (Pahl, 2005).

The organization of household money is not always consciously discussed or decided but is influenced instead by culture, gender ideologies, and especially by the relative earnings of husbands and wives. Money is not the only valued resource in the **family economy**, nor is it equally valued in all households. Studying money allocation patterns reveals important cultural differences in access and control over family resources. For example, Fleming's New Zealand research (1997) concluded that Maori and Pacific Island couples often lived within an extended family where the use of their earnings could be dictated by older relatives and the church. For couples with European origins, control over money is related to the relative amount earned by each partner and is more influenced by the notion that the husband should be the provider. In Maori and Pacific Island families, the provider role was not necessarily associated with power or authority, as other sources of male authority were available. Fleming (1999) also found that money allocation patterns in stepfamilies differed from first marriages, particularly with regard to supporting the other partner's children.

Although most wives are now employed, husbands typically earn considerably more than their wives (OECD, 2011a). In British research, most married men and women defined their personal earnings as "family money" but husbands were more likely than wives to express this view (Pahl, 1995). Although there are several different ways of managing money, most couples pool their resources, and this money can be managed jointly, by the wife, or by the husband. Increased female employment is associated with the greater pooling of earnings that are managed jointly. In fact, the higher women's earnings are relative to their husbands, the more say wives have in how their combined earnings are spent and how the household is managed (Treas and Tai, 2012; Vogler and Pahl, 1994).

Despite the increase in dual-earner households, few couples keep all their earnings in separate bank accounts, although this pattern is becoming more prevalent. In the 1990s, research found that only about 3 per cent of British couples kept all of their earnings separate but more recent research suggests that over a quarter of young British couples manage most of their earnings separately and combine only some that is designated for household expenses (Pahl, 2005). Independent money management was particularly characteristic of younger couples, those without children, and those where the woman was in full-time paid employment. Cohabitants often have different money management practices than married couples. For example, New Zealand and British studies have found that women who cohabit are more likely than married women to have their own earnings and to keep their money separate from their partner's in order to maintain their independence (Elizabeth, 2001; Pahl, 2001; Vogler et al. 2008).

Spending patterns also differ by gender. Canadian and British research suggests that wives and mothers tend to be responsible for buying food for the household, clothing for themselves and their children, and child care and school expenses. Men/fathers spent more of their earnings on meals out, alcohol, motor vehicles, repairs to the house, and gambling. Responsibility for other items of spending was more evenly distributed (Phipps and Burton, 1992; Ermisch, 2003; Pahl, 2005). With gendered differences in income, women often can raise their living standards by sharing a residence with an employed man, especially if they pool their earnings. However, if they keep their money separate and she continues to be responsible for spending in the above areas, the financial outcome might not be equitable and money could become a source of conflict (Elizabeth, 2001; Pahl, 2005). Consequently, some couples arrange to pay a percentage of their earnings rather than an equal amount into their joint account.

Another indication that relative income between partners is important for the control of household money arises out of studies of families living on state income support. In low-income households, especially those on social assistance, women tend to have more control over how the money is spent (Fleming and Easting, 1994; Christopher et al., 2001). This probably relates to the fact that women typically head lone-parent households and that their incomes are essential for the survival of these households, but are less often necessary in higher-income households. Governments often pay income support directly to the mother on behalf of the children or to both partners equally, and women generally gain decision-making power as their income approximates that of their partners. As more women work full-time, their willingness to accept male management of household resources declines.

Money has also been the source of marital conflict, regardless of who earns it (Papp et al. 2008). Despite the emphasis that economists give to rational decision-making in financial transactions, discussions of household money often involve such strong emotions as anxiety, guilt, or pride. Singh (1997) differentiated between "marriage money," which is domestic and co-operative and typically held in a joint account, and "market money," which is impersonal and subject to contract. The difference between the two is particularly important if partners divorce or if they use their family home as collateral for a husband's business loan. When the divorce settlement is finalized or the bank demands repayment of the loan, the financial arrangements that had represented trust and love suddenly become impersonal and contractual (Pahl, 2001), not to mention acrimonious and expensive. Lawton (1991: 7) uses the concept of "sexually transmitted debt" to discuss the ways that financial co-operation within marriage can end in serious problems if the trust is broken or the relationship sours.

Children learn about the social and cultural value of money from their parents early in childhood but also from their peers and the media. Increasingly, young people are using access to money and consumption to create a social identity. A 2005 New Zealand survey found that two-thirds of parents give their children allowances or pocket money (averaging $20 per week) and three-quarters of 12–19-year-olds have, or have had, part-time jobs (McFadden, 2005). Many children are expected to do household work for their allowances, such as setting the table, cleaning their rooms, and caring for younger siblings. When New Zealand teens are employed outside the home, they often work 10–20 hours a week, earning between $10 and $15 per hour. Yet, unlike previous generations, these teenagers seldom return any of this money to their parents and many see their earnings as their own. Although some save for their education or a car (especially boys), many spend their money quickly on non-essentials, such as cell phones and designer clothes, which have become status symbols, as well as magazines, CDs, and snacks. Despite youth having access to more money, McFadden argues that the current generation of New Zealand youth is falling into debt attempting to pay off their cell phone and credit card charges. Those who continue their education are also paying off student loans.

Access to credit has been increasingly important to lifestyle and always varied by age, gender, and employment status even though access to credit was restricted somewhat with the international "credit crunch" of 2008–9. However, the "easy money" that has been available to youth sometimes leads to a lifetime of poor money management and debt, especially as youth are often targeted by advertisers (ibid.). Within adult couples, men are more likely than women to acquire access to credit with their higher incomes, but wives who work full-time are more likely than homemakers to use credit cards and electronic money transactions (Pahl, 2001).

Greater use of credit cards is associated with youth, full-time employment, and higher education. Unemployed and retired people are less likely to use credit cards, but among the retired, men are more likely than women to use them, reflecting differences in income, confidence in using new technologies, or a tradition of male dominance in marital finances among this age group. Credit cards can be used as status symbols, especially when the colour gold or platinum reveals the holder's income and credit levels (ibid.). Access to financial services is clearly constrained by income, employment status, age, gender, and location of residence, as well as international credit rules and the profitability of loans for the banks and credit companies.

Although credit cards are used mainly by younger people, net worth usually increases with age. In Canadian households where a male was the main earner, net worth reached a peak between the ages of 55 and 64 years (VIF, 2010: 125). However, it declined after separation and divorce for both men and women, and was especially low for households in which a woman was the main income recipient (VIF, 2004: 122). Two incomes per family have become the norm in many countries and increasingly necessary to pay the bills. From 1980 to 2002, the after-tax incomes of most Canadians increased, even after accounting for the effects of inflation, largely because more households had acquired two earners (ibid., 91). However, personal savings are at record low levels and debt is rising relative to income in many countries (Girouard et al., 2006).

The growing gap between rich and poor households has been attributed to a number of factors, including higher rates of separation, neo-liberal restructuring of income support programs, and global labour market conditions that pay some people very high wages while encouraging low minimum wages and temporary or part-time jobs for others. Couples with two full-time incomes, high levels of education, and no children tend to have the highest incomes, while lone-mother households and large "visible minority" families tend to experience both low income and debt. In the next section, I discuss how labour markets have changed in recent years and what this means for families with children.

Changing Labour Markets

Increasingly, both men and women work for pay, but labour market conditions have changed considerably in the last 50 years. After the 1960s, the service sector of the economy expanded in many countries, wages and aspirations increased, and employers began to demand higher qualifications from new employees. As more people gained the required credentials, employers continued to raise the entry-level qualifications for many jobs. In the mid-1970s, the world economy experienced a downturn and more employers became concerned about restricting financial losses, reducing the numbers of permanent employees, maintaining national competitiveness, and/or developing new international markets. Governments also signed new trade agreements that permitted employers to make or sell their products in other countries, including places with lower production costs and higher productivity gains. Typically, this raised unemployment rates in industrialized countries with higher wages. Less often, new trade agreements permitted workers to cross borders and seek employment in other countries, such as in the European Union. Generally, the use of global markets increased the competitiveness of local labour markets as employers began to advertise nationally and internationally for new workers.

Especially since the 1980s, some manufacturing jobs that were previously unionized and nationally based have shifted outside the borders of Western economies and lost both their legislative and trade union protections. In addition, the service sector expanded, but by providing more temporary and part-time positions than full-time, year-round jobs (Banting and Beach, 1995; Edwards and Magarey, 1995; Van den Berg and Smucker, 1997; Vosko, 2009). Today, compared to the 1970s, a higher percentage of adults are working for pay, but more are also working longer hours. Nevertheless, families are not necessarily better off financially, in their quality of life, or in opportunities to spend time with family (Barrette, 2009; Sauvé, 2009). Many workers have been expected to retrain, to work in the evenings and on weekends, to become self-employed, or to take early retirement. The lives of men and women, as well as youth, continue to be influenced by these labour market changes.

At the same time, increased advertising and consumerism have heightened personal aspirations and expectations. People expect their homes to have the latest equipment—microwave ovens, dishwashers, flat-screen televisions, and personal computers—and new forms of credit were created to encourage people to aspire to higher living standards. While the cost of some consumer goods such as televisions and computers has fallen relative to average wages, the cost of housing has skyrocketed in the major cities, meaning that even those who work longer hours continue to struggle to pay for accommodation and other bills.

In late 2008, the international economy declined once again and unemployment began to rise, credit was restricted, housing prices fell, and interest rates declined. Low interest rates might be advantageous for those buying their first home but they reduce income for people living on fixed incomes, such as seniors, because these people often depend on investment income as well as pensions. Furthermore, restricted credit and high unemployment are problems for all workers. In some places, speculators and real estate investors are also suffering and many employers are in financial trouble or declaring bankruptcy. This suggests that some of the financial and labour market trends of the 1980s and 1990s could be changing, although they typically follow financial cycles.

Currently, many parents are working longer hours than parents did in the 1960s and many require their adolescents and students to earn money to contribute to their expenses. Many adolescents still expect that their post-school choices will be influenced only by their personal desires rather than being restricted by economic reforms and institutional needs, as Higgins and Nairn (2006) found in their New Zealand research. However, many young adults accrue large student loans through post-secondary education, which limit their future choices about employment, home ownership, and the accumulation of non-mortgage assets, and shape their ideas about marriage and reproduction.

In summary, work patterns have changed because employers are placing new demands on their workers with transformations in the conditions of production and trade, but also because families now need more than one wage to pay for basic living costs. However, material aspirations have also increased, and what used to be considered a luxury is now considered essential, such as two-bathroom homes, two cars per household, one or more home computers, and a personal phone. In addition, labour market changes have not impacted equally on men and women, especially if they are parents.

Gender and Work

Gendered patterns of paid work are beginning to converge as employment rates have decreased slightly for men and increased substantially for women over the past few decades. In Canada, men's labour force participation rates have fallen from 77.7 per cent in 1976 to 72 per cent in 2009, while women's have increased from 45.7 to 62.6 per cent (VIF, 2010: 79). Men's rates have decreased because youth now remain in school longer and more men work on short-term contracts, work part-time, or are self-employed. From the 1970s to the 1990s, many men were able to retire before the age of 65 with improvements to pension plans and increased savings from higher wages and interest rates (Myles, 1996). However, male wages from the 1970s to the 1990s did not always keep pace with rising living costs, and successive waves of men are now earning less than their elders at every stage in their work lives (Beaudry and Green, 1997). Consequently, the age of retirement for all workers is rising (OECD, 2009b: 83).

Although the husband still is the major breadwinner in most families, women's increased working hours and earnings are beginning to alter their expectations about marriage, children, and the household division of labour. Women's employment has increased dramatically in many countries, especially among mothers with children under six years of age (OECD, 2011a), as work patterns have been influenced by economic, ideological, and technological changes. First, the **service sector** of many national economies has expanded since the 1950s and 1960s, creating more clerical and service positions in education, retail sales, hospitality industries, health care, and the growing government bureaucracies. Many of these new jobs were thought to be appropriate for women because they were clean and safe and performed indoors. Some were also part-time, allowing mothers to retain most household duties.

Women's employment also increased because families needed wives' wages to counteract spiralling living costs after the 1960s, especially where men's real wages declined relative to living expenses in countries such as Canada and the United States (Torjman and Battle, 1999). Throughout the 1970s and 1980s, unemployment rates also increased at the same time as more families needed additional income to pay household bills. This included the consumer products that advertising campaigns induced people to buy, such as two cars and modern household appliances, as well as longer periods of formal education for the children. Furthermore, a shortage of employment opportunities encouraged more young people to stay in school, often while continuing to live in the parental home, which increased financial pressure on the entire family (Kobayashi, 2007).

The third reason for rising female employment was that feminist ideologies, revived in the 1960 and 1970s, encouraged them to continue their education and use it to contribute directly to household earnings and the larger society. North American feminists in particular argued that women should gain financial independence from their fathers and husbands to achieve equality with men, to realize their potential, and to establish an autonomous household if they so wished (Friedan, 1963; Pierson et al., 1993). At the same time, feminists in Britain, Australia, and New Zealand focused more on gaining government support for mothering at home, portraying women as different from men in their goals and experiences (Baker and Tippin, 1999). More North American women chose to seek employment to use their education, further their ambitions, earn their own money, raise their bargaining power in marriage, and contribute to household purchases and public life.

Fourth, more effective contraception permitted women to better control their pregnancies, especially after the contraceptive pill was marketed in the mid-1960s. Effective contraception enabled women to continue their education and work outside the home throughout their fertile years. Widespread use of contraception also meant that fewer employers worried about unexpected pregnancy among their female staff and were therefore more willing to hire and promote women workers. Generally, modern contraceptives have enabled women to acquire higher education, reduce their fertility, and plan for a lifetime of paid work, if they so choose.

Despite these changes, women's employment rates remain much lower than men's in OECD countries, where 72.7 per cent of men compared to 56.7 per cent of women were employed in 2010 (OECD, 2011b: 154–5). Some gender convergence is apparent in the type of jobs and the hours of work, but men and women continue to perform different kinds of work and men are more likely to work full-time, overtime, and in positions of responsibility. Women are far more likely than men to accept part-time employment in all OECD countries, as Table 6.2 indicates (OECD, 2008b), and part-time work is less likely to lead to seniority or higher lifetime wages. Instead, it creates short-term solutions and long-term problems for women. This table also shows that women tend to earn considerably less than men, even in Denmark and Sweden, and that the incidence of low-paid work varies to a significant extent by country, with the highest rate in the United States. This points to the fact that the job market and labour laws vary in different countries.

Both women's employment rates and average earnings are lower than men's. Despite anti-discrimination and pay equity legislation in most OECD countries, a gender gap remains in the wages of both full-time and part-time workers. The gender wage gap reflects not only the different jobs done by men and women but also men's longer working hours and greater acceptance of responsibility for earning family money. Women are more likely to reduce their paid work to deal with family commitments, to have lower bargaining power with employers, and to suffer discrimination when they attempt to progress through the ranks.

Although we have focused on gender differences in paid work, middle-class men of European ancestry have been most likely to experience career

Table 6.2 Labour Force Characteristics in Selected Countries, 2007–10

Country	Female Employment Rate in 2010 (% of females aged 15–64)	Women's Share of Part-Time Employment in 2007	Maternal Employment Rate in 2008 (with children under three years)	Gender Wage Gap in 2008 (% difference between median earnings of females compared to males)	Incidence of Low Pay in 2008 (% earning less than two-thirds of median earnings)
Australia	66.2	71.6	–	12	17.5
Canada	68.8	68.0	58.7	20	22.0
Denmark	71.1	62.8	71.4	12	13.0
France	59.9	80.3	58.6	12	21.5
New Zealand	66.7	72.6	45.1	8	12.7
Sweden	70.3	65.0	71.9	15	6.5 (2006)
United Kingdom	65.3	77.4	54.0	21	21.2
United States	62.4	68.4	54.2	20	24.5
OECD average	56.7	72.8	50.9	16	17.9

Source: Extracted from OECD.2010. *Employment Outlook 2010, Database on Earnings Distribution; OECD 2011d. Employment and Labour Markets: Key Tables from OECD*; OECD 2012. Towards a More Inclusive Labour Market. Paris: OECD, Extracted from Table 3.10..

advancement leading to higher earnings and better employment-related benefits (such as retirement pensions). In contrast, working-class men and members of certain cultural minorities, as well as many women, have worked with fewer expectations of advancement, pay increases, or fringe benefits, except when trade unions intervened on their behalf. Generally, men have been more likely than women to work full-time and overtime, to progress through the ranks into senior managerial or professional positions, and to earn high wages (Vosko, 2000; OECD, 2012). How do these comparative statistics relate to family responsibilities?

Employment and Parenthood

Men and women with neither spouse nor children have similar rates of full-time employment, at least in Canada, but the presence of spouse and children tends to push men and women in opposite directions (Beaujot, 2000; OECD, 2011a). Mothers tend to make more concessions than fathers to the integration of earning and caring, as unpaid domestic work is one of the important sites for "doing gender" (Beaujot, 2000; West and Zimmerman, 1987). Increasingly, mothers with young children continue to contribute to household earnings, but in some countries women opt out while their children are young. Some employed mothers accept part-time jobs, feeling that earning money is secondary to their main job as care provider and homemaker. Table 6.3 shows the percentage of mothers with children under three years of age who are in the labour force in selected OECD countries, revealing higher rates for the social democratic countries of Denmark and Sweden.

The feasibility and desirability of working part-time varies cross-nationally. Mothers are more likely to work full-time if they have attained high levels of education and earn high salaries, and if the cost of living is high, male wages are low, part-time jobs are difficult to find, separation and divorce rates are increasing, or the state provides little or no support for those outside paid work. We find considerable variation across countries among mothers employed part-time whose youngest child is under six years (OECD, 2005b:

Table 6.3 Employment Rate of Mothers with Children Under Three Years, 2008

Country	Maternal Employment Rate
Australia	–
Canada	58.7
Denmark	71.4
France	58.6
New Zealand	45.1
Sweden	71.9
United Kingdom	54.0
United States	54.2

Source: Extracted from OECD. 2012. *Towards a More Inclusive Labour Market*. Paris: OECD, extracted from Table 3.10. www.oecd.org/social/family/database>LMF1.2.

data chart SS4.3). These cross-national variations in part-time employment rates suggest that local labour market characteristics, social programs, and cultural attitudes about "good mothering" shape women's employment behaviour, rather than personal choices alone creating these patterns.

Women are also more likely than men to work in temporary jobs in almost all OECD countries (ibid., 35). The average OECD incidence of temporary employment as a percentage of all employment was 15.2 per cent for women and 13 per cent for men. However, in some countries, the rates are very high for both men and women. Although women's continuing responsibility for caring work contributes to the steady supply of part-time and temporary workers, local labour market conditions clearly influence these figures.

When women become mothers, they tend to suffer from a motherhood or child penalty in terms of their earnings, promotional opportunities, and job seniority (Crittenden, 2001; Zhang, 2009). One indicator of this penalty is that potential job applicants or actual employees who are pregnant or mothers are perceived as less qualified, less competent, and less committed to the job than childless women or men, both in experimental situations and by real employers (Correll et al., 2007). Another indicator is that the earnings gap between mothers and childless women is substantial, and it increases with women's age, educational qualifications, job experience, time outside the workforce, and the number of children they have (Zhang, 2009). In fact, this motherhood earnings gap can be higher for certain mothers than the gap between the earnings of men and women. In Canada, the earnings gap between 40-year-old childless women and comparably aged mothers with three or more years of work interruption is about 30 per cent (Zhang, 2009), compared to an earnings gap of 21 per cent between men and women.

In many countries, mothers with young children at home are more likely to work for pay and to enjoy higher household incomes if they live with a partner, as shown in Table 6.4 for Canada. Full-time work requires either unpaid child care by a family member or paid child care by a service provider. Lone mothers are less likely than partnered mothers to have either a family member available or the money to pay for care. Lone mothers' full-time employment rates also vary cross-nationally and are lower in some of the liberal states (such as Australia and the United Kingdom) because social programs permit these mothers to care for their children at home (Baker and Tippin, 1999; Baker, 2011a). In addition, demographic and socio-economic differences exist between lone and partnered mothers. For example, lone mothers tend to be younger when they bear their first child and to have lower educational attainment and less employment experience. Vast differences are also apparent among lone mothers depending on their route to lone parenthood: those who have never been married generally have the lowest socio-economic status and poorest job prospects (Dooley, 1995; Hunsley, 1997; Goodger and Larose, 1999; Millar and Rowlingson, 2001).

Table 6.4 Average After-Tax Family Income in 2007 by Family Type (in constant 2007 dollars)

Working-Aged Families	Average After-Tax Income
Couples with children	$82,000
Couples without children	$70,000
Male lone-parent families	$52,100
Female lone-parent families	$39,500

Source: Vanier Institute of the Family (2010: 99).

Parenting on a meagre income is clearly challenging, especially without a partner or affordable child care. The lone mothers in our New Zealand study (Baker, 2004a; Baker and Tippin, 2004) typically felt that being a "good mother" required constant supervision of their children, especially because so many lived in overcrowded and high-risk neighbourhoods. Many believed that paid work brought poor financial returns but left them with a myriad of household problems and child-care dilemmas, especially during school holidays or when the children were sick. The three factors of poverty, stressful work, and lack of social support seem to impede effective coping mechanisms.

Dealing with Child Poverty

Since the 1920s, most OECD countries have provided some form of income support to families with children. Early programs assisted disabled war veterans with dependants, widows, and deserted mothers with young children because governments considered these groups to be the most deserving (Bock and Thane, 1991; Baker, 1995, 2006; Gauthier, 1996). A number of countries also offered income tax relief to male workers supporting children and a financially dependent wife. These policies were intended to create some measure of equity between taxpayers with financial dependants and those without, as well as to supplement family income at a time of growing labour unrest and demand for higher wages (Baker, 1995; Ursel, 1992).

During the Great Depression of the 1930s, governments and employers' groups began to acknowledge that unemployment, accidents, and sickness could happen to the most diligent, were often beyond individual control, and required state support. In New Zealand, the first Labour government developed unemployment and sickness benefits in 1938, along with a state health-care program and extended public education. These programs were considered innovative among the liberal states at that time (Cheyne et al., 2008). In Canada, Unemployment Insurance was first paid in 1941, after years of public debate and a constitutional change that was required to overcome jurisdictional problems because employment-related programs are under provincial jurisdiction (McGilly, 1998).

By the 1940s, most of the liberal states (except the United States) also paid a universal child allowance for each child, regardless of the household income or employment status of the parents. Child allowances were paid monthly or bimonthly directly to the mother (or main care provider) in an attempt to ensure that the money was spent on children's needs (Baker, 1995). The idea behind universal child allowances was that bearing and raising children was not just something parents did for their own satisfaction but that reproduction within marriage was an expectation of citizenship, providing the nation with future workers, consumers, voters, and taxpayers.

Income support programs were also developed and/or expanded in the prosperous years of the 1960s and early 1970s for impoverished individuals and families, and family services and social housing were expanded. New social programs were created for mothers supporting children without a male breadwinner. In 1966, the Canadian federal government began to share the cost of social assistance with the provinces (with the Canada Assistance Plan), which enabled the provinces to expand services to families. In 1973, both Australia and New Zealand gave lone mothers the statutory right to state income support if they had low incomes, few assets, and needed to care for their children at home (Baker, 2006).

In recent decades, however, public discourse has changed about the purpose and value of state income support. Before universal family allowances in the 1940s, income support in the liberal states was targeted to the poorest and most deserving families to prevent them from falling into destitution. During the 1960s and 1970s, programs were expanded to keep people out of poverty and to provide equality of opportunity. After the 1990s, many governments returned to the practice of targeting social assistance to moderate- or low-income families in order to provide a "safety net" below which no family could fall (Baker, 2006). Unlike other liberal states, the United States never developed a family allowance or child benefit, and in 1972 began to place employment expectations on lone mothers receiving social assistance (Aid to Families with Dependent Children). Legislation in 1981 and 1996 created punitive "workfare" programs for lone mothers in the United States (Mink, 1998).

The United Kingdom retained its universal child benefit but the other liberal states have targeted these payments to moderate- or low-income families. In Canada, the family allowance ceased to be paid to all families with children in 1993 (Baker, 2006: 191), but federal child benefits continue to be paid to moderate- and low-income families, with a stronger emphasis on supporting the "working poor." Income support programs in some Canadian provinces have become less generous relative to living costs and average wages since the 1970s, and poor families now need to rely on charity (such as food banks) and kin to supplement state services (NCW, 2008).

In recent years, governments and international organizations have used the concept of "child poverty" rates, which are calculated as the percentage of children (under 18 years) living in households with incomes less than 50 per cent of the national median income, after taxes and government transfers. Agencies have focused on children because they cannot be held responsible for their parents' unemployment, illness, or unwillingness to work. Yet, it is actually parental circumstances and earning capacity that cause children to live in poverty and reduce their life chances.

Poverty rates for children are highest when they live in one-parent households where the parent is not working for pay and the family depends on low levels of income support, shown in Table 6.5. In one-parent households with a non-employed parent, 92 per cent of children in the United States and 89 per cent of children in Canada live in poverty. However, the comparable rate is only 20 per cent in Denmark and 18 per cent in Sweden (OECD, 2008a: 138). This table also shows that children living in two-parent households with one earner have relatively high poverty rates in North America, but rates dwindle if families have two earners (ibid.). In some countries, few mothers can afford to opt out of paid work because this would deepen the family's level of poverty.

Despite politicians' pronouncements about eliminating or reducing child poverty, these rates have actually increased since the mid-1990s in most OECD countries. The liberal states already had relatively high child poverty rates, but in Canada and New Zealand they have actually increased, by 2.2 and 2.3 per cent respectively, since 1995. However, they have been reduced in the United Kingdom, Australia, and the United States throughout the same period (OECD, 2008a: 138). One reason why child poverty increased in many countries is that income support programs were restructured to tighten expectations that

Table 6.5 Poverty Rates among Children by Household Type

Country	All Children	Children in One-Parent Households		Children in Two-Parent Households		
		Not Employed	Employed	Not employed	1 worker	2 Workers
Australia	12	68	6	51	8	1
Canada	15	89	32	81	22	4
Denmark	3	20	4	21	5	0
France	8	46	12	48	12	2
New Zealand	15	48	30	47	21	3
Sweden	4	18	6	36	14	1
United Kingdom	10	39	7	36	9	1
United States	21	92	36	82	27	6
OECD	12	54	21	48	16	4

Note: "Poverty rate" is defined as households with less than 50 per cent of national median income, after taxes and transfers, and adjusted for family size.

Source: Extracted from OECD (2009b: 93, Table EQ3.2).

beneficiaries should retrain or more actively search for work. However, the available jobs typically are insecure and pay low wages. The transition from "welfare to work" is risky for families if they must forfeit income security as well as subsidies for child care and medical expenses when they move off social assistance. If former beneficiaries lose their jobs and experience delays re-enrolling for income support, they may be worse off than remaining on social benefits. For political reasons, however, governments want to ensure that the services accompanying state income support are not more generous than those available to low-wage workers (Baker, 2011a). At the same time, they want children to grow up to become healthy and contributing citizens.

Studies concerning the long-term implications of growing up in poverty suggest that these children experience poorer health and more behaviour problems than those from higher-income families (Hobcraft and Kiernan, 2001; UNICEF, 2005). Living on a low income can permeate all aspects of child-rearing and childhood. Wealthier parents can purchase child-care ser- vices, after-school lessons, and recreational activities, counselling, and pre- ventive health care for their children. Low-income parents cannot afford to visit the doctor if they must pay for each consultation or pay to fill prescrip- tions, even if these services are partially subsidized by the state, as they are in Canada. A lack of affordable transportation also affects the ability of low- income parents to access medical services. In addition, without household savings, parents cannot prepare for emergencies. Research from several countries suggests that lone mothers with low income tend to suffer from anxiety and depression related to unpaid bills, fractious relationships, the heavy responsibility of caring for children alone, and despair about the future (Curtis, 2001; Sarfati and Scott, 2001; Baker and Tippin, 2004; Westad and McConnell, 2012).

Rapid labour market changes can lead to larger gaps between high and low earners and among those whose income derives from different sources, such as wages, salaries, state income support, or investments. With globalizing markets and increased competition, caring for children at home without earn- ing money has become a luxury affordable by fewer and fewer women, includ- ing those married to high earners or those who are independently wealthy. In many countries, households need the wages of two parents to maintain their living standards or stay out of poverty, but they also need adequate employ- ment leave for childbirth and family-related responsibilities.

Parental Leave and Child-Care Subsidies for Employed Parents

Before the 1970s, employment practices in most countries assumed that workers were men with wives at home to cook their meals, wash and iron their clothes, clean the house, and care for their children. However, the rise in maternal employment meant that laws, policies, and practices had to change to take into consideration women's child-bearing capacity, the health benefits of breast-feeding, and the care and supervision of children whose parents are employed. Offering paid leave for female employees during the interval surrounding childbirth has a long history in some European countries but is more recent in the liberal states (Baker, 2006). In 1952, the International Labour Organization (ILO) recommended that governments provide 12 weeks of paid leave and has since increased this to 14 weeks (UN, 2000: 133). Canada and most European nations have adopted this recommendation.

In Canada, employment leave is under provincial jurisdiction but maternity/parental benefits are paid by the federal government. Maternity benefits were first available in 1971 via the Unemployment Insurance program but further reforms in the 1990s improved access. Several Canadian provinces also reduced or eliminated the requirements of a lengthy employment record to enable more women to qualify for leave. In 1996, the reformed Employment Insurance (EI) program began to base eligibility for maternity/parental benefits on the number of hours previously worked rather than the number of weeks. This could help some non-standard workers to become eligible for EI, except that benefit levels were reduced in the process (Baker, 2006). The Canadian government also extended the length of parental benefits from 10 weeks to 35 weeks in 2001, which brought the combined total of maternity and parental leave to 50 weeks, paying initially up to 60 per cent of previous wages (Lawlor, 2003) but later reduced to 55 per cent.

In contrast, the United States offers no statutory right to paid employment leave for new parents at the federal level, while Australia introduced paid parental leave only in 2011 (Baker, 2011b). In 2002, New Zealand introduced 12 weeks of leave, paid at the same rate to all eligible recipients, raised this to 14 weeks in 2006, and considered raising it to 26 weeks in 2012–13. However, the duration of parental leave and the level of payment vary cross-nationally, and some European nations such as Norway and France offer generous benefits for longer periods.

If only one parent at a time is permitted to take parental leave, which is the case in most jurisdictions, the family is better able to survive on the father's higher earnings. In addition, both men and women view mothers as the logical choice because they are already taking employment leave for childbirth and recovery. Even when entitlement to childbirth leave is gender-neutral, fewer fathers take leave. According to a 2010 survey, 90 per cent of Canadian children aged 1–3 years who lived outside Quebec had mothers who took some time of leave at childbirth or adoption, but only 26 per cent of children had fathers who reported taking parental leave. The average length of time for leave was 44 weeks for mothers and 2.4 weeks for fathers. In Quebec, which has a more generous parental leave system, 99 per cent of the children had mothers who took leave (97 per cent was paid) and 76 per cent had fathers who took leave, with an average of five weeks more leave for mothers and three weeks more leave for fathers than in the rest of Canada (Findlay and Kohen, 2012). Both mothers and fathers who were self-employed took shorter periods of leave.

Most governments provide some funding for child-care services, especially if they are required for employment. Some offer tax benefits for parents who are able to show receipts for employment-related child care or they subsidize services for low-income working parents. Compared to the other liberal states, the Canadian government offers a relatively generous tax deduction for working parents using non-family child care, while the provinces subsidize care for low-income children using some federal money. In Quebec, the Parti Québécois government introduced a child-care program in 1997 that required parents to pay only $5 per day for care, whether or not parents were employed. That province also increased the number of spaces, the wages of educators, and the child-care budget at a time when other provinces were making cuts. In 2003, however, the Quebec Liberals took over the government, slowed the expansion of child care, increased parental fees, and encouraged for-profit child care (CRRU, 2003). Since then, public support for subsidizing child care remains high, although the cost was raised to $7 per day.

Conclusion: The Growing Impact of Paid Work on Family Life

Throughout much of the twentieth century, married men were the main family earners while married women cared for the home and children. Women usually worked in the formal labour force before marriage but not always afterwards, working fewer hours than men, earning lower wages, and more often earning money at home. Today, most women are employed regardless of their marital or parental status but noticeable differences remain between the work patterns of mothers and fathers.

Women's employment rates continue to be influenced by their marital status, the financial need of their households, the age of their children, ideologies about women's roles, opportunities to work part-time, and the availability of affordable child-care services, but they are also affected by national or local employment conditions. In recent decades, globalization, technological change, freer trade agreements, and new government policies have altered labour markets and employment patterns. Some workers have benefited from globalizing labour markets, including young educated men and women who are childless and geographically mobile. Yet lone mothers and certain cultural minorities remain disproportionately represented among low-wage workers and low-income households.

In the past two decades, many businesses, especially in the manufacturing sector, downsized to remain competitive in a world of freer trade and many more firms have laid off workers and/or declared bankruptcy. Governments in the liberal states no longer provide the same level of statutory protections for employees and unemployed workers, and labour forces have consequently become more polarized. Some families are "work poor" or the adults are unemployed or marginally employed, while others are "work rich" and are working long hours with insufficient time for caring activities or leisure (Torjman and Battle, 1999; OECD, 2008a). The neo-liberal restructuring of paid work and the welfare state continues to aggravate the problems of the working poor, especially youth and lone mothers. Some governments have restricted eligibility to income support, arguing that nothing should prevent the unemployed from finding and keeping work. Welfare-to-work programs imply that paid work is the answer to family poverty—but this can be true only when the job market is booming and wages are adequate relative to living costs.

Taylor-Gooby (2004) argued that new social risks have arisen from the decline of the male breadwinner family, labour market changes, and the impact of **globalization** on national policy-making. These new risks create challenges for governments as well as for youth, those without job skills, and women. They include balancing work with responsibilities for children and frail elderly family members, lacking the skills to find paid work with adequate wages, having skills that become obsolete, and using private provision that supplies insecure or inadequate services. Although balancing work and family is not exactly a new risk for women, the extent of the problem certainly has increased as more mothers have joined the workforce, male wages have not kept up with living costs, and the number of mother-led families continues to grow.

Although welfare states were established to deal with the risks of unemployment, sickness, disability, and retirement, the new risks provide complex challenges for governments (ibid.). They could expand public care for children and the elderly, promote more equal opportunities, and reduce employment poverty, but these solutions require political consensus, state intervention in the economy, and co-operation among governments, employers, unions, and voluntary organizations. New public spending would also require the political will to counteract the strong lobby from the political right that continues to argue for less state intervention and lower income taxes.

Although governments are encouraging families to derive more of their income security from paid work, parents with daily responsibilities for child care and housework enjoy fewer incentives to seek full-time employment or promotion. Many mothers cannot accept job assignments that involve relocating because they have to consider the lives of their partners and children. In addition, women's lower lifetime earnings increase their chances of poverty in old age, requiring state income support for many older unattached women. For this reason, governments are encouraging both women and men to see a lifetime of paid employment as normal; but not all women can easily do this unless family leave and caring arrangements are in place.

Questions for Critical Thought

1. Is there any research evidence that wives and husbands are entitled to the same family privileges when they become successful household earners?

2. Is the gap between the earnings of mothers and childless women higher than the gender wage gap? If so, why?

3. Do children and young people contribute their fair share to household work? Why or why not?

Questions for Debate

1. Cohabiting couples tend to organize their household money in a more equitable manner than married couples. Discuss.

2. Young people in the liberal states tend to spend their part-time earnings on frivolities while expecting their parents to finance their daily living expenses and education. Discuss.

3. Government child-care policies for working parents tend to give mixed messages to parents. Discuss.

Suggested Readings

Armstrong, Pat, and Hugh Armstrong. 2010. *The Double Ghetto: Canadian Women and Their Segregated Work*. Toronto: Oxford University Press. This is a revision and update of a classic sociology book on gender and work.

Pahl, Jan. 2005. "Individualisation in Couple Finances: Who Pays for the Children?" *Social Policy and Society* 4, 4: 381–91. This article examines how couples manage their household money, showing that it has become more individualized.

Ranson, Gillian. 2009. "Paid and Unpaid Work: How Do Families Divide Their Labour?" in M. Baker, ed., *Families: Changing Trends in Canada*, 6th edn. Toronto: McGraw-Hill Ryerson, 108–29. Ranson shows how shifts in the economy and how people earn their living affect the way that family life is organized. She also discusses the gendered division of caring work in Canada.

Suggested Websites

Childcare Resource and Research Unit
www.childcarecanada.org
> This Canadian website includes academic research and media coverage relating to child-care issues in Canada and other countries.

Organisation for Economic Co-operation and Development
www.oecd.org
> The website for this international organization contains many comparative statistics on paid work, child-care spending, and maternity benefits, especially through the project called "Babies and Bosses."

Vanier Institute of the Family
www.vifamily.ca
> The Vanier Institute site offers information about employment trends of men and women, as well as material on family spending and debt.

7 Separation, Divorce, and Re-partnering

Learning Objectives

◎ To relate the rising rates of separation and divorce to changes in the larger society.

◎ To identify the impact of family law reforms on partners, children, and parents.

◎ To discover whether re-partnering creates different kinds of families from first marriages.

Introduction

In the previous chapter, we saw that changing patterns of paid work have altered expectations about education and employment, the timing of marriage and child-bearing, and the division of labour between couples. In the liberal states, more adolescents and parents now work longer hours, including evenings and weekends, while more workers aspire for career progression and higher living standards. However, the growing percentage of the population working in insecure jobs and the increased choices about where to work also contribute to the impermanence of relationships. Even though most partners remain married for life, social researchers tend to focus on rising rates of relationship instability. Rather than spend time and money studying successful and durable marriages, researchers have focused on couple conflict, separation, and divorce, partly because governments and social agencies continue to fund such research as the social consequences can be profound.

In this chapter, we explore why a higher percentage of couples now separate, why legal marriages span shorter periods of time than in previous decades, and how the experiences of children and adults, men and women, and mothers and fathers differ in the "post-divorce family." These issues are not entirely academic ones, as many of us have experienced either parental separation or the dissolution of our own marriages, while others have witnessed the separation of friends or siblings. These personal experiences may help to shape our understandings of the consequences of separation and divorce, but we need to keep in mind that our own experiences may not be typical. However, personal knowledge might enhance our curiosity about the research findings relating to the relationship breakdowns of other people.

Why Are So Many Couples Separating?

When people get married, they usually intend to stay together for life. However, marriages are not lasting as long as they used to. A number of personal characteristics are correlated with higher rates of divorce, such as marrying someone from a different social background with varying ideas about the nature of marriage or preferable lifestyles. The probability of divorce also rises when couples marry early in life, household income is low, partners come from families with divorced parents, they have poor conflict management skills, the woman gains high levels of education and income, partners are not religious, and when couples cohabit before marriage (Bradbury and Norris, 2005; Wu and Schimmele, 2009). Bibby (2004–5) found that most Canadians look for certain characteristics in a partner and marry for a variety of reasons. However, the most prevalent reasons given for divorce were "different values and interests" and "abuse." This suggests that some partners either do not meet premarital expectations or they grow apart throughout the marriage.

In recent decades, social attitudes about marriage have also changed in the liberal states, contributing to separation and divorce. For example, the legal termination of marriage has more often been viewed as an acceptable conclusion to a relationship that has already broken down, and more people have come to appreciate that relationship dissolution does not necessarily arise from the misbehaviour of one partner. Instead, it stems from a variety of social and economic factors as well as personal and couple ones, including less economic necessity to stay together if the marriage is unhappy and both partners can support themselves. Growing time pressures and perceptions of an unfair division of labour at home also contribute to resentment (especially from employed mothers) and in some cases lead to marriage dissolution.

Couples have their own personal reasons for separating but rates of separation and divorce and the average duration of marriages that end in divorce vary regionally and cross-nationally, suggesting that societal factors alter these rates. For example, in 2008 Statistics Canada predicted that about 41 per cent of all Canadian marriages would end in divorce before the thirtieth wedding anniversary, but this varied from 25 per cent in Newfoundland to 60 per cent of marriages in Yukon (VIF, 2012). The first year of marriage is often quite satisfying for couples but the likelihood of divorce rises abruptly in Canada until the fourth year of marriage. The mean duration of legal marriages ending in divorce was 14.7 years in Canada in 2008 (ibid.), a slight increase in recent years (Ambert, 2009), while marriage duration before divorce ranges from about 10 to 15 years in other OECD countries (OECD, 2011a). Cross-national differences in divorce rates and the duration of marriage are influenced by legal restrictions, social and cultural conditions, and religious considerations (ibid.).

From 1970 to 1980, **crude divorce rates** (or divorces per 1,000 population) rose sharply in many OECD countries (OECD, 2009b). As Table 7.1 indicates, there is considerable variation in crude divorce rates by country, from a 2009 low of 0.9 per 1,000 population in Italy to a high of 3.7 in the United States. However, divorce rates have stabilized or declined slightly in recent decades in many countries as cohabitation has become more prevalent and legal marriage rates have declined. Generally, separation rates (without legal divorce) are not available from government statistics because partners can walk away from their relationships without reporting the dissolution to the authorities. Nevertheless, demographers have estimated that if separations were added to current divorce rates, the relationship breakdown rate could be four times as high as the official divorce rate, especially if we included separations from cohabitation (Beaujot, 2000: 110).

Table 7.1 Divorce Statistics in Selected OECD Countries, 1970, 1980, 2009 (per 1,000 population)

Country	1970	1980	2009
Australia	–	–	2.3
Canada	1.4	2.5	2.2
Denmark	1.9	2.7	2.7
France	0.8	1.5	2.1
Italy	–	0.2	0.9
NZ	1.1	2.1	2.3
Sweden	1.6	2.4	2.3
UK	1.1	2.8	2.4
US	3.5	5.2	3.7
OECD average	1.1	1.7	2.1

Sources: OECD, 2009b. *Society at a Glance.* Derived from Table GE 4.2; OECD 2011e. *Country Snapshots on Family and Children Policies and Outcomes.*

Higher rates of relationship breakdown have been influenced by a number of societal changes, including growing opportunities to live together outside marriage, changing attitudes about the right to happiness in marriage, and liberalized divorce laws. Before the 1950s, both men and women needed marriage in order to survive economically, but since then the expansion of women's employment opportunities, public child-care services, and state income support programs have made it possible for both women and men to leave unhappy relationships and live outside marriage. Although women are more likely than men to initiate the separation (Amato and Previti, 2003; Hewitt et al., 2005), many separated mothers with young children struggle to make ends meet without a male earner in the household. Consequently, most governments have created income support programs to enable lone parents to recover from the emotional and financial trauma that often accompanies separation and to support their children while retraining or searching for paid work. Also, separated partners can more easily live alone because of the availability of self-contained apartments and flats, household appliances, convenience food, and a variety of domestic services available on the commercial market.

Greater expectations of personal happiness and freedom of partner choice also encourage people to leave unhappy relationships. Couples now feel less obligated to stay together to fulfill their marriage vows, to please their parents, or to protect their reputations or those of their family. **Marital breakdown** has also become prevalent with increased geographic mobility and opportunities to meet people from different cultures. More **exogamy** or marriage outside one's social or cultural group means that an increasing percentage of partners enter marriage with different ideas about what constitutes a satisfactory lifestyle, a good couple relationship, or positive relations with other family members, which could augment marital conflict and eventually lead to separation.

Another reason for increased marriage breakdown is that laws in most countries now permit couples to divorce if one or both partners report that their relationship has irretrievably broken down. Previously, divorce laws in common-law countries required legal proof presented in court to show that a partner had violated the marriage contract before the other partner could petition the courts for divorce. This was a stressful, time-consuming, and expensive process. In contrast, in many places today divorce is granted if the former partners state in writing that their marriage has broken down, as long as they wait a necessary period before applying for a divorce.

Reforms dealing with the division of matrimonial property, **child custody**, and **child support** have taken place in all the liberal states. However, these legal changes have been controversial for a number of reasons. First, they highlight deep-seated resentments about the different contributions husbands and wives typically make to household management and resources. Second, children in the post-divorce family often live in low-income or impoverished households, despite recently acquired legal rights in all these countries and international conventions on the rights of the child from the United Nations. Third, parents often re-partner and scarce resources need to be shared among two or more households that include biological and stepchildren. Finally, some critics suggest that liberalized divorce laws discourage couples from working harder to make their marriages work and argue that the grounds for divorce should be tightened once again.

In summary, more relationships and marriages now end because women and men have gained more opportunities to live outside marriage and because reformed divorce laws (combined with fewer children) make it easier for couples to separate. More people believe that they have the right to a satisfying marital relationship and could be happier with a different partner. If their current marriage is unhappy, they feel that they should not be forced to stay together and should be permitted to divorce and remarry. In addition, the rise

---

> (**Box 7.1**) The Top Five Reasons Why Couples Separate and Divorce, Canada, 2004
>
> ---
>
> 1. Different values and interests
> 2. Abuse—physical and emotional
> 3. Alcohol and drugs
> 4. Infidelity
> 5. Career-oriented conflict
>
> Source: Reginald Bibby. 2004. *A Survey of Canadian Hopes and Dreams*. Ottawa: Vanier Institute of the Family. (Cited in VIF, 2010: 51).

in consensual relationships may have led to a stabilization or slight decline in divorce rates in some countries since the 1980s, but this does not mean that fewer relationships are dissolving. As we noted in Chapter 3, cohabiting couples have higher rates of separation than legally married couples. As more people cohabit, they contribute to relationship instability in the larger society (Beck-Gernsheim, 2002).

Outcomes of Separation and Divorce

Since the 1970s, the consequences of separation and divorce have become controversial and the object of considerable public debate and policy analysis. Despite widespread agreement that spouses should not be forced to live together against their wishes, marriage and divorce trends have led to a number of concerns. These include the implications for children's behaviour and emotional well-being, the high poverty rates in mother-led households, the large percentage of "fading fathers" who fail to visit their children or pay child support, and allegations of court bias against fathers in custody and access awards.

After separation, most parents make their own decisions about child custody; if the courts in the common-law countries are asked to decide, they are expected to base their decisions on "the best interests of the child." However, who decides what is best for children and how do they arrive at this decision? In practice, most children continue to reside with the mother after parental separation. Table 7.2 shows the percentage of sole-parent families headed by women in selected OECD countries. In Canada, this was about 80 per cent in 2006, down slightly from 83 per cent in 1981 (OECD, 2010: 3; VIF, 2009). The minimum child support payment required by the liberal states is usually kept at a low level to encourage and enable low-income fathers to pay, but this means that it is often too small to pay the bills for the child's household. Furthermore, in the liberal states many fathers fail to pay the required

Table 7.2 Percentage of One-Parent Households Headed by Women, Selected OECD Countries

Country	Percentage of One-Parent Households Headed by Women
Australia	87.0
Canada	80.1
France	85.3
New Zealand	83.0
United Kingdom	86.7
United States	77.5
OECD average	84.5

Source: OECD Family Database 2010, Table SF1.1A, p. 3; NZ figure from New Zealand Ministry of Social Development (2010: 13) www.oecd.org/social/family/database..

amount of child support and about one-third of fathers lose contact with their children altogether (Smyth, 2004). In most of these countries, the majority of divorced men re-partner and some produce additional children with new partners. Yet few fathers can earn enough to support two households with children.

Despite legal reform throughout the 1980s and 1990s, the courts have been unable to compensate for the gendered nature of paid and unpaid work during marriage, which clearly creates economic and social inequalities after separation. In addition, the courts are unable to compensate for the fact that two adult incomes have become necessary to cover current living expenses and that the one-earner household remains disadvantaged unless it relies on an above-average income. As we saw in Chapter 6, households led by lone mothers usually struggle on low incomes even when these mothers are employed (OECD, 2008b). Even when child-care services are unaffordable or unavailable, mothers in the liberal states are still expected to care for their children while they are earning money or to depend on relatives or neighbours to help them. This means that many mothers with young children work part-time or rely on some level of state income support that seldom pays an amount equivalent to the minimum wage (Baker, 2004a). Consequently, the average earnings of mothers supporting young children are not only lower than men's earnings but are also lower than the earnings of women without children at home (OECD, 2007a).

In most Western countries, divorce has become easier both legally and socially, especially among childless couples and those with fewer children. In countries such as Canada and New Zealand only about half of divorces involve children under 18 (Baker, 2008a); nonetheless, parents and the state need to consider their emotional and economic well-being also. Although researchers tend to focus on the harmful effects of separation and divorce on children, it is also apparent that the perpetuation of an unhappy marriage can be more detrimental than separation and divorce both to adults and to children (Amato and Booth, 1997; Pryor and Rodgers, 2001: 239; Cunningham and Thornton, 2006). Some lone mothers provide positive role models for their children with their capacity to manage the household and earn money to support the children. However, social policies and reformed family law increasingly assume that lone mothers can pay household bills on their own earnings, even when they cannot.

Family and Divorce Laws

Divorce laws vary cross-nationally but two main systems of law are used in the liberal states and in European countries. English Canada, the United States, Australia, and New Zealand originally based their legal systems on English common law, which is still used in the United Kingdom, while Quebec and many European countries use variations of civil law (Harrison, 1993). Generally, common law relies more on custom and precedents from judicial decisions while civil law emphasizes legal statutes, basic principles, and the written contracts made by cohabiting partners regarding their own wishes.

In federal states such as Canada and the United States, legal jurisdiction over family issues is further divided by province or state. In Canada, the federal government retains jurisdiction over divorce, including the legal right to remarry, and also establishes guiding principles for child custody, access, and financial support (Bala and Clarke, 1981). The provinces hold jurisdiction over marriage, the division of family assets upon the separation of spouses, and laws pertaining to the granting and enforcing of child custody, access, child support, and spousal support (Wu and Schimmele, 2009). Laws and practices relating to custody and support vary by province, as well as between Quebec and the rest of Canada. This division has led to some enforcement problems and unequal living standards for mother-led households in different parts of the country.

Marriage, child-rearing, and divorce under common law are considered to be mainly the concerns of family members rather than the broader community (Harrison, 1993: 35). Although spouses are permitted to own and control property acquired before marriage, they are expected to share the income they earn and the possessions they acquire during marriage (such as the marital home, their furnishings, and the family car). Historically, patterns of ownership differed for husbands and wives because their access to earnings and family money was not the same.

Marriage, Gender, and Property

In common-law jurisdictions, a legal wife was entitled to "dower rights" or one-third of her husband's property should the marriage dissolve. In return, a husband was expected to support his wife financially until her death or remarriage, but he retained the right to establish their legal residence (or domicile) and their standard of living. If couples divorced before the 1970s (and few did), family assets typically were divided according to dower rights, in a way that reflected who purchased them or whose name was on the deed.

A former husband could be required by the pre-1970s courts to pay **alimony,** maintenance, or lifelong financial support to his former wife if she had not committed a **matrimonial fault.** The most prevalent matrimonial fault or reason for a wife to forfeit financial support was adultery or sexual intercourse with another man. Spousal support was contingent on her fidelity during marriage, at the time of separation, and until the legal divorce—rather than on her unpaid domestic services during marriage, her caring responsibilities, or her financial need. If she left her husband, committed adultery, or remarried, she normally lost her right to his financial support (Baker, 1995: 293). Under common law, former wives also tended to receive a smaller share of marital property than husbands after divorce, which especially disadvantaged those wives who cared for their children at home rather than earning money for the household.

At the time of divorce, a portion of the family assets and/or spousal support payments could be awarded to "blameless" ex-wives (that is, women who had not committed adultery), depending on their husband's economic circumstances and the discretion of the judge overseeing the court case. Yet, enforcement procedures for this support often were ineffective and the former wife had to take her defaulting husband to court after each offence in an attempt to retrieve these payments. In Canada, the provinces were responsible for enforcing alimony, which meant that a former husband could avoid support payments by moving to another province (Baker, 2001b: 188). Spousal maintenance after divorce used to be paid to full-time homemakers and mothers, or simply to assuage a husband's guilt (Harrison, 1993). By the late 1970s, many lawyers and former partners viewed these laws as arbitrary: some husbands felt that they were paying ex-wives too much and many wives felt that their caring work and unpaid contributions to the home were undervalued.

Now, divorce terminates all marital rights and obligations in the common-law countries but *not* obligations to child support. Divorced spouses are expected to become economically self-sufficient shortly after divorce through their own earnings, and former wives are no longer awarded lifelong support although they may be granted temporary support based on financial need. While the former laws assumed that husbands were breadwinners and wives were homemakers and financial dependants, the amended laws suggest that both are equally self-supporting after separation when in fact they seldom are. The divorce laws still contain some judicial discretion with respect to spousal support, especially for older women unable to find work and long-term homemakers with few job skills, but young women are usually awarded only fixed-term support because they are seen as future employees. In 2004, for example, spousal support was ordered by the courts in only 10 per cent of Canadian cases (VIF, 2004: 37) even though labour markets were still gendered and women's average earnings were considerably less than men's, especially when they also cared for young children. This declined to 8 per cent in 2007 (Martin and Robinson, 2008).

Marital separation is emotionally difficult for both men and women but research suggests that strategies to cope with divorce are somewhat gendered. Women are more likely than men to feel relieved and liberated following a divorce, to spend time with friends, to see a counsellor for therapy, and to show greater emotional strength (Sev'er, 1992; Walker, 2005). In contrast, men are more likely than women to find solace in drinking, to return to a former girlfriend, to have casual sex, or to look for a new partner in their community or on the Internet. In addition, divorced men tend to earn higher incomes and enjoy a higher living standard, and are less likely to live with their children. Consequently, they tend to find new partners faster than women.

After a specified period of living apart, a marriage can be dissolved in most common-law jurisdictions through **no-fault divorce** even without one partner's consent, and wives can no longer delay court proceedings in an attempt to negotiate a better financial settlement. Although this appears to bring gender equality to the process, it may actually be less than equitable because women's earnings and assets tend to be lower than men's after separation (Baker, 2007). Maternal caring responsibilities clearly interfere with earning capacity, as we saw in Chapter 6. Lack of career planning, priority given to the needs of children and partners, and discrimination in the workplace further diminish women's occupational mobility and earned incomes compared to those of men.

Who should compensate for these gender differences? Should former husbands be asked to reimburse their ex-wives for raising their children, caring for the home, and therefore falling behind in their earnings? Or should the state attempt to create gender equity for girls, for women in the labour force, and especially for employed mothers with young children? The answers to these questions vary according to personal beliefs and circumstances, but have led to considerable public debate among interest groups.

Reforms in Child Custody and Residence Patterns

In the past two decades, most industrialized countries have made numerous reforms to laws relating to divorce, child custody, child support, spousal support, and the division of family assets. Generally, laws and judicial practices have rejected any implications that children could be the property of either parent after marriage breakdown or should live with a specific parent. For example, the 1985 Canadian divorce law clearly stated that either parent, or both together, could be granted "custody" or legal decision-making rights after divorce and that this decision should be based on the "best interests of the child" rather than any notion of parental rights. Yet, professionals and parents often disagree about what is the best living arrangement. Children are sometimes ambivalent when they are consulted, and young children generally prefer to live with both parents even when this is no longer possible. Despite legal changes, over three-quarters of children in the liberal states continue to live with their mothers after separation and divorce, although there is considerable variation by country (Millar and Rowlingson, 2001; OECD, 2010).

Child custody and residence arrangements after separation are currently in dispute in many jurisdictions. Although relatively few cases are contested, some lawyers and feminist activists argue that the concept of the "best interests of the child" is too vague, and that judges should instead base contested custody decisions on the "primary caregiver presumption." This means that the parent who was responsible for the primary care during marriage normally would become the custodial or resident parent after separation unless there is a good reason to alter this arrangement (Boyd, 2003). If this principle were applied, it would be relatively easy to make custody decisions and continuity would be provided for children. Also, following this principle would avoid the threat posed to women of unequal joint custody situations in which women perform most of the daily caring but men retain the power to share all decisions relating to the child's well-being (Baker, 2008b; Smart and Sevenhuijsen, 1989). However, the primary caregiver principle could reinforce both the gendered division of labour in the home and women's primary role as mothers rather than workers (Pulkingham, 1994).

Child custody used to be awarded to only one parent (usually the mother). In the 1980s, the common-law countries introduced the concept of **joint custody**, which means shared *legal* responsibility rather than physical parenting. In most families, separating parents make their own arrangements for the care of their children; custody orders were made by the Canadian courts in only 30 per cent of divorces in 2002 (VIF, 2004: 37–8). However, when the courts do intervene, the trend towards joint custody in Canada is quite evident in official statistics. The percentage of children involved in awards of custody to both parents rose from 11.6 in 1986 to 46.5 in 2004 (VIF, 2010: 66), as Table 7.3 indicates. Yet, research suggests that joint custody is most effective when it is voluntary rather than enforced by the court (Baker, 1995: 300).

A number of countries (including Australia) have amended legislation to remove the word "custody" or any other notions of child ownership from the

Table 7.3 Court-Ordered Custody Arrangements in Canada, 1986, 1995, and 2004 (% of children)

Custody Arrangement	1986	1995	2004
Mother only	72.0	67.6	45.0
Joint custody	11.6	21.4	46.5
Father only	15.3	10.9	8.1
Other	1.0	0.2	0.2

Source: Baker (1995: 300); VIF (2004: 38); VIF (2010: 67).

language of divorce and to replace them with the words "parental responsibilities" (Funder, 1996). Divorcing parents are also expected to make a parenting plan for their children with the assistance of counselling, conciliation, and mediation. Both parents now retain parenting responsibilities, yet mothers tend to remain the "resident parent" and the main provider of daily care after separation and divorce. In Canada, children experience actual shared living arrangements in only 6 per cent of court-ordered arrangements and in 12 per cent of privately settled cases. The large majority of children continue to live with their mothers even when there is shared custody (VIF, 2010: 66).

The Australian Caring for Children after Separation Project found that 79 per cent of children live with their mothers after separation (Qu, 2004). The relatively few children living with their fathers tend to be older, but no gender differences were apparent in this study. Discussing the same study, Smyth and Weston (2004) noted that less than 6 per cent of parents share the regular care of their children after separation, but that this arrangement is more likely to be preferred by fathers than by mothers, by parents already sharing care, and by non-resident parents rather than by resident parents. The attitudes of resident mothers towards **shared parenting** tend to be negative; mothers' attitudes become more positive in low-conflict parental relationships and for older children. Australian fathers reported that they *want* to be more involved in their children's lives after separation, perhaps a reaction to "the apparent shallowness of every-other-weekend contact schedules that have arisen from traditional sole (maternal) custody models of post-separation parenting" (ibid., 14).

In the same study, researchers found that about 51 per cent of non-resident parents (mainly fathers) maintain regular face-to-face contact with their children after separation but 30 per cent retain little or no contact. Higher levels of contact between fathers and children were associated with lower levels of inter-parental conflict, lower levels of **re-partnering**, less physical distance between the parents' households, and higher levels of financial resources (Smyth, 2004). Where father–child contact was tenuous, the perceptions of mothers and fathers differed. Mothers perceived that fathers lacked interest in the children while fathers felt that their former partners were cutting them out of the children's lives. This study shows that experiences and attitudes in the post-divorce family often vary by gender and social circumstances.

Reforms in Assessment and Enforcement of Child Support

Before the 1990s, fathers were expected to support their children financially, and upon divorce the courts would order them to pay an amount of child support that related more to their ability to pay rather than to the children's needs. If a father failed to pay, the children's mother was expected to take him to court to retrieve the money. This meant she had to prove he was the father, to know where he lived, to take him to court in the jurisdiction where he lived, and to pay court expenses. These procedures were impractical and too expensive for most mothers (Baker, 2008b).

As divorce rates soared in the 1970s and 1980s, policy-makers and social service workers became concerned about the high poverty rates in lone-mother households where fathers were not paying child support or not paying the full amount on time. The concern particularly focused on the long-term consequences of poverty for children's development and life chances. Government-sponsored studies in several common-law countries have found that two-thirds to three-quarters of parents required to pay child support (usually fathers) failed to pay the full amount of court-awarded support within a few years of the divorce (Trapski et al., 1994; Funder, 1996; Smyth, 2004). Consequently, most lone mothers had to rely on paid work, on loans from friends or family, or on state income support. To induce separated parents to pay child support, the Canadian government used to offer non-custodial parents (mainly fathers) an income tax deduction on support paid, but ironically required custodial parents (mainly mothers) to pay income tax on that money (Baker, 1995: 330). This proved to be an ineffective inducement for most men and payment rates remained low (Boyd, 2003).

Several jurisdictions introduced major reforms in the assessment and enforcement of child support in the 1980s, and others have followed. Child support agencies were established in some countries, such as Australia and the United Kingdom, to assess the amount to be paid by using a formula based on the number of children and the non-resident parent's income. The taxation office began collecting support money from non-resident parents (mostly fathers) and paying it to resident parents (mostly mothers) through welfare offices. These schemes involved both married and unmarried parents and generally increased the proportion of mother-led households receiving child support as well as the amounts paid (Harrison, 1993). Nevertheless, the state has been unable to collect the full amount from many separated fathers, especially those who are less affluent, unemployed, difficult to trace, never married, no longer in contact with their children, or who separated many years ago (Millar and Whiteford, 1993; Jones, 1996: 97; Smyth, 2004; Martin and Robinson, 2008).

The Canadian provinces and territories design and administer their own child support schemes and all of them have tightened enforcement procedures since the 1980s. However, awards still are set by judges in court, based on national guidelines established in 1997 and amended in 2002. Some Canadian provinces focus their enforcement on families receiving income support, while others have used the **first default principle**, which means that the government scheme is activated only when a parent makes a complaint about unpaid support. Since 1987, the federal government has provided the provinces with enforcement tools, including sharing information to locate and intercept defaulters, suspending or denying federal licences or passports, and operating an automated telephone information system (Canada, Department of Justice, 2003). Canadian provincial statistics indicate that post-reform default rates (which include partial payment, no payment, or late payment) vary from 50 per cent to 75 per cent depending on jurisdiction, and that only 43 per cent of parents pay the full amount on time (VIF, 2010: 66).

Canadian research indicates that fathers were ordered to pay child support in 93 per cent of cases, with a median payment of $435 per month in 2004 (VIF, 2004: 37). However, some researchers suggest that national child support guidelines are inequitable because they are based on the non-resident parent's income but not his net assets. They also fail to consider the resident parent's socio-economic situation or the children's financial needs (Wu and Schimmele, 2009). While default rates decreased with the new enforcement systems, an average of 65 per cent of cases are in arrears, meaning that the total amount was not paid, was not paid on time, or was not paid at all (Martin and Robinson, 2008). Nevertheless, the percentage of fathers who clearly refuse to pay is small as most "defaulters" report that they are temporarily unable to pay, are caught in administrative disputes, or are in the process of having the award adjusted in court (Lapointe and Richardson, 1994; Richardson, 2001). The reasons given for lack of payment may be legitimate, but they could also represent a more socially acceptable way of avoiding payment.

In New Zealand, more non-resident fathers now pay child support than was the case before reforms, but many pay the minimum of $16.30 NZ per week, which is merely a gesture in the direction of support and a fraction of the cost of raising children (IRD, 2012). Researchers in several countries have found that about one-third of non-resident fathers have little or no contact with their children after separation and that those with little contact are least likely to pay child support. Failure to pay is also associated with men's perceptions of access difficulties to their children (Smyth, 2002, 2004; Amato, 2004).

Australian research has shown that 41 per cent of non-resident fathers wanted to change the children's living arrangements five years after separation—two-thirds wanted the children to live with them and the remaining third wanted equal care (Smyth et al., 2001). Non-resident fathers also reported more contact with their children than the resident mothers reported that fathers have. Some non-resident fathers argued that the cost of contact should be given more weight in the process of child support assessment and that support payments should be reduced to compensate for the expenses paid when their child stays over. Although many people believe that child support legislation ought to foster and facilitate parent–child contact, legislators have argued that linking father–child contact to the amount of child support to be paid is not in the best interests of the child (Smyth, 2002).

New practices of awarding joint custody generally have given fathers or non-resident parents more access to their children after separation, but at the same time child support has been more stringently enforced. However, a number of controversial issues remain unresolved, including other ways to deal with poverty in mother-led households and the broader question of the impact of separation on children (Baker, 2008a).

Children, Separation, and Divorce

The impact of parental separation and divorce on children has been a popular research topic over the years, especially in the United States, and most researchers agree that the experience of living in a one-parent household may be quite different from living with two parents who remain happily married for life. In statistical comparisons between children living in households that have one parent and those living in "intact" households, researchers have found that children raised by one parent are more likely to experience a variety of negative outcomes. These include lower educational attainment, behavioural problems, delinquency, leaving home earlier, teenage pregnancy or parenthood, higher divorce rates when they marry, and many others (Sigal et al., 2012; Pryor and Rodgers, 2001). These differences, however, could result from many factors, such as the impact of parental **conflict** before and after the separation, loss of children's contact with their father, lack of male role models, or the drop in household income that so often accompanies parental separation.

It is important to remember that most children live with the mother most of the time after parental separation and divorce, and consequently experience reduced contact with the father or parental disputes relating to this contact. Therefore, children's well-being after parental separation could be influenced by the frequency of contact with the father and the quality of this contact. Research suggests that children who experience diminished paternal contact often suffer distress from this loss, and that paternal contact is lower with fathers who are not or were not legally married to the children's mother (Cockett and Tripp, 1994; Juby et al., 2007; Qu and Weston, 2008). However, the *quality* of time with the father and the absence of conflict in these meetings are more important than the amount of time (Amato and Rezac, 1994; Pryor and Rodgers, 2001).

Furthermore, whether or not the father continues to pay child support may influence both the children's adjustment and the socio-economic status of the child's household. Many children would resent the fact that their father is not paying for their expenses and see this as an indication of his rejection of them, but without always considering the economic constraints under which he may be operating. Children who have little or no contact with the father may not only resent his absence but have few other male role models that positively influence their lives. However, maternal grandfathers, uncles, family friends, community workers, teachers, and neighbours may fulfill this role (Harper and Ruicheva, 2004).

The low-income characteristic of lone-mother households is also a major influence on the statistical outcomes of parental separation for children. It is important to acknowledge that many of these households have experienced economic disadvantage *before* separation as well as after. People from lower socio-economic groups tend to have higher rates of bereavement (i.e., more parents die in these families), separation, and divorce (Pryor and Rodgers, 2001). When children are raised in low-income households, regardless of the number of parents present, they are more likely to suffer from certain socio-economic disadvantages that follow them into adulthood. These include delayed school readiness, lower educational attainment, more trouble with school authorities and the law, more serious childhood illnesses, higher accident rates during childhood, premature death, high rates of depression, and high rates of smoking and alcohol abuse as young adults, to name only a few (Canadian Institute of Child Health, 2002; Sigal et al., 2012).

Poverty rates remain high among mother-led households even though new procedures have been developed to enforce child support. Despite the political rhetoric about reducing "child poverty" because of its long-term consequences for children's well-being, these rates have actually increased in a number of countries since the 1990s (UNICEF, 2005; OECD, 2009b). Sporadic support or low levels of paternal child support increase the poverty rates of mother-led households, but poverty is also influenced by the inability of many lone mothers to earn sufficient incomes because they often work part-time, earn low wages, or care for their children at home on relatively ungenerous social benefits. Lone parents must also contend with a competitive job market, soaring housing costs in some urban centres, and unaffordable child-care and transportation expenses when they attempt to find paid work and become self-supporting. Yet conservative politicians and policy-makers often focus on effective ways to enforce paternal child support rather than addressing the other contributors to family poverty.

When earlier studies have controlled for household income, the negative outcomes more apparent in **lone-parent households** have declined but did not disappear (Elliott and Richards, 1991; Maclean and Kuh, 1991; Kiernan, 1997). For example, the Canadian National Longitudinal Survey on Children and Youth (NLSCY) found that about 19 per cent of children from low-income families headed by a lone mother experience a "conduct disorder" compared to 9 per cent of children from two-parent families. For those from higher-income families, this percentage drops to 13 per cent for lone-mother families and 8 per cent for two-parent families (Lipman et al., 1996). This suggests that other factors besides household income are influencing the outcomes for children living with lone parents. Never-married mothers who become pregnant before their education is completed are particularly vulnerable to low income and to behavioural problems by their children. These mothers often re-partner within a few years of the child's birth but the socio-economic disadvantages of bearing a child at a young age may linger. The children are most likely to spend their early years in one or more stepfamilies, which are not always harmonious (Marcil-Gratton, 1998; Edin and Reed, 2005). Numerous studies show that lone mothers report poorer health, more family problems, and lower incomes than partnered mothers. Dorsett and Marsh (1998) reported that British sole mothers had high rates of cigarette smoking, which augmented financial problems and poor health. Low income, poor health, and low morale all interfere with returning to paid work and improving their circumstances. Curtis (2001) found that Canadian sole mothers typically reveal poorer health than married mothers, but when they controlled for age, income, education, lifestyle factors, family size, and other recognized determinants of health, the differences diminished.

Sarfati and Scott (2001) found that New Zealand sole mothers were more likely to have lower family incomes and lower educational qualifications, to be Maori, and to live in more deprived areas. They also found poorer physical and mental health among lone mothers, but the physical health differences disappeared after controlling for socio-economic variables. My own research based on qualitative interviews with 120 lone mothers on welfare in New Zealand illustrates their concerns when they are expected to find paid work despite having sick children, poor health of their own, multiple family problems, and depression. Their stories, which coincide with research in other countries, confirm that many of the liberal states expect low-income mothers to find paid work and become self-supporting but offer them little social support to maintain their jobs and enhance their family well-being (Baker, 2002b; Baker and Tippin, 2004).

Whitehead et al. (2000) concluded that the Swedish social security system is more effective at keeping sole mothers healthier and out of poverty than the British system, yet Swedish sole mothers still report poorer mental and physical health than partnered mothers. These women may have experienced health problems before having a child, and the health issues could have contributed to marriage instability. In addition, the circumstances in which many lone mothers find themselves tend to contribute to depression and anxiety about the future. This anxiety could lead to problems disciplining children, especially if mothers have little support from family, friends, or social services. All these factors help to account for higher rates of behavioural problems in the children of lone mothers, especially those who are younger and never married.

Despite these findings, researchers have found no *direct* relationship between parental separation and children's adjustment, although many studies find differences between children from two-parent families and separated families (Amato and Keith, 1991; Burghes, 1994; Cartwright, 2008). Parental separation does add stress to children's lives through changes in relationships, living situations, and parental resources, but few studies conclude that psychological disturbance is severe or prolonged (Emery, 1994; Baker, 2007). It is difficult to determine, however, whether problems that surface later in adult life are attributable to parental divorce or other factors.

Some studies suggest that the experience of parental separation and divorce has long-term consequences for children because children's attitudes are always shaped by their home environment and their parents' relationships. However, the impact of parental marital experiences may become more apparent later in life in young people's attitudes about marriage, in their intimate relationships, and in their relationships with parents and other family members (Cartwright, 2006, 2008; Cunningham and Thornton, 2006). Woodward et al. (2000) analyzed longitudinal data from the Christchurch Health and Development Study in New Zealand. They found that exposure to parental separation was strongly associated with lower attachment to parents in adolescence and more negative perceptions of both maternal and paternal care and protection during childhood. The younger the child at the time of separation, the lower his or her subsequent parental attachment and the more likely the child was to perceive the parents as less caring but overprotective. Furthermore, other studies suggest that experiencing parental separation raises the chances of unstable relationships in adult life. This may result from poor relationship models in childhood, mistrust of the opposite sex learned from the custodial parent, or personal knowledge of divorce procedures and their aftermath.

Hughes (2005) used qualitative interviews with a small sample of Australian adults who had experienced parental separation as children to investigate some of the conclusions about the future of intimacy arising from the work of Giddens (1992) and Beck-Gernsheim (2002). These interviews suggested that experiencing parental separation may have a lasting impact by encouraging people to see intimate relationships as inherently fragile and to view the formation and termination of these relationships as part of their personal growth. Hughes's participants also saw the nuclear family as flawed and limited, especially in its potential to meet the needs of children. She concluded that if more people in the future live their lives outside the nuclear family in relatively "loose formations," this will have "monumental implications for public policy, and for the law in particular" (Hughes, 2005: 84). There is considerable evidence from OECD studies that relationship transitions are becoming prevalent as more people separate and re-partner.

Remarriage and Stepfamilies

More people are entering legal marriage for the second or third time, particularly in countries with relatively high divorce rates (OECD, 2011a). In Canada, Australia, and New Zealand, over one-third of all marriages involved at least one partner who had been previously married, and men are more likely than women to re-partner or to remarry after separation or divorce (Baker, 2008a). Remarriage rates increased in these countries from the 1960s to the early 1990s, but as cohabitation increased and first marriage rates declined, remarriage rates have also declined (Wu and Schimmele, 2009). Nevertheless, more people are creating stepfamilies or **blended families** through re-partnering.

Stepfamilies have been described as the fastest-growing family form in the last few decades (Ferri and Smith, 2003; Doodson and Morley, 2006). Because most children live with the mother after separation, the most typical stepfamily arrangement involves a mother and her new partner living with her children, who are still maintaining contact with their non-resident father. In Canada, stepfamilies with children accounted for 12.6 per cent of all families with children in 2011, up slightly from 2006 (Statistics Canada, 2012a). Most stepfamilies contain only the biological or adopted children from previous relationships, representing 7.4 per cent of all couples with children. A smaller percentage of stepfamilies include children that the remarried or re-partnered couple produced together plus at least one from previous relationships, representing 5.2 per cent of couples with children (ibid.). In Australia, 4 per cent of all families with children under the age of 18 were stepfamilies (with children brought to the relationship from either partner) and 3 per cent were blended families (with stepchildren and the biological children of the new couple) in 2006–7 (ABS, 2008c).

Despite the growth of stepfamilies, politicians, state officials, and social workers in many countries have expressed concern about the low remarriage rates among lone mothers. British research from the National Child Development Study found that 50 per cent of lone mothers re-partnered within three years if they had never been married, within about five years if divorced, and closer to eight years if they had been separated or widowed (McKay and Rowlingson, 1998). These time periods are similar to but slightly longer than those reported from earlier studies from the United Kingdom (Ermisch, 1991) and longer than those found in American research. The duration of lone parenthood appears to be lengthening but is longer for mothers than fathers, for those living in social housing, and for men who are unemployed (McKay and Rowlingson, 1997). Poor economic prospects, especially for young men, discourage marriage and remarriage among lone parents (Edin and Reed, 2005). No financial advantage can be gained by a lone mother marrying an unemployed man, as her economic hardship could increase and she might disqualify herself from state income support. In addition, re-partnering does not necessarily lead to better child development, although it usually constitutes an economic gain for the lone mother and her children if the man is employed.

Researchers have found that children in stepfamilies differ statistically from children living in lone-parent or intact families. Children in stepfamilies have been found to have higher rates of accidents, higher levels of bedwetting, more contact with the police, and lower self-esteem, and, on average, they leave school earlier without qualifications compared to children in lone-parent families (Wadsworth et al., 1983; Elliott et al., 1993; Beaupré et al., 2006). Pryor and Rodgers (2001) argue that these experiences can be explained by the lower family aspirations and expectations that step-parents have for their stepchildren compared to their own biological children, as well as by family friction in these households. Stepfamilies also involve more conflict than lone-parent families because they include more than two sets of adults (both resi-dent and absent parents) as well as children from different parents and social backgrounds, who are all supposed to live together amicably.

In addition, stepfamilies often experience more financial problems, espe-cially when fathers are supporting children in more than one household. These financial difficulties may lead to more general disputes about the fair allocation of resources, time, and attention. Researchers also note that young children fare better than older children in stepfamilies because adaptation is easier at an earlier age before allegiances are developed to the absent parent. Researchers on stepfamilies report that the role of stepmother is more ambigu-ous and stressful than the role of stepfather, and find that mothers are described as being more negative towards step-parenting than are fathers (Cheal, 1996; Doodson and Morley, 2006; Schodt, 2008).

Stepfamily formation has been viewed as another stressful event to cope with for children who were not involved with their parents' decision to separ-ate any more than they were party to their parent's decision to re-partner (Smith, 2004). While the new household members need to learn to become a functioning family unit, the relationship between the children and their non-resident father usually continues, even though it may change. Researchers agree that prolonged conflict between parents has a negative impact on the children, but they disagree about how feelings of closeness with biological fathers influence children's acceptance of stepfathers. Some studies suggest that children who develop strong bonds with their biological fathers may feel that forming a relationship with the stepfather would be disloyal to the bio-logical father. However, most researchers have found little correlation (ibid.).

The Study of Stepchildren and Step-Parenting in the United Kingdom was a large cross-sectional study of stepfamilies living in and around London from one to four years between 1998 and 2002. Marjorie Smith (2004) reported on children's views about contact with their non-resident fathers and the quality of relationships with their fathers and stepfathers using data from this study. Sixty-seven per cent of children reported contact with their non-resident parents within the past year. More frequent contact (at least monthly) was associated with children's perceptions of a "good quality relationship" and with their father behaving in a "normal way" rather than focusing mainly on treats and special activities.

Contrary to some American findings from the 1980s, Australian research found that having a good relationship with the biological father does not preclude having a good relationship with the stepfather (Smyth, 2004). In fact, the authors of this Australian Institute of Family Studies research concluded that children who have strong relationships with their mothers and non-resident fathers are more likely to develop good relationships with their stepfathers. More generally, Smyth concluded that children who are well adjusted and have a positive self-image are more likely to form positive relationships with those around them. New Zealand research reported by Pryor (2004) also confirmed this finding. As stepfamilies are a growing family type in all the liberal states, research is expanding rapidly on this topic (Pryor, 2008; Shriner, 2009).

Conclusion

Since the 1960s, the liberal states have experienced similar socio-demographic trends relating to relationship breakdown, including higher separation rates, more mother-led families, high rates of poverty in mother-led families, higher re-partnering rates, and well-publicized parental disputes over child support, custody, and access. In response to the political pressure arising from these trends, these countries liberalized their divorce laws and developed **gender-neutral** laws relating to divorce, support, and child custody. In deciding where the post-divorce child should live, these countries continue to emphasize the "best interests of the child." Co-operation between parents over access and care arrangements is encouraged, and the family courts include mediation and less adversarial practices than courts dealing with non-family matters.

Despite these reforms, controversies relating to separation and divorce continue. Mothers usually retain the daily care of their children after marriage breakdown but nearly half of mother-led households live on low incomes in Canada and some English-speaking countries (OECD, 2008a). Since the 1980s, non-resident fathers have gained more legal rights to make decisions about their children's welfare. Although more divorced fathers now maintain contact with their children, about a third of non-resident fathers lose contact. Laws enforcing child support have been tightened, making more fathers pay, but the state has been unable to retrieve the full amount of financial support from all fathers required to pay.

In the past few decades, numerous researchers from a variety of disciplines have investigated various aspects of marriage breakdown and its social and economic outcomes. They have concluded that high rates of separation and divorce reflect the rise of individualism, the greater **secularization** of society, and the growing view that relationships should last only as long as they are mutually satisfying. However, high rates of re-partnering suggest that intimate cohabitation is still desired and valued. Furthermore, it is still the case that most people aspire to committed and permanent relationships and that most couples remain married for life.

If we add together legal marriages, remarriages, consensual heterosexual relationships, and same-sex cohabitation, we could argue that the percentage of people living in intimate partnerships remains as high as ever. However, fewer partners are willing to remain in unhappy relationships for an extended time. The desire for intimacy remains strong, but more social and economic forces work against the durability of relationships, including labour market trends, greater geographic mobility, gendered patterns of paid and unpaid work, and new ideas about creating personal biographies. Both the legitimation and the rising prevalence of separation and divorce continue to present challenges to former partners, families, communities, social service agencies, and the welfare state.

Questions for Critical Thought

1. Why did divorce rates rise so rapidly after the 1960s? According to the research, why do so many separated/divorced fathers absent themselves from their children's lives and fail to pay child support, even when it is ordered by the courts?

2. Why do cohabiters have higher rates of separation than married couples?

3. Is divorce more likely to occur if young people enter marriage with the knowledge that divorce is relatively easy, both socially and legally?

Questions for Debate

1. Parental separation or divorce tends to reduce the quality of intimate relationships later in life. Discuss.

2. Living in a stepfamily is not easy. Discuss some of the issues and concerns.

3. Children are the real victims of divorce. Discuss.

Suggested Readings

Ambert, Anne-Marie. 2009. *Divorce: Facts, Causes and Consequences*, 3rd edn. Ottawa: Vanier Institute of the Family, at: <www.vifamily.ca>. This online resource summarizes a large amount of research on families in Canada and the United States.

Cherlin, Andrew J. 2010. *The Marriage-Go-Round: The State of Marriage and the Family in America Today*. New York: Knopf Doubleday. Cherlin discusses the unique pattern in which Americans marry and divorce more than couples in other developed countries, examining the contradictions between the desire for individualism and the cultural value of commitment to one person for life.

Wu, Zheng, and Christophe Schimmele. 2009. "Divorce and Repartnering," in M. Baker, ed., *Families: Changing Trends in Canada*, 6th edn. Toronto: McGraw-Hill Ryerson, 154–78. This chapter provides a historical perspective on divorce in Canada and discusses divorce outcomes for various family members.

Suggested Websites

Australian Institute of Family Studies

www.aifs.gov.au

> This organization has been carrying out research for several decades on a number of family issues, including separation and divorce and its impact on children.

Journal of Divorce and Remarriage

www.haworthpress.com

> This interdisciplinary academic journal is an authoritative resource on all aspects of separation, divorce, single parenting, remarriage, and stepfamilies.

Organisation for Economic Co-operation and Development

dx.doi.org/10.1787/soc_glance-2008-8-en

> The OECD provides cross-national statistics on marriage and divorce in some issues of its biannual *Society at a Glance: OECD Social Indicators*. This site offers information from the 2009 edition, which provides the latest statistics.

8 Mid-Life, Aging, and Retirement

Learning Objectives

◎ To realize that aging is partially "socially constructed" as its meaning varies over time, social class, gender, and culture.

◎ To acknowledge that mid-life often brings new challenges as paid work intensifies, children stay at home longer, more marriages end, and parents sometimes require care.

◎ To gain an overview of research findings about lasting marriages and grandparenting.

◎ To understand how income and assets vary by age and employment status, and how governments have supported the well-being of elderly persons.

Introduction

In this chapter, I discuss the various portrayals of aging in the media, advertising, public discourse, social programs, and academic research. The meaning of aging clearly changes with our own chronological age, but also with rising life expectancies and visible indicators of fitness, health, and activity level among middle-aged and older people. This chapter suggests that the lives of the middle-aged and elderly are often presented in somewhat misleading and biased ways. For example, recent media advertising typically presents older people as heterosexual couples who live in retirement villages, continue to enjoy a strong sex life, dote on their grandchildren, and take luxurious cruises around the world. The social and health research focuses on care problems of the frail elderly, elder abuse, and poor health and loneliness, but academic studies seldom discuss lasting marriages, unmarried elderly people, or gay and lesbian elderly. At the same time, political discourse tends to concentrate on old-age pensions, rising medical expenditures, and poverty in age, while recent discourse has discussed grandparent responsibilities for their neglected or abused grandchildren.

In reality, increasing age often brings higher incomes and assets, career progression, growing satisfaction with family and friends, and considerable emotional and material assistance to children and grandchildren. Most seniors now live in private households with a spouse or cohabiting partner and many also have children still living in the household. In Canada, for example,

92.1 per cent of seniors (aged 65 and over) lived in private households in 2011, including 56.4 per cent with a partner and/or children, 24.6 per cent who lived alone, and 11.0 per cent who had other arrangements such as living with relatives. The remaining 7.9 per cent lived in collectives such as nursing homes or seniors' residences (Statistics Canada, 2012a). The percentage of three-generation households has been rising slightly with increasing immigration, and 3.8 per cent of children under 14 years also live with their grandparents on a full-time basis (VIF, 2010: 74). This suggests that many households are providing mutual support and care for partners, parents, children, and grandchildren. However, elderly women are much more likely than men to live alone or share a collective dwelling with their children. In 2011, 31.5 per cent of elderly women in Canada lived alone compared to 16.0 per cent of elderly men (Statistics Canada, 2012a).

More men and women also delay retirement from paid work until older ages than in the 1970s, and most remain active and enjoy good health well beyond their sixties and seventies. Although older couples are now slightly more likely to divorce than in the past, the majority of marriages still last a lifetime. Most people over the age of 60 are parents and grandparents, but a growing minority live alone, have re-partnered, or live as same-sex couples. Some of the social myths about mid-life and old age are addressed in this chapter, but I first examine the changing social meanings attributed to aging.

The Changing Meaning of Aging

Ideas about appropriate behaviour, appearance, and relationships for older people have changed considerably over the centuries and especially in the last few decades. As life expectancy has increased, so have the meanings of "old age" and "elderly," although the definitions of these concepts seem to vary with our own age. For example, when we were children, a 25-year-old seemed old, but when turning 50 our definition of old age might rise to 70 or 80 years. When you are 90, a person aged 75 might be considered a "youngster." So perceptions of aging are related to our personal circumstances. However, social scientists can also see patterns in aging and the social circumstances of the elderly based on gender, social class, culture, and socio-economic changes in the larger society. Furthermore, some organizations and agencies continue to profit from focusing on the needs of youth, the middle aged, or the elderly, and adjust their advertising, publicity, or lobbying towards the interests of these age categories.

The fashion and cosmetics industries have convinced many women (and a growing number of men) to spend large amounts of time, effort, and money attempting to look younger than their chronological age. Although physical attractiveness, fitness, and fashionable clothing have always been important to some people, a youthful appearance seems to be valued more for women than men in today's society (Abu-Laban and McDaniel, 1998; Winterich, 2007). Some women attempt to maintain the appearance and feeling of youthfulness with the assistance of hair colouring, skin treatments, Botox injections, cosmetic surgery, designer clothing, hormone replacement therapy, diets, and exercise. Furthermore, advertisers often use images of youthful and sexy women to sell a variety of products, especially those targeted to men.

Women are encouraged to believe that a youthful and glamorous appearance is essential for their self-esteem, their friendships, and their ability to find and retain (heterosexual) intimate relationships. The "marriage gradient" actually shows that older men often cohabit with and marry much younger women but the reverse seldom occurs, which indicates that a man's older age may actually become an asset (especially if he is also rich and famous) while a woman's advanced age may become a liability on the dating or marriage market. However, social class, education, and culture tend to be intervening variables in the quest for eternal youth.

In some occupations requiring wisdom or expertise, women and men might attempt to look older than their chronological age or at least settle for looking their age. In contrast, older people working in the fashion industry or aspects of the media might want to look younger than they really are. Affluent people seem better able to use their financial resources and education to remain healthier, more active, and to live longer than those on lower incomes, who often look older through years of hard work, poor nutrition and health care, or stressful lives. Those with higher incomes are able to live in spacious and well-heated houses in safer communities, and are able to buy more nutritious food, preventive health-care services, and supervision for their children and other family members in need of care. Richer people are also less likely to work outdoors or to smoke and to drink alcohol to excess, which contributes to a younger appearance (Wister, 2005). Certain cultural groups also place a higher value on "active aging," take regular exercise, keep their weight down, enjoy adequate leisure time, and travel widely in later life, although this may partially relate to their social class as well as their culture.

Generally, sociologists would argue that the meanings associated with chronological age are socially constructed, and the outcomes of chronological aging reflect the socio-economic and cultural circumstances of people's earlier lives. However, many older people also seem to look younger and more fit than they did a few generations ago. This has led people to revise some of the earlier ideas about typical patterns of family life and aging.

Life Expectancy, the Life Cycle, and Aging

Since the 1930s, life expectancy has increased in most developed countries as a result of improvements in sanitation, accommodation, diet, and health care. Health improvements particularly include the development of inoculations against contagious diseases, the invention of antibiotics, and advances in maternal health. Life expectancy at birth varies by country but in industrialized nations such as Canada and the United States, women tend to live longer than men. The gender gap in life expectancy was 4.7 years in 2006 in the OECD countries (OECD, 2009b: 103) but life expectancies also vary by social class (Whitehouse and Zaidi, 2008).

The gender gap in life expectancy can be attributed to the decline of maternal death rates or safer childbirth, as well as higher premature death rates among males, which are influenced by lifestyle factors, use of health-care services, and cultural practices. In most countries, girls and boys are socialized to develop different interests and activities, and boys are often encouraged to take more risks, first in play and later in work and leisure. Therefore, gendered patterns are apparent in activities reducing life expectancy, such as cigarette smoking, the use of illegal drugs, excessive alcohol consumption, reckless driving of motor vehicles, dangerous recreational activities, and working in dangerous jobs. The gender differences in life expectancy are augmented further within households because men tend to marry or cohabit with younger women, and wives normally outlive their husbands.

Stages in the life cycle are now becoming less distinct than in previous decades. Prior to World War II, many people left school, worked for several years, married, raised children, saw their children grow up and leave home, retired from paid work (or saw their partner retire), and helped raise their grandchildren. Now, more people reproduce outside of marriage, they partner and re-partner, begin new families in mid-life or old age, bring stepchildren together, move in and out of jobs, retire and return to paid work, or retain their paid jobs as long as possible.

These new trends suggest that generational differences will be apparent in typical patterns of aging. For example, people born after World War II (the post-war baby boomers) tend to be better educated than previous generations. On average, their post-secondary degrees and diplomas enabled them to find higher-paying jobs than their parents had and, with the assistance of credit cards and the dual-earner couples, they came to expect higher living standards. They are more likely than their parents to travel internationally, to engage in regular exercise, to have experienced more than one marriage or partnership, to take adult education courses, to question authority, and to become more articulate about their needs as they grow older.

The post-war generation (born 1945–65) grew up with a variety of social security programs. Unlike their parents, they felt less need to save their money in case of unemployment, ill health, or disability in old age. This generation continued to consume at a higher rate than their parents' generation, with the expectation that social security benefits would continue and that credit would always be available. The post-war generation may live longer and healthier lives than their parents' generation, as they were fortunate to grow up with better nutrition, sanitation, and health services, and with an increased knowledge of the relationship between fitness, nutrition, smoking, and health. On the other hand, environmental pollution, higher rates of obesity, cigarette smoking and substance abuse, and new strains of viruses could curtail this optimistic scenario.

Throughout the 1980s and 1990s, many men retired before age 65, earlier than previous generations, and lived off private savings and investments, employer-sponsored pension benefits, and public pensions. Now, more men and women are remaining in the labour force longer, with increasing uncertainty about incomes and pensions, declining house prices in some places, lower interest rates, fewer private savings, and higher levels of household debt. In the near future, many people will continue working until their mid-sixties or seventies, either to acquire adequate retirement incomes or because they enjoy their work and the social interaction with their workmates.

Post-war baby-boomers will probably place less emphasis than previous generations on "rugged individualism" or self-reliance in their old age because many have relied throughout their lives on government assistance or formal services as well as their own initiative. With fewer children than their parents' generation, they may need to purchase more assistance in old age. With higher levels of education and more experience with hiring help, they may become more demanding about the quality of services than the elderly in the past. With the international downturn in the economy after 2008, however, many older workers are being made redundant before they have paid off their mortgages or saved enough money for a comfortable retirement.

In contrast, the cohort of people born after the 1970s will likely experience a different scenario of aging. They may be less able to afford retirement from paid work because they have worked part-time for larger portions of their lives, changed jobs more frequently, saved less money, separated from partners and divided joint assets, and accrued substantial personal and household debt. Many of those with low incomes will be unable to depend on home ownership as a form of retirement savings, and they may be less likely to have acquired work-related pensions or personal savings to permit retirement. In addition, they may have less confidence in the future of public pensions or state-sponsored services for the elderly.

In the twenty-first century, most adults still reproduce and later become grandparents when their adult children reproduce (Mann, 2007). Relationships between grandparents and their grandchildren could become more salient as life expectancies rise and these relationships have longer to develop. On the other hand, the trend towards delayed childbirth will mean that some children will be relatively young when their grandparents die, as the years between generations lengthen. Furthermore, young people are now more mobile and often move far away from their birthplace or parents' community. In addition, the divorce and re-partnering of adult children prevents many grandparents from developing close relationships with their grandchildren. Some social scientists have suggested that rapid social change and population aging could encourage intergenerational conflict between the young who are competing for jobs and resources and the older workers who want to hold onto their jobs. However, the young and the middle-aged ultimately have a vested interest in improving pensions and services for the elderly. The real conflict is more likely between organizations and especially commercial companies whose interests lie with youth and those whose interests lie with seniors. Many of our social organizations such as schools and universities, which have based their funding policies on growing numbers of students (or "bums on seats"), will fight to change the funding formulas when these are no longer to their advantage. Improved conditions for the elderly will eventually benefit individuals, families, and communities, but not necessarily all public or private organizations.

Even a generation ago, social scientists talked about "the family life cycle" as though everyone went through the same stages of personal and family development at the same time. Now, rising rates of cohabitation, separation, divorce, re-partnering, lifelong learning, and the need to find new ways to earn a living have disrupted the typical life stages of the past.

Mid-Life: Is It a Time of Security or Crisis?

In popular culture, mid-life has been associated with aging "crises" for both men and women, but in reality these are myths for most people (Pool and Feldman, 1999). Typically, mid-life is a time of greater financial security and relationship stability. Increasingly, both men and women are employed during their middle years and their earnings often peak just before retirement. Household assets tend to be at their peak in mid-life and household debt generally declines with older age. Rates of home ownership are the highest in the 55–64 age category, as Table 8.1 shows for Canada, but vast differences exist by household income. While low-income Canadians were *less* likely to own their own home in 2006 than 1971, the highest-income earners were more likely to own their home in 2006, suggesting a growing gap between the rich and the poor.

In the past when men typically worked for one employer for life, they might be tiring of their job by the time they reached their fifties. Now, fewer men stay in the same occupation for life, with less employment permanence, and more need and opportunities to seek better jobs elsewhere. Middle-aged women are also likely to be in the full-time workforce, especially in North America, and most of these women are stable workers who are gaining in seniority and earnings and making an important contribution to household income. Households with two full-time earners are likely to have the most financial security (Sauvé, 2009).

Table 8.1   Percentage of the Population Owning Their Home, by Age Category and Highest and Lowest Household Income Quintiles, 1971 and 2006

Age Category and Income Quintile	1971 Percentage	2006 Percentage
Age 20–34: Bottom income quintile	31	19
Top income quintile	38	77
Age 35–54: Bottom income quintile	62	46
Top income quintile	74	90
Age 55–64: Bottom income quintile	68	55
Top income quintile	76	93
Age 65–74: Bottom income quintile	63	53
Top income quintile	72	92
Age 75 or more: Bottom income quintile	60	49
Top income quintile	70	85

Source: Adapted from Hou, Statistics Canada. 2010. *Home Ownership over the Life Course of Canadians: Evidence from Canadian Censuses of Population*, Table 1. www.statscan.gc.ca.

For women, mid-life also corresponds with menopause, which involves not only physiological changes but may also contribute to thoughts and concerns about aging and loss of attractiveness. When more middle-aged women devoted their lives to child-bearing and child-rearing, menopause and children leaving home could more readily be perceived as synonymous with the end of their usefulness. Now, mid-life for mothers often means a reduction of responsibilities for child supervision, and if the children are no longer living at home it could mean less daily housework such as food shopping, meal preparation, and laundry. At the same time, a reduction of domestic work permits women to spend more time and effort on other activities, such as their paid jobs.

Clearly, both men and women look and feel different as they grow older. Men are less likely than women to colour their greying hair or to have anti-aging treatments such as Botox or cosmetic surgery, but many men are nevertheless concerned about their weight, physical fitness, sexual prowess, the quality of their intimate relationships, their relationships with their children and friends, job satisfaction, and their financial future. However, the concepts of "mid-life criss" and "empty nest syndrome," which were often used in social science literature to describe middle age, with their suggestions of depression and anxiety about lost youth and children leaving home, seem less relevant today than in the past.

When parents are in their forties and fifties, their children are now more likely than in the 1970s to live at home because educational requirements for employment and independent living costs continue to increase. Parents often feel compelled to give advice to teenage children and help them finance their education because part-time jobs seldom provide students with sufficient income to become self-supporting (Mitchell, 2007). The prolonged financial dependency of adult children could lead to more companionate relationships between parents and their adult children. Continuing education and job retraining are becoming more necessary, not only for youth but also for all adults, so both adults and children in the same household might be studying or retraining, which could serve as a common bond. However, prolonged financial dependency among young people could also increase family conflict, especially when intergenerational values or lifestyles differ, or parents attempt to enforce "old-fashioned" household rules. Parents may also gain new responsibilities to assist or care for their frail elderly parents while they retain some responsibility for the supervision and mentoring of their own children (Neal, 2007).

The trend to delay parenting until women are over 30 years old, which is apparent among a growing minority, delays the "post parental" stage in many contemporary families; those who become parents later in life could easily be in their late fifties or sixties when their children leave home. In Canada, 42.3 per cent of young adults aged 20 to 29 lived in the parental home in 2011 compared to 26.9 per cent in 1981 (Statistics Canada, 2012a). The trend for young adults to remain living at home with their parents and the trends towards delayed marriage and first births, which are most noticeable among middle-class educated women, also can postpone parents' retirement age. Particularly, unattached mothers who entered the workforce later in life (such as after a separation or divorce) may have difficulty accruing adequate pension credits from their employers to enable them to retire from paid work before their mid-sixties.

With rising life expectancies, mid-life can mean more responsibilities for aging parents and parents-in-law, and women are often expected to become the primary caregivers for both children and elderly relatives. As more middle-aged women become employed and are unavailable to provide personal care, they tend to become managers of care rather than actual care providers (Connidis, 2009; McDaniel, 2009). In other words, these women retain the responsibility for hiring service providers and negotiating with them on behalf of their elderly parents or other relatives. Furthermore, as birth rates decline, fewer adult children are available to care for elderly parents and more community services will be needed.

The greater prosperity of older dual-career families and early retirement incentives continue to allow some mid-life couples to travel, spend more money on entertainment, and choose early retirement. At the same time, efforts to restructure workplaces and growing competition from younger workers may squeeze older employees out of their jobs and encourage others to cease working as employees and instead to establish their own businesses. Becoming self-employed is an occupational gamble that is most feasible when there are no children to support or when a spouse already has a steady income. The growing employment and financial instability may actually contribute to marital stability in later life because the costs of separation (including dividing combined assets) can prove too high for some couples.

Throughout the 1980s and 1990s, higher disposable incomes and more generous early retirement programs encouraged many workers to retire in their fifties and spend more time on leisure activities. However, the age of retirement in the liberal welfare states is now rising again with insecure employment, lower interest rates, and higher living costs (OECD, 2009b). Especially women accept early retirement, as Table 8.2 shows, although the percentage of workers who exit from the labour force before pension entitlement varies by country (as does the age of pension entitlement). Women tend to retire earlier than men despite their longer life expectancy and lesser pension entitlement. This pattern reflects official retirement ages (which used to permit women to retire earlier than men), women's marriage to older partners, the synchronization of retirement decisions within couples, and lower pressure on women to be family earners. In the OECD countries, the average official retirement age in 2009 was 62.7 for women and 63.6 for men, although the actual age of retirement is rising in many countries, especially for women (ibid., 82).

Table 8.2 Percentage Exiting Labour Force before Official Age of Retirement*, by Country and Sex, 2007

Country	Women (%)	Men (%)
Australia	64.4	62.2
Canada	63.3	61.9
Denmark	63.5	61.3
New Zealand	66.5	63.9
Sweden	65.7	62.9
United Kingdom	63.2	61.9
United States	64.6	63.9
OECD average	63.5	62.3

*The most common official age of retirement is 65, although some jurisdictions have abolished mandatory retirement.

Source: OECD. 2009. *Society at a Glance*. Paris: OECD, p. 83. www.oecd.org/social/indicators

Not all people are married in mid-life; some have already separated or divorced while others never cohabited or married. By mid-life, single people who wanted to partner have probably accepted their circumstances and created an acceptable lifestyle outside marriage. Single lifestyles are more visible and socially acceptable now than they used to be, as marriage rates have declined, separation and divorce rates remain high, and cohabitation has become prevalent. In addition, gay and lesbian networks and singles organizations provide social support for many people living outside couple or family households. These factors contribute to improving the quality of life for singles and probably create more public tolerance towards non-family lifestyles among older people.

With age, some of the social pressure to marry diminishes, either because single people have learned how to cope without being married or partnered or because they have developed a network of friends in similar circumstances. Furthermore, pressure to marry and bear children lessens for both heterosexual and gay/lesbian people as they pass the age when their cohort has married and produced children. Yet, some gays and lesbians do not "come out" until after they have been married and produced children. Especially lesbian mothers who have experienced custody problems with the children's father may be better able to live their lives after their children have grown up (Nelson, 1996).

Life Satisfaction and Marriage Stability

Researchers have tried to understand how relationship satisfaction varies throughout the duration of marriage and what makes some relationships last while others end in separation. It is difficult to assess the merits of some of the research because many of the earlier studies were based on retrospective reporting and involved couples in therapy rather than a random selection of the population (Parker, 2002). It is widely accepted in family research that marital satisfaction tends to follow a U-shaped trajectory: satisfaction is usually high in the early years but often declines during the middle or parenting years, rising again after children leave home and in old age (Van Laningham et al., 2001; Lavner and Bradbury, 2010). In fact, satisfaction seems to decline in the middle years even when there are no children present (Clements et al., 1997), although exceptions have been found to this trend.

Gender, individual differences, and cross-national variations in life satisfaction are also evident (Blanchflower and Oswald, 2008). Having a high income does not necessarily make people happier (Kahneman et al., 2006) but perceptions of "adequate" income, relatively good health, and supportive friends and relatives seem important for older people's life satisfaction. While people don't have to be married to have supportive relationships, those who have been married for 25 years or longer typically report more satisfying lives. Despite the research focus on marriage instability, a number of studies over the years have investigated the factors leading to marriage longevity.

Mackey and O'Brien (1995) identified five factors that appear to be important for marital longevity: containment of conflict; mutuality of decision-making; quality of communication; relational values of trust, respect, understanding, and equity; and sexual and psychological intimacy. Their research was based on interviews with 60 American couples who married from the 1940s to the 1960s, and whose youngest child had completed high school. The themes of adaptability, resilience, and commitment recurred throughout the interviews. While some of the attitudes and values of these people changed over the years, their views of marriage as a permanent commitment of love and fidelity held fast.

Alford-Cooper (1998) collected data on 576 American couples living on Long Island in New York, whose marriages were intact for 50 years or more.

Based on questionnaires, as well as interviews with a smaller sub-sample, they found that only 56 per cent reported being "very happily married" but a further 37 per cent reported being "happily married." Although 21 per cent had at some point concluded that their marriages had failed, they had stayed together because they wanted to remain with their children, they did not believe in divorce, or they lacked the financial resources or social support to leave. When asked which relationship characteristics helped them stay together, the most common ones were trust, a loving relationship, and willingness to compromise. They also reported mutual respect, a need for each other, compatibility, children, and good communication.

Sharlin, Kaslow, and Hammerschmidt (2000) conducted a study of non-clinical couples (i.e., couples not in therapy, counselling, or crisis) from eight countries (United States, Canada, Israel, Chile, Germany, Netherlands, Sweden, and South Africa) who had been married, or in the case of Sweden had been living together, from 20 to 46 years. The study included 610 couples obtained through the authors' networking, which created a sample somewhat biased to the middle or upper middle classes. Love, mutuality, and sharing emerged as bases for long-term marital satisfaction, and a number of qualities such as mutuality of trust, respect, support, give and take, and the sharing of values, beliefs, interests, philosophies, fun, and humour all arose across cultures. Couples said that they stayed in the relationship because of commitment to the partnership and love of their spouse, but those who expressed lower levels of happiness reported staying together for the children and to honour their commitment to a lifelong relationship.

More recent studies from the United States indicate that older women report lower levels of marital happiness, marital interaction, and marital power than older men (Bulanda, 2011). In another study, Dush and Taylor (2012) found that respondents who believed in lifelong marriage, shared decisions equally with their spouse, and couples where the husband shared the housework reported less marital conflict and higher levels of marital happiness in later life.

These studies often focus on a set of circumstances, characteristics, or attributes influencing marriage stability, but Wallerstein and Blakeslee (1996) describe happy and lasting marriages as the product of a series of processes. Based on interviews with 50 married couples in the United States who reported their marriages as "very happy," the researchers identified four different types of marriage that were not necessarily mutually exclusive, which they called "romantic," "rescue," "companionate," and "traditional" marriages. Each of these was based on different assumptions and dynamics, suggesting that there is no single way to create a happy and lasting marriage. Wallerstein and Blakeslee argue that marriage is "always a work in progress" (1996: 269) that requires ongoing maintenance, including negotiation and compromises.

Most marriages still last for life but more long-term relationships now end in divorce compared to 20 years ago, although the percentage of divorces is still larger in the 35–45 age category. Because older men often marry younger women, women's marriage and divorce rates at older ages are lower than men's. More women than men still petition for divorce, although joint petitions are on the rise (Ambert, 2009; ABS, 2008). In addition, more separated and divorced people re-partner and establish new households without legally marrying. Nonetheless, remarriage remains more popular than cohabitation among older couples, especially those who are more affluent and have children and grandchildren. Older re-partnering parents often experience concerns about joint property, pension entitlement, inheritance, and providing role models of committed relationships for their children.

Part of the reason for rising separation and divorce rates among older couples relates to economic opportunities. Having individual earnings provides new options for women in mid-life, and those in unhappy marriages are able to separate and divorce because both they and their former partner have more financial resources to live independently. Nevertheless, we saw in Chapter 7 that former wives are less likely than former husbands to prosper economically after divorce, and they are less likely to re-partner and do not re-partner as rapidly. Neither children's living arrangements nor women's incomes relative to those of men have changed much in recent decades, and custodial or resident mothers continue to live on lower incomes than their male counterparts. The shortage of suitable male partners and women's time spent caring for children reduce the probability of female remarriage in later life.

In addition, women appear less eager than men to remarry, perhaps because more women experienced non-reciprocal experiences as partners and carers throughout marriage (Poole, 2005; Ranson, 2009). Although more middle-aged and older people now leave unhappy marriages, most couples stay together regardless of the quality of their marriage—out of loyalty, concern about their children, fear of loneliness, or from financial pressures. Many who leave marriages later in life or who are widowed continue to look for new partners, with some turning to Internet dating, as shown in Box 8.1.

Grandparenting and Widowhood

About three-quarters of the population of countries such as the United Kingdom and Canada become grandparents during their lifetime, and they remain grandparents for an average of 25 years (Mann, 2007). Many people become grandparents when they are in their forties or fifties, when they are still employed or involved with other activities. Grandparenting is often described as an "affective role" but it has become more heterogeneous over the decades, especially with high rates of separation, divorce, and re-partnering. Most

Box 8.1   Excerpts from Various Dating Websites for Seniors

Dating services are available online that specialize in finding partners for older people or "seniors." Below are some excerpts from various websites.

Female, age 68: "Happy, fun loving lady. Work full time in a job that I enjoy very much. I like to dance and listen to lively music (and sing along). I have three adult children and 7 grandchildren, we are all close. I look forward to meeting someone. . . ."

Male, 67 years old: "Young looking bilingual and non smoker man, 6'1" 205 lbs, attractive, sensitive and curious to learn. Earlier a programmer-analyst and business man, now retired and secure. I like wine tasting and good food. I am a quiet person and much prefer a friendly setting over a loud bar and night club. I exercise at the gym 3 times a week and am in shape. I love to plan last minute getaways"

Female, aged 71: "I am fit and well but get a bit lonely sometimes. I would love an occasional companion for outings and holidays, perhaps. I love to travel (Did so with both my late husbands . . . at separate times!) I have recently taken up writing . . . ."

Male (photo looks very elderly): "I am an athletic attractive, educated, very polite international man who fluently speaks several languages, that likes the nice things. I enjoy sharing and the companionship of a similar and . . . ."

Source: Various online websites for dating/relationships, retrieved and compiled September 2012.

grandparents see their grandchildren regularly but a small minority (about 10 per cent in the United States) take over the daily care of their grandchildren because the children's parents are unable to care for them, a consequence of alcohol or drug abuse or work-related pressures (ibid.). Other grandparents remain detached and distant. Increasingly, adult children move away from their parents for education and work, and some grandparents rarely see their grandchildren because of the geographic distance. However, they may still remain in regular communication with them. Levels of involvement with grandchildren seem to be greater when grandchildren are very young compared to when they are teenagers but they may also vary by the grandparents' age, health, other activities, class background, and geographic proximity (Gauthier, 2002; Harper, 2005).

Much of the research on grandparenting focuses on grandmothers, either implicitly or explicitly (Harper, 2005), partly because grandmothers have served as the principal grandparent and spent more time in physical and emotional care of their grandchildren. Grandmothers often expect to spend time with both their children and grandchildren, especially during holidays and celebrations, and frequently babysit their grandchildren for at least some of the time while the children's mothers work for pay or simply to give the parents a break. Some immigrant parents sponsor the immigration of their own parents to help care for their grandchildren while the parents work.

Becoming a grandmother seems to be very important to the well-being of many older women, but styles of grandparenting vary considerably by individual as well as by gender. Studies have found that grandmothers want to "be there" for their children and grandchildren but also do not want to "interfere" with their children's parenting. This "norm of non-interference" may create some degree of ambivalence with grandparenting (Mason et al., 2007) as disagreements over the correct way to bring up children represents the major source of intergenerational conflict (Mann, 2007). The older generation often expresses concern about grandchildren's apparent lack of respect for authority, their unruly behaviour, their eating habits, and their consumerism.

Earlier American studies reported that grandfathers were more remote and formal than grandmothers (Bengston, 1985), but recent research has found that grandfathers often see themselves as emotionally close to their grandchildren and heavily involved in mentoring and transferring values. In addition, grandfathers can serve as replacement partners for lone mothers, serving as the primary male role model for the children (Harper and Ruicheva, 2004). Compared to fatherhood, grandfathering often involves more leisure, enjoyment, and nurturing, although grandmothers continue to be more involved in care activities and maintain more contact with grandchildren.

One of the reasons why people marry and reproduce is to widen their social networks, create companionship and emotional support for life, and reduce the fear of loneliness in later life. However, about one-quarter of people in the liberal states do not become parents or grandparents. Researchers have asked if older parents are more socially integrated or whether older childless couples simply replace their lack of children with more friends. Dykstra (2006) found in her research in Germany and the Netherlands that people who never had children had smaller social networks in old age but more contact with peers of the same generation, including siblings, friends, colleagues, cousins, and neighbours. However, over time, these networks diminish as age peers die or move away. In contrast, parents become grandparents and develop expanding networks of younger relatives, especially after their partner dies.

The experience of widowhood varies by personal experiences, gender, socio-economic status, and cultural background, as do other phases in the family life cycle. In Canada, half of all marriages end with the death of a husband but only one-fifth with the death of a wife. Therefore, widowhood is primarily associated with older women. In addition, the proportion of elderly people who are widowed and have not re-partnered is declining in many countries as more older people are never-married, are separated or divorced, and/or have re-partnered (Connidis, 2010; Martin-Matthews, 2011). At the same time, the age of widowhood is rising in the liberal states with increased life expectancy.

Earlier research on widowhood centred on role theory, especially focusing on role loss and role exit (Lopata, 1996). Current studies tend to examine how past and current experiences and events shape widowhood, viewing it as a process of transition rather than a status, as partners often witness the gradual decline of their partner well before their death. Researchers also focus on resilience, coping measures, and compensation, generally relying on interpretive perspectives to understand how both widows and widowers interpret and give meaning to the death of the partner, to living alone after sharing a home for many years, and to creating new lives for themselves with support from family and friends (Chambers, 2005; van den Hoonaard, 2009, 2010).

Retirement Income and Pensions

Both national governments and supra-governmental organizations such as the OECD do research on population aging and its implications to national governments. For example, they calculate "dependency ratios" or the percentage of the population aged 65 and over compared to the estimated working-age population to project future populations of seniors and their service needs. In 1960, the average old-age dependency ratio in OECD countries averaged 14 per cent but it increased to 24 per cent in 2005 and is expected to reach 52 per cent by 2050 (OECD, 2001: 27, OECD, 2007b: 42). The populations of developed countries are aging because birth rates are falling and life expectancy is rising, which means that people aged 65 and over form a growing percentage of national populations (OECD, 2007b: 99).

Some demographers and politicians see an aging population as a social problem, but most elderly couples maintain high levels of independence and provide services for friends and family, including financial assistance and child-minding for their grandchildren. In addition, many wives care for their husbands in their old age (McDaniel, 2009), as do some husbands for their wives. However, older unattached women are particularly vulnerable to poverty if they were not employed throughout their earlier years, did not own a home or inherit other assets, or if they suffer from health problems or disabilities.

State concern about old-age "dependency" focuses on the rising cost of social programs serving a growing elderly population, especially public pensions, but also the high cost of medical care during the last few years of life. Consequently, a major reason for restructuring social programs has been the rising numbers of elderly in the society or the expectation of this in the future (Beaujot, 2000: 317). Many governments are trying to prevent these higher costs through a variety of policy changes and educational campaigns. Policy changes include raising or attempting to raise the age of receiving state-funded old-age pensions, increasing the contribution rates to retirement pensions financed through social insurance (such as the Canada Pension Plan), encouraging more private retirement plans and services, reforming long-term care facilities, and rationing certain medical operations (such as hip replacements) to those below a certain age.

Living on a fixed income in times of inflation has been a major concern of older people, their families, and seniors' groups and governments. Whether or not people can live on their pensions and savings has become an important factor in decisions about retirement now that many countries have abolished mandatory retirement from paid work. High interest rates are usually beneficial for older people living on fixed incomes because many are living on their investments as well as pensions, but they are considered unfortunate for younger couples who are borrowing money to set up a new home. More elderly people already own a home, although they may have lower incomes. Some governments offer universal old-age pensions to those of normal retirement age (often 65 and older) but other jurisdictions expect employers to provide retirement pensions for their former employees or expect employees to contribute to their own retirement through a state-supported retirement savings plan, such as the Canada Pension Plan or Kiwi Saver in New Zealand. This means that the incomes of elderly persons are typically influenced by pension entitlements, the generosity of public and private pensions, interest rates, home ownership, personal savings, and living costs.

Old-age poverty rates have generally declined in the liberal states in recent decades with improvements to state pensions and employer-sponsored pensions. Nevertheless, poverty rates continue to vary considerably by country, and are largely affected by whether or not an elderly household member is employed, the generosity of public pensions, interest rates, and whether or not seniors are living alone, as Table 8.3 indicates. Both Canada and New Zealand have relatively generous public pensions that are universal or available to everyone aged 65 and over (but with residency requirements that are more generous in New Zealand). In contrast, old-age pensions in Australia and the United States are based on work-related retirement contributions (as well as benefits targeted to lower-income households). In most countries, the highest poverty rates for elderly people are among unattached older women who did not work full-time for pay in their earlier years.

Political discourse about population aging includes promoting healthier lifestyles among seniors, encouraging continued participation in paid work and community activities ("active aging"), and limiting expectations about entitlement to public pensions and social services. However, Hantrais (2004) clearly demonstrates that the European Union countries most affected by population aging are not necessarily the ones where political debate and

Table 8.3 National Poverty Rates among People Living in Households with a Retirement-Age Head, by Household Characteristics, Mid-2000s

Country	All	Working for Pay	Not Working for Pay	Singles	Couples
Australia	27	4	32	50	18
Canada	7	2	10	16	4
Denmark	10	2	12	17	4
Finland	14	11	11	28	4
France	9	1	9	16	4
Germany	8	2	9	15	5
Italy	13	3	17	25	9
Japan	21	13	30	48	17
New Zealand	4	1	2	3	1
Sweden	6	3	7	13	1
United Kingdom	10	1	12	17	7
United States	24	9	34	41	17
OECD average	14	7	17	25	9

Source: OECD. 2008a. *Growing Unequal? Income Distribution and Poverty in OECD Countries*. Table 5.3: p. 140. www.oecd.org/social/inequality.htm

media interest are most prevalent. Political concern about population aging sometimes masks other social concerns, such as declining birth rates among educated women, hospital overcrowding, the rising cost of public pensions, or concerns about disability and long-term care.

Becoming Frail or Disabled

At the time when many individuals and couples are still responsible in some way for their own children and may be feeling old themselves, their parents can become widowed, less able to care for themselves, or in need of some emotional or material assistance. Because home-care services, retirement homes, and seniors' apartments are not fully developed in some of the liberal states, much of the organizational work and actual care of frail elderly parents and those with disabilities fall on the shoulders of their children. However, the rate of disability tends to increase with age. In Canada, 43.4 per cent of persons aged 65 and over and 56.3 per cent of those 75 and over report an activity limitation or problems with pain, mobility, and agility (VIF, 2010: 9). While some of these concerns may be mild, others are severe. Because women normally outlive men, many women need some social and community support later in life, and more women than men end their lives in nursing homes or hospitals. Nevertheless, only 3 to 6 per cent of the population aged 65 years and older were living in long-term care institutions in OECD countries in 2004, and this percentage has fallen in recent years with more home-care services, especially in the Nordic countries (OECD, 2007b: 96).

Traditionally, a considerable amount of care for elderly people was provided by older wives who outlived their husbands, and by middle-aged women, daughters, and daughters-in-law who were not engaged in the paid labour force (Martin-Matthews, 2007). Now, older wives (and some husbands) still provide a considerable amount of care for their partners but most daughters or daughters-in-law are expected to provide or manage family care work even when they also have full-time jobs (Lashewicz et al., 2007; Martin-Matthews and Phillips, 2008). Some families are able to hire care providers for their elderly parents or may assist their older parents or relatives to find home-care services from governments or the private sector.

Many of today's seniors are not used to relying on formal services because they grew up in an era without the money to hire assistance and without government benefits such as public health insurance, unemployment benefits, or visiting homemakers. Even when they are in need and eligible for assistance, they may be reluctant to ask for help. They may feel that other people are more deserving or that they should be able to manage on their own. Adult children may be more adept at finding which formal services are available for their parents and to bring someone into their home to assist them. However, this may be perceived as interference rather than needed assistance. Many seniors who had been self-reliant and had their own ways of doing things may resent someone else trying to arrange their affairs in their own household.

A traditional solution to the problem of caring for frail elderly parents is to bring them into the adult children's home. While this may be the best arrangement for some families, it is an option only for those seniors with adult children and often only for those whose children live nearby. Increasingly, adult children are living in another region or country and it is not feasible or possible to bring elderly parents to another jurisdiction, especially if it involves immigration to another country. Families who sponsor elderly parents as immigrants sometimes have to guarantee the government that they will not rely on the state for health care or social services. Furthermore, elderly parents may not choose to leave their friends and social network behind, or feel that living with their offspring would strain their children's marriage and cause friction with any grandchildren. Yet there are few alternatives for many lower-or middle-income families. Retirement or nursing homes are not always suitable, available, or affordable. Furthermore, many families, especially those in certain cultural communities, feel that using these services would be the same as abandoning their parents to an uncaring and inflexible living arrangement.

Rising life expectancies, smaller families, and re-partnering have broadened the responsibilities of some people in mid-life. While young people are remaining in their parents' home for longer, some people have responsibilities for their partner's children and parents, and many seniors are living well into their eighties and nineties. This means that more middle-aged parents may retain some responsibility for two generations—their children and their parents. But they may also retain some responsibility for their partner's parents as well (or even their ex-partner's parents). Adults may begin by helping out their older relatives gradually, such as cutting the lawn or helping with financial decision-making, and then take over more tasks such as driving them grocery shopping or to have a haircut, and finally doing housework and assisting with personal care.

Although governments and private agencies have developed home and community care services, such as visiting homemakers and meals-on-wheels, these tend to be underfunded by governments in the liberal states. The majority of public funding still is allocated to acute-care hospitals and medical services rather than community or home care. Although more senior residences are being built, some with meals, entertainment, and personal care services, many are privately run, expensive, and have long waiting lists. Also, many seniors prefer to remain in their own homes without moving to age-homogeneous accommodation, especially if they feel that they are relatively healthy and able to cope with personal care. Yet their children or younger relatives may not agree that they can adequately care for themselves and may feel obligated to help out.

Easing the family's responsibilities for the care of frail elderly parents or other relatives may require the reallocation of government funding into long-term care and community and home-care services rather than hospital-based medical services. In addition, more respite care programs are needed to allow family carers to leave their parent with an alternative care provider for the day while they attend to other matters. Programs to assist family caring need to focus on perceptions of need as well as actual requirements, and encourage and enable elderly people to retain their independence for longer. Some governments already provide a range of services for seniors, such as home renovations for persons with disabilities, home repair services, cleaning services, and home security checks. The cost to the user is sometimes based on one's ability to pay, which means they are subsidized by the taxpayer. However, the liberal states seem less willing to pay for these services than the social democratic states such as Sweden and Denmark (Cates, 1993; Caro, 2006; OECD, 2007b).

Does Aging Make People More Conservative?

For decades, sociologists have questioned whether people become more conservative as they grow older or if each **cohort** experiences aging differently because of earlier circumstances and life events. Most sociological studies of aging compare different generations living at the same time rather than several generations throughout their entire lifespan, so it is difficult to know whether social and attitudinal differences between age groups are the result of the aging process. Intergenerational variations could be caused by the political, economic, and social conditions during childhood, adolescence, or early adulthood. Certainly the generation that is now over 65 years of age has grown up in a different social and economic world than today's youth, who will be the elderly of the future.

The lives of many of today's seniors, or those who have recently died, were greatly influenced by the Great Depression of the 1930s and World War II. The Depression may have curtailed education, delayed marriage, or forced them to accept financially secure but unchallenging work. Trying to make ends meet during those years encouraged thrift, financial anxiety, and caution. Travelling overseas during wartime may have been their first opportunity to see the world, to leave their hometown, and make some money, as well as to serve their country. Yet many surviving veterans and refugees, as well as their families, were changed forever by the destruction of war, the death of relatives and friends, food rationing, loneliness, and subsequent injuries or disabilities. Both the Depression and World War II made lasting impressions on today's elderly, altering their attitudes, expectations, behaviour, and relationships.

Past generations needed to be prepared for life's unexpected events in a way that young people born after the 1960s find difficult to comprehend. Today's seniors had to prepare themselves for the future by saving money, maintaining a support network of friends and family, or cultivating an attitude of resignation because they lacked social security programs, health insurance, bank credit, reliable birth control, or personal choices. Many of today's elderly relied on hard work and family loyalty, and hoped that their children would feel a reciprocal responsibility to assist them later in life. Nevertheless, most elderly couples live independent lives and many provide volunteer work for their communities as well as child care and financial assistance for their adult children.

In contrast, those born in the liberal states after World War II were raised to take income security programs, private insurance, government medical insurance, inflation, and financial credit for granted. They felt less compelled to save for the future, to "defer gratification," or to stay in unsatisfying jobs or unhappy marriages out of duty or obligation. They were more likely to flaunt social rules, to move in and out of jobs and relationships, to live for the present rather than the future, and to live for themselves rather than their children (if they had any). The acceptance of government supports and employment fringe benefits is well entrenched in the psyche of this generation, and this affects their present lifestyle as well as their outlook on the future.

The generation born after the mid-1970s, however, seems to be experiencing far less income security than their "baby boomer" parents or grandparents, and may be less able to finance their education or buy a home without incurring substantial debt. They are more likely to accept the insecurity of marriage and the desirability of cohabitation but may crave more security as they become older. Although many reject legal marriage when they are in their twenties, research suggests that most will eventually marry and buy a home, although they may carry their household debt well into their senior years.

This suggests that each generation tends to view old age differently from their parents but also to feel that they have more control over their lives, more personal choices, and more right to express their views. Today's middle-aged and elderly women are more likely to have their own jobs, interests, and earnings, and often see their families as important parts of their lives but not their entire lives. More of the current middle-aged and elderly have been divorced and have grandchildren and other relationships from previous marriages and remarriages, further blurring the boundaries of families. But the higher rates of separation and divorce and the increasing percentages of one-parent households could mean that poverty among older women will continue despite the increases in women's employment.

Conclusion

As life expectancies have increased, job markets expanded, and living standards improved, the lives of the middle-aged and elderly have also changed. Although more older women than men become widowed, live alone, and survive on low incomes, many seniors now remain active until their eighties and nineties, which means that the age of 60 now seems younger. Many jurisdictions have abolished mandatory retirement and both men and women are working longer for pay, after a period of earlier retirement for men and increased labour market participation rates for women in the 1970s and 1980s.

With more cohabitation, separation, and re-partnering, many people are beginning new intimate relationships or creating stepfamilies and blended families in mid-life and beyond, although remarriage rates remain higher for men than women. Family structures and activities have become more complex, and seniors may now be participating in family celebrations that include their new partners, their biological children, their children's partners, stepchildren, grandchildren, and step-grandchildren (or even great-grandchildren), parents, in-laws, and former in-laws. For the sake of family peace, older people may feel that it is necessary to accept all these new relationships and to remain friendly with their former partners as well as their children's former and current partners. The social networks of most seniors include their children and their grandchildren, providing regular social contact with younger generations, but childless older people tend to have more peer-related social networks. Although grandchildren can be a great source of joy, they can also be a source of family conflict, especially if grandparents disapprove of their upbringing.

Life satisfaction remains relatively high for older people and is influenced by the perception of good health, adequate income, and supportive social networks. The material well-being of seniors continues to vary considerably by country and is influenced by retirement laws, the generosity of public and private pensions, and interest rates, as well as the employment status of elderly persons and their household income, savings, and assets. The highest poverty rates among households with a head aged 65 and older are among those who are single and outside the workforce, a category that includes a disproportionate percentage of women.

Rising life expectancies and changing values about aging mean that young people often anticipate a more active old age than their parents' generation. As the larger baby boom generation ages, older people could acquire more political power to demand improved services and facilities, although popular culture and consumer advertising continue to focus on youth. Some of these seniors will be financially secure with continued employment earnings, retirement pensions, and personal savings, and will create the need for new services and facilities that cater to older people. In doing so, they will probably challenge present notions about the capabilities and interests of elderly people. Our stereotypes about old age tend to be based on our perceptions of relatives, friends, and acquaintances, as well as images in the media. There are many reasons to believe that elderly people in the future will be different from past generations and even different from today's seniors. Therefore, policymakers should be wary of relying on predictions based solely on demographic projections, without considering socio-economic and cultural influences.

Questions for Critical Thought

1. If we did a content analysis of popular women's magazines and men's magazines, what might we conclude about aging and gender?

2. Is aging a different experience for gays and lesbians than for heterosexuals? What evidence can you find to support your answer?

3. Is there any evidence that older people are lonelier than younger people, especially after widowhood? Is there any evidence that childless people are lonelier than parents in old age?

4. Which kinds of pensions are better for women: universal old-age pensions or retirement pensions? Why?

Questions for Debate

1. People tend to become more conservative with age. Debate.

2. The expression that a woman looks like "mutton dressed as lamb" suggests that trying to look younger through hair dyes or fashionable clothing is counterproductive, and perhaps even plays into the hands of capitalism. Discuss.

3. Children should be responsible for their aging parents rather than expecting the welfare state to provide long-term residential care.

Suggested Readings

McDaniel, Susan. 2009. "The Family Lives of the Middle-Aged and Elderly in Canada," in M. Baker, ed., *Families: Changing Trends in Canada*, 6th edn. Toronto: McGraw-Hill Ryerson.

Mann, Robin. 2007. "Out of the Shadows? Grandfatherhood, Age and Masculinities," *Journal of Aging Studies* 21: 281–91.

Martin-Matthews, Anne. 2011. "Revisiting 'Widowhood in Later Life': Changes in Patterns and Profiles, Advances in Research and Understanding," *Canadian Journal on Aging* 30, 3: 359–75.

Mason, Jennifer, Vanessa May, and Lynda Clarke. 2007. "Ambivalence and Paradoxes of Grandparenting," *Sociological Review* 55, 4: 687–706.

Suggested Websites

Institute of Aging
www.cihr-irsc.gc.ca
> This virtual research institute is part of the Canadian Institute of Health Research and is dedicated to the advancement of knowledge in the field of aging to improve the quality of life and the health of older Canadians.

Vanier Institute of the Family
www.vifamily.ca
> The Vanier Institute website includes a particularly relevant paper by Anne Martin-Matthews, "The Ties That Bind Aging Families" (2005).

Australian Institute of Family Studies
www.aifs.gov.au
> This website provides an annotated bibliography about grandparents' role in families and child care, their contact with grandchildren after divorce, and grandparents raising grandchildren.

9

Constraints on Personal Choices

Learning Objectives

◎ To learn how sociologists predict future patterns in family life based on demographic and social trends.

◎ To understand the socio-economic and cultural constraints on personal choices relating to intimacy and family life.

◎ To identify trends in family studies as a discipline.

Introduction

Two central questions underlie this book. The first asks which aspects of family and intimate relations are new and differ from previous patterns and which have remained relatively similar over recent decades. The second question asks which changes in the larger society have most constrained people's choices about how they live in their personal and family life. Throughout the previous chapters, I have shown that, at least in the liberal states, more young people now cohabit rather than marry in their first union and more couples delay legal marriage and reproduction. More dating, sexual activity, and cohabitation occur between partners from different socio-cultural backgrounds, as well as between couples of the same sex. Cohabiting and marital relationships last for shorter time periods, separation and re-partnering is more prevalent, children continue to live with their mothers after separation, more children live in stepfamilies, and more people find a new partner later in life. Nevertheless, most people marry, produce children, and eventually become grandparents.

These family trends, which are apparent in all the liberal states and many other Western countries, are created by large numbers of people behaving in similar ways at the same time, which suggests that personal choices are shaped by some of the same ideas and structural changes. For example, new ideas about equity and human rights, changing employment opportunities, and increased living costs influence our desires and decisions about choosing a partner, getting married, buying a house, having children, leaving a relationship, or experiencing old age. At the same time, the types of work we do—both paid and unpaid—continue to be shaped by gendered and class-based ideas and practices, even though labour market practices are changing rapidly.

Because personal life is influenced by so many social, psychological, cultural, and economic factors, efforts to alter family demography through social policies have not always had the desired effort. These policies include "wedfare" programs, which are designed to encourage lone mothers to marry so that they can be supported by a male breadwinner rather than welfare payments, and "baby bonuses," which are benefits paid to parents at childbirth to encourage reproduction and to help with birth-related expenses. Governments have always experienced difficulties trying to control sexuality, reproduction, and marriage.

In this book, I have used both a political economy framework and interpretive theory to demonstrate the ways that socio-economic forces influence and shape our personal choices. I have argued that current labour market trends tend to create an insecure environment for family formation, child-rearing, home ownership, and marital stability. Job requirements shifted when more governments deregulated the economy and signed free trade agreements with other countries, and more companies exported internationally, created branch plants in countries with cheaper production costs, and advertised globally for higher-level positions.

Employment conditions worsened when the international economy began to take a downturn in 2008. The trend to hire a portion of lower-level staff on short-term contracts continues to help corporate managers maximize their profits and to cushion their business interests against international economic downturns because these workers can be laid off more easily when their labour is no longer required. In some jurisdictions, employers are given temporary tax exemptions and are also permitted to pay lower wages and benefits to temporary and part-time staff. Although some workers use casual jobs to enable them to improve their skills or education or to care for their children, many find that current employment practices reduce their income security, complicate their relationships, and limit their opportunities to buy a home.

Working in another country may bring new excitement and opportunities, but it also alters lifestyles and relationships, placing constraints on the activities of parents, partners, and children. Working from home or outside the main workplace permits employees to make more choices about how and when to work, but it may also alter domestic arrangements such as who does most of the household work. Furthermore, the decision to pursue **telework** is often made by management rather than being the personal choice of individual employees. Generally, employees and the self-employed are working longer hours in the liberal states, and higher percentages are working on contracts and in the evenings and on weekends (Bittman, 2004; Crompton, 2004; OECD, 2011c: 55). Mobile telephones and laptop computers enable people to "work anywhere," but this blurs the distinction between work time and family/leisure time, and may improve neither the economic circumstances of the household nor personal relationships.

The 24-hour economy requires special initiatives to maintain a work/life balance because working long hours tends to be stressful, imposes on the personal time of couples, and often requires one partner to manage the household work or to pay for these services. Family practices such as eating the evening meal together are becoming less prevalent because more family members are employed and more are working non-standard hours. These changing work patterns gradually shape preferences about family practices, education, and future occupational choices as students learn to anticipate the need for computer skills, post-secondary education, national and international experience, working long hours, or accepting contract work to gain the necessary experience to further their careers.

Changing work patterns modify our personal lives but so do media representations. Young persons are increasingly subjected to both subtle and explicit forms of advertising that encourage them to look slim and fashionable in order to find friends or sexual partners, to indulge themselves with consumer goods, and to expect to create comfortable material lives. To afford this lifestyle, however, people require paid work, secure incomes, and few dependants. With readily available credit and insecure jobs, young people, especially, are encouraged to live beyond their means, accruing higher levels of personal debt that impact on the ability to build family assets throughout their lives. Increasingly, young couples respond to these pressures by delaying marriage, childbirth, and home ownership (Baker, 2009b).

Many middle-class youth now live with their parents longer than was common a few decades ago. In addition, cohabiting couples tend to delay marriage, buying a home, and having a child while they establish their careers and financial security and strengthen their relationship. However, marriage and child-rearing continue to be viewed as desirable and long-term commitments. Fathers are still expected to be the primary earners and mothers are encouraged to find paid work but also to make employment sacrifices in order to create a comfortable home and provide child care. At the same time, relationships become vulnerable to conflict and separation with more residential mobility, precarious income security, the need to accommodate two careers, and higher levels of personal and household debt. Personal life is altered in many ways by current labour market demands, new educational requirements, higher material aspirations, and higher levels of debt.

Technological innovations also have influenced personal choices and family life. More effective birth control enables people to engage in sexual intercourse outside a secure relationship with fewer risks of pregnancy, and to limit their family size within marriage, but new advances in assisted conception permit more couples and individuals to try to reproduce (Ford et al., 2003; Baker, 2005b). The ability to freeze sperm means that conception can happen after the donor or father's death. In addition, "designer babies" are possible, post-menopausal women can have babies, and wealthy couples can commission low-income women to produce children for them (Eichler, 1997). Although these new reproductive practices are not yet widespread, they are frequently discussed in the media, and the very possibilities alter our ways of thinking about sex, reproduction, and childbirth.

Innovations in transportation technology also shape family life. The invention of automobiles early in the twentieth century permitted more privacy and intimacy for "courting" couples. The widespread use of automobiles also altered patterns of residence, allowing people to live farther from work in suburban or rural communities and to purchase a holiday home. It also encouraged more travel for both work and leisure. Now, more households own more than one car, which increases costs but enables couples to work in different locations farther from home. International travel is also more feasible with lower airfares relative to wages. Affordable and faster international travel permits more people to take overseas holidays, to maintain contact with friends and family abroad, and to study or work in other countries. It also enables them to flee from family conflict or abusive partners and to find a safe haven in other jurisdictions. However, new computerized surveillance technologies and multilateral agreements between governments assist officials to apprehend parents who cross borders to shirk their family responsibilities (Baker, 2006).

Members of some families are now spread throughout the world and immigrants arrive from a larger range of countries with varying family practices (OECD, 2005b). Although this increases cultural diversity, research suggests that especially young migrants and the second generation modify their family demography to make it more consistent with patterns in their adopted country (Albanese, 2009a). Nevertheless, more young people in Western countries now have parents and grandparents living in arranged marriages, dressing in traditional clothes, and eating a wider variety of foods. Many migrants maintain regular contact with relatives back home through e-mail, texting, Skype, long-distance telephone calls, electronic financial transfers, and frequent air travel. Some parents even earn money in one place and raise children in another, and small percentages become "transnational citizens" or "cosmopolitans" who are equally comfortable living in several countries.

Cell phones, texting, and e-mail help family members and friends to maintain contact and permit parents to "supervise" their children from a distance, even while working. Television and the Internet bring international news and advertising into our homes, encouraging a more cosmopolitan outlook but also introducing us to new forms of consumerism that tend to raise our material aspirations, as well as engendering negative responses to the homogenization of culture and lived experience. In addition, the Internet enables global marketing, the rapid spread of news, international lobbying, chat groups, sexual encounters, and new dating practices, but also bullying and the dissemination of pornography and stalking. Technology increasingly permeates our sexual practices, child-rearing, the maintenance of relationships, the design of our homes, and patterns of work and leisure, introducing new ideas and irritations into our lives.

Increasingly, people around the world watch the same television programs and videos, read the same books and material on the Internet, and view the same images and advertisements, although the "globalization of culture" consists largely of Western ideas from North America, the United Kingdom, and Europe circulating to the rest of the world (Baker, 2006). Young people in remote or less developed areas can be enticed by these images and ideas, and may try to simulate the fashions and lifestyles of the West. Consequently, more people expect to choose where they live and with whom, what they buy, how they will earn a living, and how they spend their leisure time. Westernization tends to encourage contraceptive use, freer choice of marriage partners, nuclear family living, a greater acceptance of cohabitation and divorce, and the desire for more gender equality within marriage (Giddens, 1992).

New ideas about human rights, gender equity, family obligations, and entitlement to social benefits also shape expectations and patterns of personal life in subtle ways (Baker, 2006). Policy reforms initially force people to conform but they also tend to modify social expectations over time and eventually alter behaviour. Restructuring social programs may also help shape the meaning of "good parenting," gender relations, and women's occupational aspirations, as well as expectations about future social provision. Recently, governments in the liberal states have encouraged both mothers and fathers to view paid employment as the normal activity for all adults, even though they have not always provided the necessary facilities or subsidies for child care.

Throughout this book I have argued that even though we can now exercise more choice in our personal lives, few of the new patterns in relationships are entirely matters of individual choice. Our behaviour and even our personal ambitions tend instead to be shaped by social and economic activities and events in the larger society, and these are difficult for individuals to control. Constraints on relationships may relate to lack of money or power, new legal requirements, technological changes, pressures from family and friends, and feelings of obligation or entitlement. Personal constraints can arise simply from the wishes, actions, or inactions of an intimate partner. For example, we might choose to live in an egalitarian relationship but if our partner refuses to share the household earning, material resources, or the domestic work, we cannot have what we want. We may choose to grow old with our partner, but if he or she leaves us, our own personal preferences may no longer be relevant.

It is difficult to anticipate how we would react to particular changes in our personal lives, such as an unexpected pregnancy or a marital separation, or how or where we will be living in 20 years. It is even more challenging for social scientists to predict future patterns in personal and family life.

Predicting Future Family Patterns

Two important goals of science are to identify patterns and accurately predict future trends. Within the social sciences, predicting human behaviour seems complicated because so many factors are involved, such as new ideas, technological changes, economic and political transformations, labour market transitions, legal and policy changes, emotions, and personal choices. Researchers attempting to predict trends in personal and family life have often ignored some of these factors and relied instead on past and current demographic patterns as social indicators of the future, but human beings also can choose to resist prevailing patterns and contravene socially acceptable behaviour. Consequently, predictions have not always been accurate, especially when researchers rely mainly on past demographic trends. A successful prediction of personal and family life requires some knowledge of social psychology, political movements, policy reform, economic trends, technological innovations, and popular culture.

Despite the challenges of prediction in the social sciences, the rest of this chapter suggests some family patterns that are likely to continue into the future. These ideas, portrayed in Table 9.1, have been garnered from a wide variety of research on family demography, new forms of relationships, changing labour market trends, and the restructuring of public policy. However, the trends pertain only to people living in Western industrialized countries and especially the liberal states. In addition, these predictions stretch only a few decades into the future because it is so difficult to know how socioeconomic and political life might change. Nevertheless, this exercise should enable us to draw some conclusions about the nature of personal and family life, and the power of certain constraints on our choices.

Will People Still Get Married?

Compared to the 1950s, more people are now sexually active outside marriage, more couples cohabit without legal ceremony, and the average age of marriage has been rising. At the same time, we have seen that live-in relationships without legal ceremonies tend to have a shorter duration and more end in separation. In the next two decades, these trends will likely continue and even accelerate. More people will come to believe that their personal and intimate life is their own affair, with little relevance to religious leaders or civil authorities.

Young people pursuing higher education will continue to live with their parents until they are well into their twenties, although many will also have intimate partners. When they leave the family home many will need to share accommodation as housing costs rise relative to income, especially in the major cities. This means that more young people will live with various roommates and sexual partners but will not necessarily "settle down" with one

Table 9.1 Future Trends in Family Life

Area of Family Life	Future Trend
Cohabitation	• Rates will rise among all age groups.
Age of Marriage	• Average age will rise as more first unions are consensual and more older couples remarry.
	• The age will remain higher for males and higher-income couples.
Marriage Rate	• The rate will decline with more consensual unions.
	• It will remain above-average for non-Christian religious groups and fundamentalist Christians.
Fertility Rate	• Fertility will continue to decline for younger and more educated women.
	• It will remain higher for low-income groups and certain cultural minorities.
Duration of Marriage	• Length of marriage will decline with the normalization and legitimation of divorce and more focus on self-development.
	• But older remarriages will remain more stable.
Re-partnering and Remarriage Rate	• Remarriage will rise as more people divorce but higher cohabitation rates reduce remarriage.
	• Non-legal re-partnering will be higher among younger people, low-income groups, and divorced people.
Housework and Child Care	• More employed couples will hire home-cleaners and child-minders.
	• But women will continue to take responsibility for most indoor household tasks, child care, and elder care.
	• Fathers will do more cooking, shopping, and child care but will retain responsibility for household and car repairs.
Labour Force Participation	• More mothers will work full-time and increase their contributions to household finances.
	• More fathers will work overtime or at two jobs.
	• Many parents will work longer hours to support their children, while others will experience unemployment or under-employment.

partner until they complete their education, develop some work stability, repay their debts, and acquire financial assets. With the decline in the economy and rising unemployment, however, some individuals will become more security-conscious and choose to legalize their intimate relationships in an attempt to protect their financial assets and enhance their personal stability. With less job security, rates of separation and divorce might also decline as fewer people will be able to afford separate dwellings and will have to make the best of their relationships.

As both men and women pursue busy careers and older people seek new partners, more individuals will rely on introductions by friends, dating agencies, organized activities, and self-advertising in newspapers and especially on Internet relationship websites to find partners. Many of these relationships will become sexual soon after the individuals meet and some will lead to cohabitation without much consideration about permanence. Advanced birth control technology will continue to enable heterosexual couples to enjoy sexual activity without pregnancy, and the social and legal differences between cohabitation and legal marriage will likely diminish even further. In addition, ideas about the right to privacy and personal happiness will continue to pervade much of Western culture, shaping patterns in sexuality and relationship formation.

It also seems realistic to suggest that in the coming decades fewer adults will be living with relatives such as parents and siblings, but more will be creating non-traditional households based on neither the nuclear family nor the extended family models. Also, more adults will avoid legal marriage in the future as sexuality becomes even more separated from marriage and reproduction, and men and women can easily live—both socially and financially—without a legal partner. However, the social pressure and personal desire to partner, marry, and reproduce will remain strong. Most people will either cohabit or marry at least once in their life, as shared living provides greater opportunities for love, regular sex, and companionship while reducing loneliness and accommodation expenses. Considering current rates of separation, however, more people will cohabit with several consecutive partners over their lifetime but spend time between relationships with casual intimacies, roommates, living alone, or sharing a home with their children.

Judging from current trends in some European countries as well as in the liberal states, a growing minority of intimate couples will "live apart together" for specific periods of time while they study, work, or raise their children in separate locations. This will be especially prevalent among university-educated couples where out-of-province or overseas training and work are expected to bring higher occupational returns and where two high-level business or professional jobs are difficult to find in the same place. However, it will also remain a pattern favoured by some re-partnered couples with adolescent children, or migrant couples where one partner returns to work or to oversee the family business in their country of origin. Commuting couples might live together on the weekend or even less frequently but will be free to devote considerable amounts of time and energy to paid work, child-rearing, or leisure activities when they are apart. In many cases, this "choice" will be influenced by higher rates of unemployment or under-employment, more international migration, the difficulties of blending families, and the growing importance of financial security for both men and women in a globalizing economy and during economic hard times.

Same-sex couples sharing a home will become more prevalent in the future, and more will live openly and choose to formalize their personal commitment. The formalization of same-sex relationships through "civil union" or "civil partnership" legislation or the extension of marriage rights has already occurred in some jurisdictions and continues to be under discussion in others. However, not all same-sex couples will choose to live in "marriage-like relationships." Gay men, especially, will be more likely than lesbian women to opt for a series of intimate partners while living alone close to a community of like-minded friends, or will choose to cohabit for short periods without any expectation of a lifelong partnership.

If a higher percentage of the population lives outside nuclear families, lifestyle and housing preferences will change as more people choose low-maintenance apartments or flats rather than single-family houses with gardens to maintain. With fewer family responsibilities and less household work, singles and child-free couples will likely spend less time at home and more time eating out, enjoying time with friends, attending leisure events, and travelling. In addition, these individuals and couples will be more likely to work full-time and overtime, to earn higher incomes, to spend less on home ownership and child-related expenses, and therefore to have more discretionary income for entertainment, recreation, and travel.

Generally, relationships will become more consensual and less permanent, although most people will continue to marry and produce children and grandchildren (Cherlin, 2010). Giddens (1992) talked about the possibility of "pure relationships" that would be unclouded by feelings of obligations, dependencies, and inequalities. Although this may be possible for some people, most couples will still depend on each other for companionship, financial support, and domestic chores. Although wives will increasingly earn household money, economic dependencies will continue as two incomes become essential to pay the household bills. In addition, economic inequalities and power differentials will continue between husbands and wives, reflecting gender inequalities in paid and unpaid work, including the responsibility for housework and the daily care of children. The probability of a "pure relationship" could increase as more women become economically self-supporting, fewer children are born, and more fathers actively engage in child care. However, most couples will marry and produce at least one child, and more mothers than fathers will become economically dependent on their partners.

As women expect more control over their lives, they will be more likely to initiate sexual and cohabiting relationships. Nonetheless, vestiges of the double standard of sexuality will linger, penalizing women—through social stigmatization and the possible negative impact on prospects for marriage and job promotion—who appear to be too obvious in their sexual needs or who openly seek recreational sex. With more consensual unions and liberal divorce laws, relationships will also last for shorter periods of time but people will be seeking new partners throughout the lifespan. Current patterns suggest that men will continue to prefer women who are attractive, "petite," and unencumbered with children at home, and the age gap will become larger as older men seek new younger partners. Most children will continue to live with their mothers after separation, but these mothers will be expected to combine paid work and caring obligations, managing on lower female earnings. Although more women are gaining higher education and are working full-time, **neo-liberal restructuring** in the labour force continues to reward those who are willing and able to work overtime. Many lone mothers will be unable to meet this expectation. As rates of legal marriage and fertility continue to fall, separation will become less complicated and more prevalent but it will still be emotionally and financially draining for all involved.

These predictions suggest that relationships in the future will be formed more easily and dissolved with less social disapproval and legal intervention. Fewer people will live in families but when they do, families will become smaller, with fewer children and fewer relatives sharing households. Although some new immigrants will initially live in extended family households, those who are wealthier, more educated, and fluent in the language of the host country will be more likely to prefer to live in nuclear family households. Increasingly, the liberal states are accepting educated immigrants with middle-class backgrounds. The children of recent migrants, especially those born and educated in the host country, will be less likely to see extended family living as desirable when they reach adulthood. In the future, more people in the general population will live alone, which will counteract any trend for recent immigrants to share accommodation. The percentage of couples who remain childless will also increase as contraception becomes more effective and abortion is made easier, although a strong anti-abortion backlash remains apparent in countries such as the United States, where abortion laws could also be tightened. In addition, as young people raise their material aspirations, many will yearn for fewer family responsibilities, especially women who anticipate a life of full-time employment.

Social conservatives will continue to worry about low marriage rates and the impermanence of couple relationships, but policies to encourage legal marriage and permanent relationships will have limited success. State inducements to marry, such as income tax benefits, seldom compensate for the perceived reasons to avoid marriage, such as concern about legal entanglements, lifetime responsibilities, restrictions on mobility, expectations of monogamy and parenthood, and gendered patterns of paid and unpaid work.

Research shows that heterosexual legal marriage is most likely to occur when men gain secure jobs with adequate incomes to support the household, and where couples and their children are severely disadvantaged if they cohabit but do not marry. As more women become self-supporting, the importance of living with a male breadwinner diminishes, although a steady male income continues to provide a better standard of living even for high-earning women. At the same time, living outside marriage or cohabitation will

Box 9.1   The Deep-Seated Concern over "The Family"

Family change is very complicated. It is not necessarily a cause for "worry," although most academics and political commentators would, I think, be prepared to say that the pace of such change warrants careful attention. What to do in the face of such change is more contentious still. For the most part, the nostalgia for the traditional family has not translated into firm policies designed to put the clock back, for example by returning working mothers to the home, or by making divorce much harder to obtain. Indeed, at least in the English-speaking countries, politicians on the right, who are most likely to wax eloquent on the subject of family values, are also usually the most loath to accept state intervention in the family.

Source: Lewis, 2003. *Should We Worry about Family Change?* Toronto: UTP: p.12–13.

become easier as more services are developed for those without the time or skills to care for themselves, their homes, and their children. Furthermore, as non-marital cohabitation begins to look more like legal marriage, there are fewer social and legal reasons to marry, although the symbolic reasons remain for many couples.

Will People Still Have Children?

In earlier chapters, I noted that fertility decline is influenced by economic and social changes in the larger society as well as personal preferences. Raising children has become more costly for parents and combining paid work with child-rearing is increasingly difficult without heavy state subsidies for child care. In the past, people were taught that the purpose of marriage was reproduction but they also expected that their children would contribute to their household resources and support them in old age, as well as bring them love, companionship, and personal satisfaction. In addition, women used to be encouraged to see child-rearing as a career but they are now pressured to become educated and help support the household, which means that they are more likely to want to limit their family size. Educated women tend to be more knowledgeable about contraception and more inclined than less educated women to believe that they have the right to use it. Forfeiting household income is also more consequential when educated women leave the labour force for child-bearing and child-rearing.

Fertility rates will continue to decline in the liberal states but cultural and class differences will remain visible in these rates. For example, young women with disadvantaged backgrounds or from certain cultural groups will continue to experience higher rates of pregnancy and childbirth before completing their education, before marriage, and at younger ages within marriage. Generally, however, birth rates will continue to decline among younger age groups, although they will decline faster among "white" or "European" women and wealthier women. Certain religious groups (such as fundamentalist Christians and Muslims) and some "visible minorities" (such as American blacks and Hispanics, and New Zealand Maori and Pacific Islanders, who are often fundamentalist Christians) will be less likely to use contraception and will therefore produce more children.

In general, women will continue to delay child-bearing and more first births will occur when women are in their late twenties and early thirties. As women reach their late thirties, conception problems will increase and more women will turn to physicians and clinics for advice and treatment about conception and fertility. Now that more women produce their first child at older ages, doctors will see these women as "high-risk patients" requiring technological interventions in childbirth, such as induced births and Caesarean deliveries. With high levels of medical intervention as well as lifestyle-related risks, more women could experience miscarriages and more births could lead to infants and children with disabilities that require ongoing medical treatment. However, the older average age of women at first birth also means that more women will have completed their education and established themselves in paid work before pregnancy. Therefore, more employees will require paid parental leave, breast-feeding breaks, infant child-care services, and flexible working arrangements.

Fewer babies will be born in the future but more of them will be born to unmarried mothers, lesbian couples, and older women. Most children will continue to be conceived within cohabitation or legal relationships but fewer of these relationships will include two heterosexual partners. As in the present, lesbians will be more likely to become parents than gay men, and lesbian co-mothers will continue to be more engaged in parenting than heterosexual fathers. Among heterosexual couples, fewer of these relationships will last until the child reaches school age, which implies that more children will spend a portion of their childhood living with only one parent, usually their mother. More children will also live in stepfamilies, most likely with the mother and her new partner. Mothers will remain the resident parent after most cases of separation, although more fathers will have legal access to their children and will share joint custody or legal decision-making.

As more people cohabit rather than marry, relationships will become shorter and less stable. A greater number of men will conceive children with more than one woman over their lifetime. Most of these children will continue to live with their mothers while their fathers move on to new partners, some of whom will be mothers living with children from their previous relationships. As more children live in stepfamilies, governments will experience problems enforcing paternal child support, ensuring that fathers remain engaged with their biological children, and resolving disputes about child-rearing in the post-divorce family.

How Will Couples Combine Earning and Caring?

Recent labour market trends indicate that fewer workers in the future will retain one full-time job with the same employer throughout their working lives. Occupational transitions will become prevalent, with more adults returning to formal education and upgrading their skills, as well as moving from employment to self-employment, accepting contract jobs, and searching for better employment opportunities and conditions elsewhere. At the same time, more family members will be employed, although finding work and keeping it may become more difficult if international economic conditions do not improve. In the past decade, more wives and adolescents have been working for pay compared to the 1960s. In the future, fewer adults will be working the former nine-to-five workday and more will be working in the evenings, on the weekends, and on statutory holidays. With so much time devoted to paid work, family schedules will be difficult to co-ordinate and family meals, discussions, negotiations, activities, and celebrations will become complicated to manage. This could have negative implications for cohesion and communication within the household.

"Globalized" labour markets and freer trade arrangements will encourage more workers to follow employment opportunities to different regions of the country and across international borders. The European Union now permits workers to move freely among some member countries. Workers can also move between Australia and New Zealand, and Canadians and Americans can cross borders for specific jobs but with more restrictions (Baker, 2006). Free trade agreements and integrated markets will continue to encourage employment mobility, but it is not always easy for workers to persuade their partners and children to follow, especially if the partner is already employed. There may also be settlement problems related to schooling, employment, and language in a new jurisdiction or country.

When families migrate for employment purposes, partners need to be recognized, which will still be difficult in some countries, especially if they are of the same sex or living in consensual unions. If partners or adult children expect to find employment, their credentials need to be recognized by potential employers and authorities in the new host country and all family members need to be able to speak the local language. More children will need to adapt to local schools and find new friends in a foreign country. Nuclear families crossing international borders often leave behind the support of grandparents and other extended family members, who might have offered financial and emotional support as well as child-care services. Geographical mobility in the future will expand employment opportunities for parents and provide adventures (or problems) for partners and children, but these changes could also heighten family conflict and lead to disruption and marital dissolution.

As employment becomes less secure for a greater number of people, many adults will continue working until older ages than a few decades ago. The trend towards early retirement, noticeable in the 1970s and 1980s, has already started reversing in many countries as both men and women work long hours but do not necessarily increase their prosperity or household assets. Self-employment, short-term contracts, and part-time work may not provide access to the same retirement plans as permanent employees enjoy. Therefore, more workers in the future will be forced to remain in the labour force for financial reasons, perhaps taking gradual retirement at older ages in order to maintain their income security. This could restrict the employment opportunities of younger workers, especially in tightening labour markets, but it might make retirement more feasible for older workers, both financially and psychologically. Other older workers may be edged out of their jobs by tightening economic conditions before they are ready for retirement.

Will Couples Stay Together?

Separation and divorce have become normalized and legitimized as they grow more prevalent, but the rising insecurity of intimate relationships will become more consequential in the future. First, the insecurity of legal marriage could discourage some young people from making public commitments because they will be afraid that their relationships might end in divorce, which could be legally complex, costly, and stigmatizing. Yet statistically, cohabiting relationships have higher rates of separation than legal marriages, suggesting that relationship instability will continue to increase at a societal level (Wu, 2000; Lichter and Quian, 2008).

Second, relationship instability will discourage young girls from accepting the idea that they can rely in the future on a male breadwinner and will encourage them to prepare for a lifetime of personal earning and greater independence. More job-oriented education and career planning will reduce the gendered nature of paid work, raise the earnings of women relative to men, and increase wives' incomes relative to those of their husbands. However, the pattern for women to marry older men with higher incomes will also continue. Furthermore, by becoming more financially independent, women will also increase their chances of relationship instability because women who are self-supporting tend to feel less obliged to stay in unhappy relationships. Not only do they have fewer economic reasons to stay, but their male partners may also feel less guilt about separating from women who are self-supporting or who easily could become so.

More children will experience the dissolution of parental relationships, and when their parents are between partners, some children will begin to normalize living with one parent (usually the mother). If the mother re-partners, the children may initially feel some personal disruption but more children will view living in one-parent households and stepfamilies as normal. The boundaries of children's families tend to become more complex in stepfamilies, including both resident and non-resident parents and their new partners and parents, as well as step-siblings and grandparents from several relationships. Adapting to this complexity will undoubtedly challenge some children and parents, but it will not necessarily lead to serious problems for them. Children will learn to become more flexible about their parents' intimate relationships, but parents and step-parents will also need to remain sensitive to children's perceptions and needs. No child or adolescent wants to feel displaced by her or his parent's new lover or new step-siblings, and more parents will be required to work at creating social cohesion within stepfamilies or blended families.

As more adults re-partner later in life, the average age in all new marriages will rise, dynamics will change in many families, and images of middle age and aging will gradually be refashioned. For many older couples, their new intimate relationships will provide a new lease on life, altering daily routines and prevalent images of sexuality, maturity, and parental obligations. The fact that some of the same transitions experienced by parents could simultaneously be happening to their mature children might help to bridge the generation gap even though the years between generations will be growing longer.

Will Aging Be a Problem?

Many demographers and policy-makers see the "aging population" as a social problem and assume that more seniors in the population will burden society with higher public costs. However, if the average age of retirement and pension eligibility is raised and older workers continue to earn a living and pay taxes, this may become less of a problem. Furthermore, aging will not necessarily become a personal or family concern. After all, older individuals and couples typically maintain high levels of independence but also provide services for friends and family, including lending money to their adult children and caring for their grandchildren while the parents are working. In addition, many wives care for their husbands in their old age and some men care for their aging wives (Martin-Matthews, 2007, 2011; McDaniel, 2009). Nevertheless, some seniors are more vulnerable than others. For example, older unattached women are particularly vulnerable to poverty if they did not work for pay in their earlier years, if they suffer from health problems or disabilities, or if they did not own a home or inherit other assets.

Life expectancy has been rising for centuries but some researchers now predict that it could begin to fall within the next two decades because of the high rates of obesity and its related diseases in developed countries such as Canada, the United States, and New Zealand (Walsh, 2005). Widespread obesity, especially among low-income people, will raise the already high rates of diabetes, heart disease, and strokes, as well as increase fertility problems. Researchers and policy-makers are particularly concerned about childhood obesity, which will undoubtedly cause future health problems and shorten lives. In addition, environmental pollution and continued use of tobacco, caffeine, and other drugs are expected to reduce life expectancy in the future (ibid.).

As fertility declines and mothers are older when they produce their first child, the spacing between generations will become larger in the future. This may mean that fewer children and young adults will know their grandparents, although with higher living standards and improvements in health care some of their grandparents will live longer. These demographic changes also suggest that many parents will reach the age of 65 before their children reach maturity and leave home, forcing some parents to work longer to help finance their children's living and educational expenses. This could delay the retirement of more parents, which might provide a further opportunity for governments to increase the eligibility age for retirement benefits or old-age pensions in order to save public money.

Although governments often reform social programs to make them more consistent with current lifestyles, they also use changing family demography to justify forms of restructuring that save public money or downsize the welfare state. Studying family trends is therefore essential for governments. It is also useful to business people who are trying to predict or manipulate market trends in order to sell more of their consumer products. For academics, studying patterns in intimate experiences and family life reveals the impact of transformations occurring in the wider society on personal life and sheds light on the diversity and adaptability of family experiences.

The Future of Family Studies

We have seen in this book that researchers and theorists have been studying family life for over a hundred years but the academic field of family studies, and especially the sociology of the family, has changed considerably over the decades. These studies are certain to develop further in the future. While early research made false assumptions about the extent of uniformity, consensus, and co-operation within families, current research highlights diversity and conflict in personal life and family experiences. This includes a focus on gendered differences in domestic labour, power differentials and conflict in relationships, new patterns of family formation (including same-sex unions and cohabitation), cultural variations in marriage systems and family dynamics, and the impact of marital separation on various family members. Current studies also address the impact of politics, technology, and the media on the creation of "personal biographies," new ways of finding sexual relationships, and cosmetic work on the body.

While social class was always a predominant variable in family research, gender, age, sexual preference, and **ethnicity** have also become central to current analyses of personal and family life. However, more studies continue to focus on couples with young children rather than on families in mid-life and old age. Women's family-related experiences have been researched more than men's but new studies on masculinity, fathering, and grandfathering are beginning to correct this imbalance (Dudley et al., 2012; Mann, 2007).

Current research on family and personal life acknowledges the large differences in income, lifestyle, and family composition based on race, ethnicity, and culture. With higher rates of immigration and international travel, more researchers are focusing on cultural variations in finding partners, marriage systems, and perceptions of family obligations, as well as the intergenerational differences between immigrants and their native-born children. The meaning of marriage and prevalent assumptions underlying family life are becoming especially relevant with immigration from Islamic and Hindu countries, as well as renewed interest in indigenous families. This indicates that the previous overemphasis on the Eurocentric, nuclear, and middle-class family is diminishing.

Despite this new focus, I argue in this book that social class continues to be a central variable shaping aspirations, achievements, and lifestyle. Studies with social policy implications continue to see household income and wealth accumulation as crucial variables influencing all aspects of personal life, although they seldom use the sociological concept of social class. Many researchers continue to use the political economy approach to analyze the impact of global markets and social policy restructuring on family life, often combining it with feminist analysis. At the same time, new researchers also draw on the post-structuralist theoretical perspective, which gives primacy to the power of ideas and media representations. This approach, widely used in feminist analyses and cultural studies, emphasizes the importance of personal choice, agency, identity, and consumerism, without always giving adequate consideration to the social and economic constraints on personal choices and identity creation.

In this book, I have used a theoretical perspective that I label the "feminist political economy" approach because I focus on the impact of changes in the economy and social policies on patterns of work and gender relations. This approach reminds us that personal relationships are influenced by changes in the larger society, including patterns of education, employment, and state support, but this impact is often different for men and women, and for mothers and fathers. These societal forces tend to shape our aspirations, expectations, the division of labour at home, the amount of time available for family life, and the resources we have to spend on living standards and family activities.

Hours and conditions of paid work can be partly a personal choice. However, they are also typically organized and modified by employers, unions, and governments, depending on their ideologies, political alliances, and power.

Furthermore, the emphasis on the importance of paid work and the "long-hours culture" is more prevalent in the liberal states than in some European countries with shorter working hours, more holidays, and stronger support for parenting. We need to know more about the impact of working long hours on relations between partners and between workers and their children. Future research could also help us to understand how the new consumerism that accompanies **neo-liberalism** shapes the aspirations of young people and influences their future lifestyles and intimate relationships.

The study of family and personal life has a long academic history, forming a significant portion of research and theorizing in sociology, anthropology, social work, gender studies, social psychology, and cultural studies. In recent years, researchers have been analyzing the impact of globalization and new efforts to restructure welfare states on employment patterns, on the growing gap between the rich and the poor, and on rising levels of household debt. However, social scientists are only beginning to explore the consequences of these economic transformations, as well as the impact of consumerism and advertising, on intimacy and family life.

Throughout this book I have argued that labour market constraints, increased migration, new technologies, and global ideas about equity and human rights are shaping intimate relationships. Although we may have acquired more choice to create our own personal biographies, we continue to live with some of the same socio-economic constraints, as well as several new limitations on our relationships.

Questions for Critical Thought

1. What evidence do sociologists have for the future prediction that most people will eventually marry at some point in their lives?

2. Do social policies actually influence the way that people live in their personal lives or do people normally disregard the expectations of their governments?

3. How could we explain the growing interest in fathering and masculinity within family studies?

Questions for Debate

1. As more women work full-time and overtime, household work will be shared more equitably between male and female partners. Discuss.

2. A deepening recession could encourage more couples to legally marry or remain together. Discuss.

3. We can create any kind of family life we want, if we have the will to do so. Discuss.

Suggested Readings

Beck-Gernsheim, Elisabeth. 2002. *Reinventing the Family: In Search of New Lifestyles.* Cambridge: Polity Press. This book discusses recent changes in family life, analyzes concerns about loss of stability, and argues that new forms of family life are expanding choices and opportunities.

Lewis, Jane. 2003. *Should We Worry About Family Change?* Toronto: University of Toronto Press. Lewis discusses the main policy debates about the family, outlining current socio-demographic changes and different views about how they should be interpreted.

OECD. 2012. *The Future of Families to 2030.* Paris: OECD. This report was produced from international OECD statistics and discusses the social, economic, and political factors that could influence family life in the future.

Suggested Website

The Future Families Project
www.vifamily.ca
> *The Future Families Project: A Survey of Canadian Hopes and Dreams* by Reginald Bibby (2004) is discussed on the website of the Vanier Institute of the Family.

Glossary

Abuse Deliberate maltreatment of another person that could be verbal, emotional, physical, or sexual.

Access The legal arrangement for contact between a non-custodial parent and his/her offspring following separation or divorce.

Alimony Spousal support awarded to divorced women before the enactment of no-fault divorce legislation.

Arranged marriage A marriage in which the partner is selected by elder family members but the young people may have the right to veto the choice.

At-risk families Families with a high probability of going hungry or having inadequate accommodation, or in which the likelihood of abusive behaviour is higher than normal.

Bilateral descent Lineage traced through the families of both the bride and groom.

Blended families Stepfamilies formed through post-marital cohabitation or remarriage that include step-siblings, half-siblings, or both.

Census family A term used by Statistics Canada to refer to a married or cohabiting couple living with or without never-married children, and a lone parent living with never-married children.

Child custody The guardianship of a child and the authority to make decisions about the child's welfare and upbringing.

Child poverty The percentage of children living with impoverished parents, a concept designed to enhance sympathy for the plight of blameless children.

Child support The privately arranged or court-ordered financial support a non-custodial parent must pay to support his/her offspring.

Civil code Law, as in Quebec and many European countries, based largely on written statutes rather than previous court cases or custom (like common law).

Civil union Marriage approved by the state but not necessarily by the church.

Cohabitation An intimate union between a couple who share a household and live together in marriage-like circumstances; also called common-law marriage.

Cohort A category of people either born at the same time or experiencing certain life stages or events at the same time.

Common law The body of general, largely unwritten legal conventions based on prior judicial rulings and traditional customs.

Common-law relationships Cohabitation without legal marriage.

Complementary roles Separate spheres for men and women in marriage.

Conflict Non-violent or violent disagreements or arguments within a relationship.

Corporatist states States whose social security is based on social insurance programs funded by employers, employees, and government, with higher benefits for those with higher incomes.

Crude divorce rates The annual number of divorces per 1,000 marriages (or per 1,000 population) within a specific jurisdiction, such as a country or province.

Developmental theory Learning theory that assumes that children pass through stages of cognitive, motor, and psychological development, and that particular tasks or concepts must be adequately learned before a child passes through the next stage of development.

Double standard The differential evaluation for men and women of identical situations and behaviours.

Endogamy Marriage within one's group, which may be race, ethnicity, religion, caste, or socio-economic status.

Ethnicity Process of awareness of a shared historical and cultural tradition, and therefore group belonging, used as a basis for differential distribution of recognition, rewards, and relationships.

Exogamy Marriage outside the group.

Extended family Several generations, or siblings and their spouses and children, who share a household and resources.

Family economy The waged and unwaged contributions of all family members to ensuring the survival of the household.

Family policies The pursuit and attainment of collective goals and values in addressing problems of families in relation to the state.

Family preservation A principle governing child welfare that relies on the extended family and social support to keep children living with family members rather than placing them in foster homes or institutions.

Family values Beliefs and attitudes that emphasize the (patriarchal) nuclear family as the basic unit of society and the importance of raising children.

Family wage A single wage, normally earned by a breadwinner father, sufficient to support the entire family, hence avoiding the need for the paid labour of the wife or children.

Feminist political economy perspective An analytical framework focused on women's viewpoint and experiences, as well as on how labour markets, social structures, and cultural understandings impact on women.

First default principle The enforcement by the state of child support only if the non-custodial parent fails to make the necessary payments.

Gender roles The ways that males and females interact in a society, considering their different socialization and life experiences.

Gender-neutral Something that could pertain equally to male or female.

Generation The time between the birth of a mother and her offspring, now about 30–35 years.

Globalization The world scale of economic and other activity made possible by the spread of information and telecommunications technology, as well as improved and relatively low-cost transportation.

Homogamy The similarities in the age, social class, race, and ethnicity of couples.

Incest taboos Rules preventing couples from marrying or reproducing with those who are too closely related due to concerns about inbreeding, congenital abnormalities, and family jealousy.

Industrialization The process by which manufacturing industries become dominant in a country's economy.

Intersectionality A concept suggesting that life circumstances may be influenced by a combination of factors such as age, gender, marital status, sexual preference, ethnicity, culture, race, or occupation.

Joint custody The legal situation where both parents share authority over decisions regarding child welfare and upbringing after divorce.

Kinship care Alternative care by grandparents or other relatives instead of foster care by strangers.

Labour force Those who are either engaged in formal paid employment or seeking paid employment.

Liberal states States in which social security is based largely on need and benefits are targeted to low-income and "problem" families.

Lone-parent households Circumstances where one parent shares a residence with his or her never-married children.

Male breadwinner family A two-parent family with the father as principal earner and the mother as care provider.

Marital breakdown The legal grounds for divorce based on circumstances that impair marital functioning, such as spousal desertion or long-term separation.

Marriage market A term that applies an economic analogy to describe the availability of potential marriage partners and how they are valued in a particular culture or period.

Maternity leave The official time away from paid employment taken by a mother for childbirth or adoption.

Matriarchy A system that gives women more authority than men.

Matrifocal family A family focused around the mother.

Matrilineal Tracing family descent through the mother's side of the family.

Matrilocality The custom of the groom living with the bride's family or in her community.

Matrimonial fault An act considered to violate the marriage contract and therefore to be a justification for divorce.

Medicalization The tendency within the medical profession to extend the reach of doctors into society and the lives of individuals, for example, in childbirth through technological monitoring, hospitalized birthing, and other medical interventions.

Monogamy A system of marriage in which each adult is allowed only one spouse at a time.

Monolithic bias Assumption that all families are similar, with an overemphasis on uniformity of experience and structure at the expense of diversity.

Neo-liberalism Political rationality that supports the restructuring of societies to better meet the demands of a global market economy, emphasizing competition, individual self-enhancement, and personal responsibility for problems.

Neo-liberal restructuring Organizational changes within large firms to increase efficiency and save costs, usually involving layoffs resulting from outsourcing of work processes, contract labour, and the movement of manufacturing processes offshore to low-wage countries with weaker environmental standards and less stringent labour standards.

Neo-local residence The custom of the bride and groom living in a separate location from both of their birth families.

No-fault divorce The legal provision for marital dissolution through a non-acrimonious process, as opposed to fault-based divorce that involves proving a spouse guilty of a matrimonial offence or fault.

Nuclear family A husband and wife and their children sharing the same household and co-operating economically.

Parental leave Official time away from paid employment that may be taken by either the mother or father at childbirth or adoption.

Participant observation Fieldwork methodology in which the researcher is or seeks to become part of the group under study.

Patriarchy Social or family system giving men more authority than women.

Patrilineal societies Societies in which lineage or family relationships are traced through the male side of the family.

Patrilocal systems Social systems in which the bride moves into or near her husband's family home.

Political economy perspective Analytical approach emphasizing the links among economic changes, the work people do, policy decisions, and personal life.

Polyandry A system of marriage in which women are allowed more than one husband at a time.

Polygamy A system of marriage in which adults are allowed more than one spouse at a time.

Polygyny A system of marriage in which men are allowed more than one wife at a time.

Post-structuralism Theoretical perspective that explains social change through personal choices, the power of ideas, and public discourse rather than laws, rules, or access to power and money.

Psychoanalytic theory An approach to socialization that stresses the importance of early childhood experiences and subconscious emotions in shaping personality.

Re-partnering The transition into cohabitation or remarriage after divorce or separation.

Rites of passage Events that symbolize changes in maturity and elevate community status, such as marriage or child-bearing.

Role models Persons whose behaviour is patterned by others.

Roles Patterns of behaviour governed by social expectations, rights, and duties, and associated with a specific position in a social situation (such as a husband in a family).

Same-sex marriage Gay and lesbian marriage.

Secularization The process of becoming less constrained by religious writings or authorities, or involving the separation of church and state.

Serial monogamy Marriage to or cohabitation with one partner at a time but involving several partners over a lifetime.

Service sector The part of the economy that provides services rather than goods; also called the tertiary sector. The secondary sector is the goods-producing or manufacturing sector; the primary sector involves primary resources, such as mining, forestry, and agriculture.

Shared parenting Both parents share the physical care and decision-making regarding the child during marriage or after divorce, regardless of who has legal custody.

Significant others Those people we love or value, who also influence our lives.

Social class A category of people who share a similar social and economic position and who are conscious of their similarities.

Social constructionism A theoretical framework that argues that social reality and meaningful behaviour is created through social interaction and cultural understandings.

Social democratic states States that seek to prevent poverty and inequality by providing state services and income support for everyone, regardless of family income.

Social exchange theory Use of economic analogies from cost–benefit analysis to explain marriage and family relations, which are assumed to involve a process of negotiation and the assessment of time/emotional investments.

Social institution An established set of roles, norms, and relationships organized around some central activity or social need.

Social insurance The pooling of the risk of unemployment, disability, or sickness among employers, employees/ citizens, and the state, financed through contributions from all three groups.

Socialization The complex learning process through which individuals develop their personality and acquire the knowledge, skills, and motivation necessary for participation in social life.

Social learning theory The view that development occurs when children process social and cultural information from their environment by observing others, interpreting what they see, and then acting.

State The government as well as the public agencies that support and enforce its policies.

Structural functionalism An analytical approach focusing on how social structure influences individual behaviour and assuming that behaviour is governed by rules, laws, and expectations that maintain the structure of society.

Surrogate mothers Women who gestate and give birth to a child for another couple.

Survey research Questionnaire-based collection of a large sample of quantitative data.

Symbolic interaction perspective An analytical approach that assumes people create their own social reality by defining and interpreting the symbolic meanings of those responding to them.

Systems theory An analytical perspective that sees the family as a system of interactions and relationships in which the behaviour of one member influences all others and behavioural patterns recur.

Telework Work (often at home) through telecommunication or computer links to the main workplace.

Violence Unwarranted physical or verbal force, or sexual aggression against another person.

Welfare state The laws and social programs designed to protect citizens in times of unemployment, illness, old age, or insufficient income.

References

Abercrombie, Nicholas, Stephen Hill, and Bryan S. Turner. 1994. *The Penguin Dictionary of Sociology*, 3rd edn. London: Penguin Books.

Abu-Laban, Sharon M., and Susan A. McDaniel. 1998. "Beauty, Status and Aging," in N. Mandell, ed., *Feminist Issues: Race, Class, and Sexuality*, 2nd edn. Scarborough, Ont.: Prentice-Hall Allyn and Bacon, 78–102.

Adair, V., and C. Rogan. 1998. "Infertility and Parenting: The Story So Far," in V. Adair and R. Dixon, eds, *The Family in Aotearoa New Zealand*. Auckland: Addison-Wesley Longman.

Akyeampong, Ernest B. 1998. "Work Absences: New Data, New Insights," *Perspectives on Labour and Income* 9, 1: 9–17.

Albanese, Patrizia. 2009a. "Ethnicity, Immigration, and Family Life," in Baker (2009a: 130–53).

————. 2009b. *Children in Canada Today*. Toronto: Oxford University Press.

Alford-Cooper, F. 1998. *For Keeps: Marriages That Last a Lifetime*. New York: M.E. Sharpe.

Al-Krenawi, Alean, and Vered Slonim-Nevo. 2008. "Psychosocial and Familial Functioning of Children from Polygynous and Monogamous Families," *Journal of Social Psychology* 148, 6: 745–64.

Amato, Paul. 2004. "Parenting through Family Transitions," *Social Policy Journal of New Zealand* 23 (Dec.): 31–44.

————. 2005. "The Impact of Family Formation Change on the Cognitive, Social and Emotional Wellbeing of the Next Generation," *The Future of Children* 15, 2: 75–96.

————. 2012. "The Well-Being of Children with Gay and Lesbian Parents," *Social Science Research* 41: 771–4.

Amato, Paul R., Alan Booth, David R. Johnson, and Stacy J. Rogers. 2007. *Alone Together: How Marriage in America Is Changing*. Cambridge, Mass.: Harvard University Press.

———— and A. Booth. 1997. *A Generation at Risk: Growing Up in an Era of Family Upheaval*. Cambridge, Mass.: Harvard University Press.

———— and B. Keith. 1991. "Parental Divorce and the Well-being of Children: A Meta-analysis," *Psychological Bulletin* 110, 1: 26–46.

———— and D. Previti. 2003. "People's Reasons for Divorcing: Gender, Social Class, the Life Course and Adjustment," *Journal of Family Issues* 24: 602–26.

———— and S.J. Rezac. 1994. "Contact with Nonresident Parents, Interparental Conflict, and Children's Behavior," *Journal of Family Issues* 15, 2: 191–207.

Ambert, Anne-Marie. 1997. *Parents, Children and Adolescents: Interactive Relationships and Development in Context*. New York: Haworth Press.

————. 2005a. "Cohabitation and Marriage: How Are They Related?" Ottawa: Vanier Institute of the Family. At: <www.vifamily.ca>.

————. 2005b. "Same-Sex Couples and Same-Sex-Parent Families: Relationships, Parenting and Issues of Marriage." Ottawa: Vanier Institute of the Family. At: <www.vifamily.ca>.

————. 2009. *Divorce: Facts, Causes and Consequences*, 3rd edn. Ottawa: Vanier Institute of the Family.

Arie, Sophie. 2003. "EU Goes Dutch on Gay Rights," *The Guardian*, 26 Sept. At: <www.guardian.co.uk>.

Armstrong, P., C. Amaratunga, J. Bernier, K. Grant, A. Pederson, and K. Willson. 2002. *Exposing Privatization: Women and Health Care Reform in Canada*. Toronto: Garamond Press.

Asthana, Anushka. 2005. "Too Posh to Push Births under Fire," *The Observer*, 4 Sept. At: <observer.guardian.co.uk>.

Australian Bureau of Statistics (ABS). 2007a. "Census Shows Marriage Still the Norm of Couples." Canberra: ABS. At: <www.abs.gov.au/ ausstats/>.

————. 2007b. *Marriages, Australia*, 2006. Canberra.

————. 2008a. *Births, Australia*, 2007. Canberra. At: <www.abs.gov.au/AUSSTATS/ abs@.nsf/mf.3301.0>.

————. 2008b. *Divorces, Australia*, 2007. Canberra. At: <www.abs.gov.au/ausstats/abs@ .nsf/mf/3307.0.55.001?OpenDocument>.

———. 2008c. *Family Characteristics and Transitions, Australia 2006–7*. Catalogue # 4442.0. At: <www.abs.gov.au>.

———. 2008d. *Marriages, Australia, 2007*. Canberra: ABS.

———. 2010. "Measures of Australia's Progress: Levels of Housing." Canberra: ABS. At: <www.abs.gov.au/ ausstats/>.

———. 2011. *Births, Australia, 2011*. Canberra. At: <www.abs.gov.au/ausstats>.

Australian Institute of Family Studies. 2008. *Family Facts and Figures*. Canberra: Commonwealth of Australia.

Baker, Maureen. 1982. "Finding Partners in the Newspapers: Sex Differences in Personal Advertising," *Atlantis* 7, 2: 137–46.

———. 1993. *Families in Canadian Society*, 2nd edn. Toronto: McGraw-Hill Ryerson.

———. 1995. *Canadian Family Policies: Cross-National Comparisons*. Toronto: University of Toronto Press.

———. 2001a. "Child Care Policy and Family Policy: Cross-National Examples of Integration and Inconsistency," in G. Cleveland and M. Krashinsky, eds, *Our Children's Future: Child Care Policy in Canada*. Toronto: University of Toronto Press, 275–95.

———. 2001b. *Families, Labour and Love: Family Diversity in a Changing World*. Sydney and Vancouver: Allen & Unwin and University of British Columbia Press.

———. 2002a. "Child Poverty, Maternal Health and Social Benefits," *Current Sociology* 50, 6: 827–42.

———. 2002b. "Poor Health, Lone Mothers and Welfare Reform: Competing Visions of Employability," *Women's Health and Urban Life* 1, 2 (Dec.): 4–25.

———. 2004a. "Devaluing Mothering at Home: Welfare Restructuring and 'Motherwork'," *Atlantis* 28, 2: 51–60.

———. 2004b. "Families," in Lorne Tepperman and James Curtis, eds, *Sociology*. Toronto: Oxford University Press, 162–85.

———. 2004c. "The Elusive Pregnancy: Choice and Empowerment in Medically Assisted Conception," *Women's Health and Urban Life* 3, 1 (May): 34–55.

———. 2005a. *Families: Changing Trends in Canada*, 5th edn. Toronto: McGraw-Hill Ryerson.

———. 2005b. "Medically Assisted Conception: Revolutionizing Family or Perpetuating a Nuclear and Gendered Model?" *Journal of Comparative Family Studies* 36, 4: 521–44.

———. 2005c. "Childbirth Practices, Medical Intervention and Women's Autonomy: Safer Childbirth or Bigger Profits?" *Women's Health and Urban Life* 4, 2 (Dec.): 27–44.

———. 2006. *Restructuring Family Policies: Convergences and Divergences*. Toronto: University of Toronto Press.

———. 2007. "Managing the Risk of Childhood Poverty: Changing Interventions by the State," *Women's Health and Urban Life* 6, 2: 8–21.

———. 2008a. "Lingering Concerns about Child Custody and Support," *Policy Quarterly* 4, 1: 10–17.

———. 2008b. "Low-Income Mothers, Employment and Welfare Restructuring," in N. Lunt, M. O'Brien, and R. Stephens, eds, *New Zealand, New Welfare*. Auckland: Cengage Learning, 69–77.

———. 2009a. *Families: Changing Trends in Canada*, 6th edn. Toronto: McGraw-Hill Ryerson.

———. 2009b. "Working Their Way Out of Poverty? Gendered Employment in Three Welfare States," special issue "Patterns of Change and Continuity: Understanding Current Transformations in Family Life," ed. Janeen Baxter, *Journal of Comparative Family Studies* 40, 4: 617–34.

———. 2010a. "Career Confidence and Gendered Expectations of Academic Promotion," Journal of Sociology 46, 3: 317–34.

———. 2010b. "Choices or Constraints? Family Responsibilities, Gender and Academic Careers," *Journal of Comparative Family Studies* 41, 1: 1–18.

———. 2010c. "Motherhood, Employment and the 'Child Penalty'," *Women's Studies International Forum* 33: 215–24.

———. 2011a. "Gendering 'Child' Poverty: Canadian Policies for a Deepening Recession," special issue on "The Politics of Childhood," *International Journal of Canadian Studies* 42: 25–46.

———. 2011b. "Key Issues in Paid Parental Leave Policy," *Policy Quarterly* 7, 3: 56–63.

———. 2011c. "Revisiting the 'Dual Welfare State': Sickness, Injury and Unemployment Programs in Two 'Liberal' Regimes," special issue, ed. Toba Bryant, *Women's Health and Urban Life* 10, 1: 10–31.

————. 2011d. "The Political Economy of Child Care Policy: Contradictions in New Zealand and Canada," *Policy Quarterly* 7, 1: 39–47.

————. 2012a. *Academic Careers and the Gender Gap.* Vancouver: University of British Columbia Press.

————. 2012b. "Fertility, Childrearing and the Academic Gender Gap," *Women's Health and Urban Life* 11, 2: 9–25.

————. 2012c. "Gendered Families, Academic Work and the 'Motherhood Penalty'," *Women's Studies Journal* 26, 1: 11–24.

———— and Vivienne Elizabeth. 2012a. "'A Brave Thing to Do' or a Normative Practice? Marriage after Long-Term Cohabitation," *Journal of Sociology.* Published online 22 Oct.

———— and ————. 2012b. "Negotiating 'Marriage': Comparing Same-Sex and Different-Sex Cohabiting Couples," *New Zealand Sociology* 27, 2: 1–20.

———— and ————. 2012c. "Second-Class Marriage? Civil Union in New Zealand," *Journal of Comparative Family Studies* 43, 5: 633–45.

———— and ————. 2014. *Marriage in the Age of Cohabitation: How and When People Are Tying the Knot in the Twenty-First Century.* Toronto: Oxford University Press.

———— and David Tippin. 1999. *Poverty, Social Assistance and the Employability of Mothers: Restructuring Welfare States.* Toronto: University of Toronto Press.

———— and ————. 2002. "When Flexibility Meets Rigidity: Sole Mothers' Experience in the Transition from Welfare to Work," *Journal of Sociology* 38, 4: 345–60.

———— and ————. 2004. "More Than Just Another Obstacle: Health, Domestic Purposes Beneficiaries, and the Transition to Paid Work," *Social Policy Journal of New Zealand* 21 (Mar.): 98–120.

Bakker, Isabella, and Rachel Silvey, eds. 2008. *Beyond States and Markets: The Challenges of Social Reproduction.* London: Routledge.

Bala, Nicholas, and Kenneth L. Clarke. 1981. *The Child and the Law.* Toronto: McGraw-Hill Ryerson.

Banting, Keith G., and Charles M. Beach, eds. 1995. *Labour Market Polarization and Social Policy Reform.* Kingston, Ont.: Queen's University, School of Policy Studies.

Barber, Jennifer S., and William G. Axinn. 1998. "The Impact of Parental Pressure for Grandchildren on Young People's Entry into Cohabitation and Marriage," *Population Studies* 52, 2: 129–44.

Barker, John. 2003. "Dowry," in Ponzetti (2003: 495–6).

Barnes, Gordon E., Leonard Greenwood, and Reena Sommers. 1991. "Courtship Violence in a Canadian Sample of Male College Students," *Family Relations* 40 (Jan.): 37–44.

Barrette, Jacques. 2009. "Work/Family Balance: What Do We Really Know?" Ottawa: Vanier Institute of the Family.

Battle, Lee Smith. 2012. "Moving Policies Upstream to Mitigate the Social Determinants of Early Childbearing," *Public Health Nursing* 29, 4: 1–11.

Bauman, Zygmunt. 2003. *Liquid Love: On the Frailty of Human Bonds.* Cambridge: Polity.

Baxter, Janeen. 1994. *Work at Home: The Domestic Division of Labour.* Brisbane: University of Queensland Press.

————. 2002. "Patterns of Change and Stability in the Gender Division of Household Labour in Australia, 1986–1997," *Journal of Sociology* 38, 4: 399–424.

———— and Michael Bittman. 1995. "Measuring Time Spent on Housework: A Comparison of Two Approaches," *Australian Journal of Social Research* 1, 1: 21–46.

————, Michele Haynes, and Belinda Hewitt. 2010. "Pathways into Marriage: Cohabitation and the Domestic Division of Labor," *Journal of Family Issues* 31, 11: 1509–29.

————, Belinda Hewitt, and Michele Haynes. 2008. "Life Course Transitions and Housework: Marriage, Parenthood and Time Spent on Housework," *Journal of Marriage and Family* 70, 2: 259–72.

————, ————, and Mark Western. 2005. "Post-Familial Families and the Domestic Division of Labour," *Journal of Comparative Family Studies* 36, 4: 583–600.

Baxter, Jennifer, and Peter McDonald. 2004. "Home Ownership among Young People in Australia: In Decline or Just Delayed?" conference paper prepared for NLC Workshop, University of Queensland, 29–30 June.

Beach, Jane, Martha Friendly, Carolyn Ferns, Nina Prabhu, and Barry Forer. 2009. *Early Childhood Education and Care in Canada*, 8th edn. Toronto: Childcare Resource and Research Unit.

Beaudry, Paul, and David Green. 1997. "Cohort Patterns in Canadian Earnings,"

Working Paper #96. Toronto: Canadian Institute for Advanced Research.

Beaujot, Roderic. 2000. *Earning and Caring in Canadian Families*. Peterborough, Ont.: Broadview Press.

Beaupré, P., P. Turcotte, and A. Milan. 2006. "When is Junior Moving Out? Transitions from the Parental Home to Independence," *Canadian Social Trends* (Statistics Canada Catalogue 11–008), 28 Aug., 8–13.

Beck-Gernsheim, Elisabeth. 2002. *Reinventing the Family: In Search of New Lifestyles*. Cambridge: Polity Press.

Beeby, Dean. 2006. "Legalize Polygamy, Federal Study Urges," *GlobeandMail.Com*, 13 Jan.

Bélanger, Alain, Yves Carrière, and Stéphane Gilbert. 2001. *Report of the Demographic Situation in Canada 2000*. Statistics Canada Catalogue 91–209-XPE. June. Ottawa: Ministry of Industry.

Bengston, V. 1985. "Diversity and Symbolism in Grandparental Roles," in V.L. Bengston and J.F. Robertson, eds, *Grandparenthood*. Beverly Hills, Calif.: Sage, 11–25.

Benoit, Cecilia, Dena Carroll, and Alison Millar. 2002. "But Is It Good for Non-Urban Women's Health? Regionalizing Maternity Care Services in British Columbia," *Canadian Review of Sociology and Anthropology* 39, 4: 373–96.

Berger, Peter, and Thomas Luckmann. 1967. *The Social Construction of Reality: A Treatise in the Sociology of Knowledge*. Garden City, NY: Doubleday.

Bernard, Jessie. 1972. *The Future of Marriage*. New York: World Publishing Company (revised in 1982).

Bezanson, Kate. 2006. *Gender, the State and Social Reproduction: Household Insecurity in Neo-Liberal Times*. Toronto: University of Toronto Press.

Bibby, Reginald. 2004. *The Future Families Project: A Survey of Canadian Hopes and Dreams*. Ottawa: Vanier Institute of the Family. At: <www.vifamily.ca>.

———. 2004–5. "Future Families: Surveying Our Hopes, Dreams, and Realities," *Transition* 34, 4: 3–14.

Bittman, Michael. 1991. *Juggling Time*. Canberra: Australian Bureau of Statistics.

———. 1998. "The Land of the Lost Long Weekend? Trends in Free Time among Working Age Australians," Social Policy Research Centre Discussion Paper #83. Sydney: University of New South Wales.

———. 2004. "Sunday Working and Family Time," paper presented to "Work–Life Balance across the Lifecourse" conference, University of Edinburgh, 2 July.

——— and Jocelyn Pixley. 1997. *The Double Life of the Family: Myth, Hope and Experience*. Sydney: Allen & Unwin.

——— and James Rice. 1999. "Is the End of the Second Shift in Sight? The Role of Income, Bargaining Power, Domestic Technology, and Market Substitutes," paper presented at the Australian Sociological Association annual meeting, Melbourne, Monash University, 9 Dec.

Black, D., et al. 2000. "Demographics of the Gay and Lesbian Population in the United States: Evidence from Available Systematic Data Sources," *Demography* 37: 139–54.

Blanchflower, David G., and Andrew J. Oswald. 2008. "Is Well-Being U-Shaped over the Life Cycle?" *Social Science and Medicine* 66, 8: 1733–49.

Bock, Gisela, and Pat Thane, eds. 1991. *Maternity and Gender Policies: Women and the Rise of European Welfare States 1880s–1950s*. London and New York: Routledge.

Boden, Sharon. 2003. *Consumerism, Romance and the Wedding Experience*. New York: Palgrave Macmillan.

Bogle, Kathleen A. 2008. *Hooking Up: Sex, Dating, and Relationships on Campus*. New York: SUNY Press.

Bosch, Xavier. 1998. "Spanish Doctors Criticised for High Tech Births," *British Medical Journal* 317, 7170 (21 Nov.): 1406.

Bowlby, J. 1953. "Some Pathological Processes Set in Train by Early Mother–Child Separation," *Journal of Mental Science* 99: 265–72.

———. 1958. "The Nature of the Child's Tie to His Mother," *International Journal of Psycho-Analysis* 39: 350–73.

———. 1969. *Attachment*. New York: Basic Books.

Boyd, Susan B. 2003. *Child Custody, Law, and Women's Work*. Toronto: Oxford University Press.

Bradbury, Bettina. 2005. "Social, Economic, and Cultural Origins of Contemporary Families," in Baker (2005a): 71–98.

———. 2012. *Wife to Widow: Lives, Laws, and Politics in Nineteenth-Century Montreal*. Vancouver: University of British Columbia Press.

Bradbury, Bruce, and Kate Norris. 2005. "Income and Separation," *Journal of Sociology* 41, 4: 425–46.

Braithwaite, Dawn O., and Leslie A. Baxter. 2005. *Engaging Theories in Family Communication: Multiple Perspectives.* Thousand Oaks, Calif.: Sage.

Brennan, Deborah. 1998. *The Politics of Australian Child Care: Philanthropy, Feminism and Beyond.* Melbourne: Cambridge University Press.

———. 2007a. "Babies, Budgets, and Birthrates: Work/Family Policy in Australia 1996–2006," *Social Politics* (Spring): 31–57.

———. 2007b. "The ABC of Child Care Politics," *Australian Journal of Social Issues* 42, 2 (Winter): 213–25.

Broude, G. 1994. *Marriage, Family, and Relationships.* Denver: ABC-CLIO.

Brown, Judith. 1988. "Iroquois Women: An Ethnohistoric Note," in B. Fox, ed., *Family Bonds and Gender Relations.* Toronto: Canadian Scholars' Press, 83–98.

Brownridge, Douglas A. 2003. "Male Partner Violence against Aboriginal Women in Canada: An Empirical Analysis," *Journal of Interpersonal Violence* 18: 65–83.

———. 2008. "The Elevated Risk for Violence against Cohabiting Women: A Comparison of Three Nationally Representative Surveys of Canada," *Violence Against Women* 14, 7: 809–32.

Budig, Michelle, and Paula England. 2001. "The Wage Penalty for Motherhood," *American Sociological Review* 66, 2: 204–25.

Bulanda, Jennifer R. 2011. "Gender, Marital Power, and Marital Quality in Later Life," *Journal of Women and Aging* 23, 1: 3–22.

Bulbeck, Chilla. 2005. "'Women are Exploited Way Too Often': Feminist Rhetorics at the End of Equality," *Australian Feminist Studies* 20, 46 (Mar.): 71–2.

Burghes, L. 1994. *Lone Parenthood and Family Disruption.* Occasional Paper #18. London: Family Policy Studies Centre.

Butler, Judith. 1990. *Gender Trouble: Feminism and the Subversion of Identity.* New York: Routledge, Chapman and Hall.

———. 1997. *The Psychic Life of Power: Theories of Subjection.* Stanford, Calif.: Stanford University Press.

Callan, Victor J. 1982. "How Do Australians Value Children? A Review and Research Update Using the Perceptions of Parents and Voluntarily Childless Adults," *Australian and New Zealand Journal of Sociology* 18, 3: 384–98.

Cameron, Jan. 1990. *Why Have Children? A New Zealand Case Study.* Christchurch: Canterbury University Press.

———. 1997. *Without Issue: New Zealanders Who Choose Not to Have Children.* Christchurch: Canterbury University Press.

Canada, Department of Justice. 2003. "Child Support." At: <canada.justice.gc.ca/en/ps/sup/index.html>.

Canadian Fertility and Andrology Society. 2011. "Assisted Reproduction and Live Birth Rates for Canada," press release. At: <www.cfas.ca>.

Canadian Institute of Child Health. 2002. *The Health of Canada's Children*, 3rd edn. Ottawa: Canadian Institute of Child Health.

Caro, Francis G., ed. 2006. *Family and Aging Policy.* London: Haworth Press.

Cartwright, Claire. 2006. "You Want to Know How It Affected Me? Young Adults' Perceptions of the Impact of Parental Divorce," *Journal of Divorce and Remarriage* 44, 3 and 4: 125–43.

——— and Heather McDowell. 2008. "Young Women's Life Stories and Accounts of Parental Divorce," *Journal of Divorce and Remarriage* 49, 1 and 2: 56–77.

Castellano, Marlene Brant. 1991. "Women in Iroquois and Ojibway Societies," *Transition* 21, 4: 6–10.

Castles, Francis G. 1985. *The Working Class and Welfare: Reflections on the Political Development of the Welfare State in Australia and New Zealand, 1890–1980.* Sydney: Allen & Unwin.

———. 2002. "Three Facts about Fertility: Cross-National Lessons for the Current Debate," *Family Matters* 63 (Spring/Summer): 22–7.

——— and Ian F. Shirley. 1996. "Labour and Social Policy: Gravediggers or Refurbishers of the Welfare State?" in F. Castles, R. Gerritsen, and J. Vowles, eds, *The Great Experiment: Labour Parties and Public Policy Transformation in Australia and New Zealand.* Auckland: Auckland University Press, 88–106.

Cates, Norman. 1993. "Trends in Care and Services for Elderly Individuals in Denmark and Sweden," *International Journal of Aging and Human Development* 37, 4: 271–6.

Cavanagh, Shannon E. 2008. "Family Structure History and Adolescent Adjustment," *Journal of Family Issues* 29, 7: 944–80.

CBC News. 2013. "'Exhausted' Parents Leave Autistic Son at Government Office," 1 May. At: <www.cbc.ca/news/canada/ottawa/story/2013/05/01/ottawa-autism-son-left-government-services.html>.

Chambers, P. 2005. *Older Widows and the Life Course: Multiple Narratives of Hidden Lives.* Aldershot, UK: Ashgate.

Cheal, David. 1991. *Family and the State of Theory.* Toronto: University of Toronto Press.

———. 1996. "Stories about Step-families," in *Growing Up in Canada: National Longitudinal Survey of Children and Youth.* Ottawa: Human Resources Development Canada and Statistics Canada, 93–101.

———, ed. 2010. *Canadian Families Today: New Perspectives*, 2nd edn. Toronto: Oxford University Press.

Che-Alford, Janet, and Brian Hamm. 1999. "Under One Roof: Three Generations Living Together," *Canadian Social Trends* 53 (Summer): 6–9.

Cherlin, A.J. 1996. *Public and Private Families: An Introduction.* New York: McGraw-Hill.

———. 2004. "The Deinstitutionalization of American Marriage," *Journal of Marriage and Family* 66, 4: 848–61.

———. 2010. *The Marriage-Go-Round: The State of Marriage and the Family in America Today.* New York: Knopf Doubleday.

Cherniak, Donna, and Jane Fisher. 2008. "Explaining Obstetric Interventionism: Technical Skills, Common Conceptualisations, or Collective Countertransferance?" *Women's Studies International Forum* 31: 270–7.

Chesnais, J.C. 1992. *The Demographic Transition: Stages, Patterns, and Economic Implications.* Oxford: Clarendon Press.

Cheyne, Christine, Mike O'Brien, and Michael Belgrave. 2008. *Social Policy in Aotearoa New Zealand*, 4th edn. Melbourne: Oxford University Press.

Childcare Resource and Research Unit, University of Toronto (CRRU). 2003. "Childcare in the News" (online), 11 Dec.

Chodorow, Nancy. 1978. *The Reproduction of Mothering: Psychoanalysis and the Sociology of Gender.* Berkeley, Calif.: University of California Press.

———. 1989. *Feminism and Psychoanalytic Theory.* New Haven: Yale University Press.

Christopher, K., P. England, S. McLanahan, K. Ross, and T.M. Smeeding. 2001. "Gender Inequality in Affluent Nations: The Role of Single Motherhood and the State," in K. Vleminckx and T.M. Smeeding, eds, *Child Wellbeing, Child Poverty and Child Policy in Modern Nations.* Bristol: Policy Press, 199–220.

Clark, Warren. 2006. "Interreligious Unions in Canada," Ottawa: Statistics Canada. At: <www.statcan.gc.ca/pub/11-008-x/2006003/pdf/9478-eng.pdf>.

Clements, M., A. Cordova, H. Markman, and J. Laurenceau. 1997. "The Erosion of Marital Satisfaction Over Time and How to Prevent It," in R.J. Stern and M. Hojjat, eds, *Satisfaction in Close Relationships.* New York: Guilford Press.

Cockett, M., and J. Tripp. 1994. *The Exeter Family Study.* Exeter, UK: University of Exeter.

Collins, Simon. 2005. "Sperm Donors Could Become 'Third Parents'," *New Zealand Herald*, 21 Apr., A3.

Coltrane, Scott. 1998. *Gender and Families.* Thousand Oaks, Calif.: Pine Forge Press.

Connidis, Ingrid. 2010. *Family Ties and Aging*, 2nd edn. Thousand Oaks, Calif.: Pine Forge Press.

Connolly, Ellen. 2004. "You've Come Almost No Distance At All, Baby," *Sydney Morning Herald*, 15 Dec. (online).

Connolly, Marie. 2003. "Kinship Care—A Selected Literature Review," paper prepared for the Department of Child Youth and Family Services, Wellington, NZ.

Cook, Kay E. 2011. "Social Support in Single Parents' Transition from Welfare to Work: Analysis of Qualitative Findings," *International Journal of Social Welfare.* Published online 27 Oct.

Cooley, Charles H. 1902. *Human Nature and Social Order.* New York: Charles Scribner's Sons.

Coontz, S. 2005. *Marriage, A History: From Obedience to Intimacy, or How Love Conquered Marriage.* New York: Penguin.

Correll, S., S. Benard, and I. Paik. 2007. "Getting a Job: Is there a Motherhood Penalty?" *American Journal of Sociology* 112, 5: 1297–338.

Couch, Danielle, and Pranee Liamputtong. 2008. "Online Dating and Mating: The Use of the Internet to Meet Sexual Partners," *Qualitative Health Research* 18, 2: 268–79.

Coveney, Peter. 1982. "The Image of the Child," in C. Jenks, ed., *The Sociology of Childhood*. London: Batsford, 42–7.

Cowan, Carolyn, et al. 1985. "Transition to Parenthood: His, Hers, and Theirs," *Journal of Family Issues* 6: 451–81.

Craig, Lyn. 2006. "Parental Education, Time in Paid Work and Time with Children: An Australian Time-Diary Analysis," *British Journal of Sociology* 57, 4: 553–75.

————— and Michael Bittman. 2008. "The Incremental Time Costs of Children: An Analysis of Children's Impact on Adult Time Use in Australia," *Feminist Economics* 14, 2: 59–88.

Crittenden, A. 2001. *The Price of Motherhood: Why the Most Important Job in the World Is Still the Least Valued*. New York: Metropolitan Books.

Crompton, Rosemary. 2004. "Women's Employment and Work/Life Balance in Britain and Europe," plenary address at "Work/Life Balance across the Life Course" conference, University of Edinburgh, 1 July.

Crouter, Ann C., and Alan Booth. 2006. *Romance and Sex in Adolescence and Emerging Adulthood: Risks and Opportunities*. New York and London: Routledge.

Cuneo, Carl. 1979. "State, Class and Reserve Labour: The Case of the 1941 Unemployment Insurance Act," *Canadian Review of Sociology and Anthropology* 16, 2: 147–70.

Cunningham, Mick, and Arland Thornton. 2006. "The Influence of Parents' Marital Quality on Adult Children's Attitudes toward Marriage and Its Alternatives: Main and Moderating Effects," *Demography* 43, 4: 659–72.

Curtis, Lori J. 2001. "Lone Motherhood and Health Status," *Canadian Public Policy* 27, 3: 335–56.

Dalley, Bronwyn. 1998. *Family Matters: Child Welfare in Twentieth Century New Zealand*. Auckland: Auckland University Press.

Davis, S.N., T.N. Greenstein, and J.P. Marks. 2007. "Effects of Union Type on Division of Household Labor," *Journal of Family Issues* 28, 9: 1246–72.

DeKeseredy, Walter. 2005. "Patterns of Family Violence," in Baker (2005a: 229–57).

Dempsey, Ken. 1997. *Inequalities in Work and Marriage: Australia and Beyond*. Melbourne: Oxford University Press.

————— and David De Vaus. 2004. "Who Cohabits in 2001? The Significance of

Age, Gender and Religion," *Journal of Sociology* 40, 2: 157–78.

De Vaus, David. 2002. "Marriage and Mental Health," *Family Matters* 62 (Winter): 26–32.

Devereux, Monique. 2004. "Religious Leaders Say Wearing Veils Is a Personal Choice," *New Zealand Herald*, 2 Nov. At: <www.nzherald.co.nz>.

Dewson, Emma. 2004. "Off to the Dance: Romance in Rural New Zealand Communities, 1880s–1920s," *History Australia* 2, 1 (Dec.).

Dickason, Olive Patricia. 2006. A *Concise History of Canada's First Nations*. Toronto: Oxford University Press.

Doodson, Lisa, and David Morley. 2006. "Understanding the Roles of Non-Residential Stepmothers," *Journal of Divorce and Remarriage* 45, 3 and 4: 109–30.

Dorsett, Richard, and Alan Marsh. 1998. *The Health Trap: Poverty, Smoking and Lone Parenthood*. London: Policy Studies Institute.

Doucet, Andrea. 2006. *Do Men Mother?* Toronto: University of Toronto Press.

Douthitt, Robin A., and Joanne Fedyk. 1990. *The Cost of Raising Children in Canada*. Toronto: Butterworths.

Doyal, L. 1995. *What Makes Women Sick? Gender and the Political Economy of Health*. New Brunswick, NJ: Rutgers University Press.

Dranoff, Linda Silver. 1977. *Women in Canadian Life*. Toronto: Fitzhenry & Whiteside.

Drolet, Marie, and René Morissette. 1997. "Working More? What Do Workers Prefer?" *Perspectives on Labour and Income* 9, 4: 32–8.

Dudley, James R., Melvin H. Herring, Keith Cradle, and Melanie Rose Pace. 2012. "Fathering the Children of Teenage Mothers: The Need for Procreative Consciousness and Responsibility," *Families in Society* 93, 2: 123–32.

Dumas, Jean, and Yves Péron. 1992. *Marriage and Conjugal Life in Canada*. Ottawa: Statistics Canada (Catalogue no. 91–534E).

Duncan, S., A. Barlow, and G. James. 2005. "Why Don't They Marry? Cohabitation, Commitment and DIY Marriage," *Child and Family Law Quarterly* 17: 383–98.

Dunne, G. 2000. "Opting into Motherhood: Lesbians Blurring the Boundaries and Transforming the Meaning of Parenthood and Kinship," *Gender and Society* 14: 11–35.

Dush, Claire M.K., and Miles G. Taylor. 2012. "Trajectories of Marital Conflict across the Life Course: Predictors and Interactions with Marital Happiness Trajectories," *Journal of Family Issues* 33, 3: 341–68.

Dwyer, Angela E. 2006. "From Private to Public Bodies: Normalising Pregnant Bodies in Western Culture," *Nexus: Newsletter of the Australian Sociological Association* 18, 3: 18–19.

Dykstra, Pearl A. 2006. "Off the Beaten Track: Childlessness and Social Integration in Later Life," *Research on Aging* 28: 749–67.

———— and T. Fokkema. 2007. "Social and Emotional Loneliness among Divorced and Married Men and Women: Comparing the Deficit and Cognitive Perspectives," *Basic and Applied Social Psychology* 29, 1: 1–12.

Eaton, Asia A., and Suzanna Rose. 2011. "Has Dating Become More Egalitarian? A 35 Review Using Sex Roles," *Sex Roles* 64: 843–62.

Edin, Kathryn. 2003. "Work Is Not Enough," plenary address to Australian Social Policy Conference, University of New South Wales, Sydney, 10 July.

———— and Maria J. Kefalas. 2005. *Promises I Can Keep: Why Poor Women Put Motherhood before Marriage.* Berkeley: University of California Press.

———— and Laura Lein. 1997. *Making Ends Meet: How Single Mothers Survive Welfare and Low-Wage Work.* New York: Russell Sage Foundation.

———— and Joanna M. Reed. 2005. "Why Don't They Just Get Married? Barriers to Marriage among the Disadvantaged," *Marriage and Child Wellbeing* 15, 2: 117–36.

Edlund, Jonas. 2007. "The Work–Family Time Squeeze: Conflicting Demands of Paid and Unpaid Work among Working Couples in 29 Countries," *International Journal of Comparative Sociology* 48, 6: 451–80.

Edwards, Anne, and Susan Magarey, eds. 1995. *Women in a Restructuring Australia: Work and Welfare.* Sydney: Allen &Unwin.

Edwards, Peter. 2011. "This Is Not Just an Aboriginal Issue. It Is a Canadian Issue," 10 June, *thestar.com*.

Eichler, Margrit. 1988. *Families in Canada Today*, 2nd edn. Toronto: Gage.

————. 1997. *Family Shifts: Families, Policies, and Gender Equality.* Toronto: Oxford University Press.

————. 2005. "Biases in Family Literature," Baker (2005a): 52–68.

————, Patrizia Albanese, Susan Ferguson, Nicky Hyndman, Lichun Willa Liu, and Ann Matthews. 2010. *More Than It Seems: Household Work and Lifelong Learning.* Toronto: Canadian Scholars' Press (Women's Press).

Einarsdottir, Anna. 2011. "'Marriage' and the Personal Life of Same-Sex Couples," in V. May, ed., *Sociology of Personal Life.* London: Palgrave Macmillan, 48–58.

Elizabeth, Vivienne. 2000. "Cohabitation, Marriage, and the Unruly Consequences of 'Difference'," *Gender and Society* 14, 1: 87–100.

————. 2001. "Managing Money, Managing Coupledom: A Critical Investigation of Cohabitants' Money Management Practices," *Sociological Review* 49: 389–411.

———— and Wendy Larner. 2009. "Racializing the 'Social Development' State: Investing in Children in Aortearoa New Zealand," *Social Politics* 16, 1: 1–27.

Elliott, J., and M. Richards. 1991. "Parental Divorce and the Life Chances of Children," *Family Law*: 481–4.

————, ————, and H. Warwick. 1993. *The Consequences of Divorce for the Health and Well-Being of Adults and Children.* Final Report for Health Promotion Trust #2. Cambridge, UK: Centre for Family Research.

Emery, R. 1994. "Psychological Research on Children, Parents, and Divorce," in Emery, ed., *Renegotiating Family Relationships: Divorce, Child Custody, and Mediation.* New York: Guilford Press, 194–217.

Engels, Friedrich. 1972 [1884]. *The Origin of the Family, Private Property and the State.* New York: Pathfinder.

England, Paula. 2010. "The Gender Revolution: Uneven and Stalled," *Gender and Society* 24, 2 (Apr.): 149–66.

Erfani, Amir, and Roderic Beaujot. 2006. "Familial Orientations and the Rationales for Childbearing Behaviour," *Canadian Studies in Population* 33, 1: 49–67.

Erikson, E. 1963. *Childhood and Society*, 2nd edn. New York: Norton.

————. 1968. *Identity: Youth and Crisis.* New York: Norton.

Ermisch, John. 1991. *Lone Parenthood: An Economic Analysis*. Cambridge: Cambridge University Press.

———. 2003. *An Economic Analysis of the Family*. Princeton, NJ: Princeton University Press.

Esping-Andersen, Gøsta. 1990. *The Three Worlds of Welfare Capitalism*. Cambridge: Polity Press.

———, ed. 1996. *Welfare States in Transition: National Adaptations in Global Economies*. London: Sage.

Evenson, Ranae, and Robin W. Simon. 2005. "Clarifying the Relationship between Parenthood and Depression," *Journal of Health and Social Behaviour* 46: 341–58.

Evertsson, Marie. 2006. "The Reproduction of Gender: Housework and Attitudes toward Gender Equality in the Home among Swedish Boys and Girls," *British Journal of Sociology* 57, 3: 415–36.

Featherstone, M. 1991. "The Body in Consumer Culture," in M. Featherstone and B.S. Turner, eds, *The Body: Social Process and Cultural Theory*. London: Sage.

Ferri, E. 1984. *Step Children: A National Study*. Windsor, UK: NFER-Nelson.

——— and K. Smith. 2003. "Partnerships and Parenthood," in E. Ferri, J. Bynner, and M. Wadsmith, eds, *Changing Britain, Changing Lives*. London: Institute of Education.

Findlay, Leanne C., and Dafna E. Kohen. 2012. "Leave Practices of Parents after the Birth or Adoption of Young Children," *Canadian Social Trends*, 30 July. At: <www.statcan.gc.ca/pub/11-008-x/2012002/article/11697-eng.pdf>.

Fisman, R., S. Iyengar, E. Kamenica, and I. Simonson. 2006. "Gender Differences in Mate Selection: Evidence from a Speed Dating Experiment," *Quarterly Journal of Economics* 121, 2: 673–97.

Fleising, Usher. 2003. "Bride-Price," in Ponzetti (2003): 175–6.

Fleming, Robin. 1997. *The Common Purse*. Auckland: Auckland University Press.

——— with Toni Atkinson. 1999. *Families of a Different Kind*. Waikanae, NZ: Families of Remarriage Project.

——— and S.K. Easting. 1994. *Couples, Households and Women: Report of the Pakeha Component of the Intrafamily Income Study*, Wellington Intrafamily Income Project. Palmerston North, NZ: Social Policy Research Centre, Massey University.

Fletcher, G. 1978. "Division of Labour in the New Zealand Nuclear Family," *New Zealand Psychologist* 7, 2: 33–40.

Fletcher, R. 1973. *The Family and Marriage in Britain*. Harmondsworth: Penguin.

Ford, Jane, Natasha Nassar, Elizabeth Sullivan, Georgina Chambers, and Paul Lancaster. 2003. *Reproductive Health Indicators, Australia, 2002*. Sydney: Australian Institute of Health and Welfare.

Foucault, Michel. 1979. *The History of Sexuality*. London: Allen Lane.

Fox, Bonnie. 2001. "The Formative Years: How Parenthood Creates Gender," *Canadian Review of Sociology and Anthropology* 38, 4: 373–90.

———. 2006. "Motherhood as a Class Act: The Many Ways in Which 'Intensive Mothering' Is Entangled with Social Class," in Kate Bezanson and Meg Luxton, eds, *Social Reproduction: Feminist Political Economy Challenges Neo-Liberalism*. Montreal and Kingston: McGill-Queen's University Press, 231–62.

———. 2010. *When Couples Become Parents: The Creation of Gender in the Transition to Parenthood*. Toronto: University of Toronto Press.

Friedan, Betty. 1963. *The Feminine Mystique*. New York: Norton.

Friendly, Martha, and Jane Beach. 2005. *Early Childhood Education and Care in Canada*, 6th edn. Toronto: Childcare Resource and Research Unit.

——— and Susan Prentice. 2009. *About Canada: Childcare*. Toronto: Fernwood.

Funder, Kathleen. 1996. *Remaking Families: Adaptation of Parents and Children to Divorce*. Melbourne: Australian Institute of Family Studies.

——— and Margaret Harrison. 1993. "Drawing a Longbow on Marriage and Divorce," in K. Funder, M. Harrison, and R. Weston, eds, *Settling Down: Pathways of Parents after Divorce*. Melbourne: Australian Institute of Family Studies, 13–32.

Funk, Laura. 2012. "Living Apart Together (LAT) Relationships: An Emerging Family Form," paper presented to the Canadian Sociology Association annual meeting, Waterloo, Ont., Wilfrid Laurier University, 29 May.

Furstenberg, F., F. Morgan, and P. Allison. 1987. "Paternal Participation and Children's Well-Being after Marital Dissolution," *American Sociological Review* 52: 695–701.

Gaffield, Chad. 1990. "The Social and Economic Origins of Contemporary Families," in M. Baker, ed., *Families: Changing Trends in Canada*, 2nd edn. Toronto: McGraw-Hill Ryerson, 23–40.

Gauthier, Anne Hélène. 1996. *The State and the Family: A Comparative Analysis of Family Policies in Industrialized Countries*. Oxford: Clarendon Press.

Gauthier, A. 2002. "The Role of Grandparents," *Current Sociology* 50, 2: 295–307.

Gazso-Windle, Amber, and Julie Ann McMullin. 2003. "Doing Domestic Labour: Strategising in a Gendered Domain," *Canadian Journal of Sociology* 28, 3: 341–66.

Gershuny, Jonathan, and Oriel Sullivan. 2003. "Time Use, Gender, and Public Policy Regimes," *Social Politics* 10, 2: 205–28.

Gibbons, Luz, José M. Belizán, Jeremy A. Lauer, Ana P. Betrán, Mario Merialdi, and Fernando Althabe. 2010. *The Global Numbers and Costs of Additionally Needed and Unnecessary Caesarean Sections Performed per Year: Overuse as a Barrier to Universal Coverage*. World Health Report, Background Paper, 30.

Giddens, Anthony. 1992. *The Transformation of Intimacy: Sexuality, Love and Eroticism in Modern Societies*. Cambridge: Polity Press.

———. 2006. *Sociology*, 5th edn. Cambridge: Polity Press.

Gilding, Michael. 1997. *Australian Families: A Comparative Perspective*. Melbourne: Addison Wesley Longman.

———. 2002. "Families of the New Millennium," *Family Matters* 62 (Winter): 4–10.

———. 2005. "Families and Fortunes: Accumulation, Management Succession and Inheritance in Wealthy Families," *Journal of Sociology* 41, 1: 29–46.

Gillespie, R. 1999. "Voluntary Childlessness in the United Kingdom," *Reproductive Health Matters* 7, 3: 43–53.

———. 2003. "Childfree and Feminine: Understanding the Gender Identity of Voluntarily Childless Women," *Gender and Society* 17, 1: 122–36.

Girouard, Nathalie, Mike Kennedy, and Christophe André. 2006. "Has the Rise in Debt Made Households More Vulnerable?" OECD Working Paper #535. Paris: OECD.

Glenn, Noval D., and Charles N. Weaver. 1988. "The Changing Relationship of Marital Status to Reported Happiness," *Journal of Marriage and the Family* 50: 317–24.

Glick, Paul. 1984. "Marriage, Divorce and Living Arrangements: Prospective Changes," *Journal of Family Issues* 5 (Mar.): 7–26.

Goffman, Erving. 1959. *The Presentation of Self in Everyday Life*. Garden City, NY: Doubleday Anchor.

Goldscheider, Frances, and Gayle Kaufman. 1996. "Fertility and Commitment: Bringing Men Back In," *Population and Development Review* 22, suppl.: 87–92.

Goldthorpe, J.E. 1987. *Family Life in Western Societies*. Cambridge: Cambridge University Press.

Goode, W.J. 1964. *The Family*. Englewood Cliffs, NJ: Prentice-Hall.

Goodger, Kay, and Peter Larose. 1999. "Changing Expectations: Sole Parents and Employment in New Zealand," *Social Policy Journal of New Zealand* 12: 53–70.

Goodnow, J.J. 1989. "Work in Households: An Overview and Three Studies," in D. Ironmonger, ed., *Households Work*. Sydney: Allen & Unwin.

——— and D. Susan. 1989. "Children's Household Work: Task Differences, Styles of Assignment, and Links to Family," *Relationships: Journal of Applied Developmental Psychology* 10: 209–26.

González-López, Maria José. 2002. "A Portrait of Western Families: New Modes of Intimate Relationships and the Timing of Life Events," in A. Carling, S. Duncan, and R. Edwards, eds, *Analysing Families: Morality and Rationality in Policy and Practice*. London: Routledge, 21–48.

Graham-Bermann, Sandra, and Jeffrey Edleson. 2001. "Introduction," in Graham-Bermann and Edleson, eds, *Domestic Violence in the Lives of Children: The Future of Research, Intervention and Social Policy*. Washington: American Psychological Association.

Gray, Matthew, Lixia Qu, and Ruth Weston. 2007. "Fertility and Family Policy in Australia," Melbourne: Australian Institute of Family Studies.

Greenwood, Gaye A. 1999. "Dissolution of Marriage: Public Policy and 'The Family-Apart'," Master's thesis, Auckland: School of Social Policy and Social Work, Massey University at Albany.

Gross, N. 2005. "The Detraditionalization of Intimacy Reconsidered," *Sociological Theory* 23, 3: 286–311.

Guest, Dennis. 1997. *The Emergence of Social Security in Canada*, 3rd edn. Vancouver: University of British Columbia Press.

Hagestad, G.O., and V.R.A. Call. 2007. "Pathways to Childlessness: A Life Course Perspective," *Journal of Social Issues* 28: 1338–61.

Hakim, Catherine. 2000. *Work-Lifestyle Choices in the 21st Century*. Oxford: Oxford University Press.

Haley, Kirstin. 2008. "How Do Teenagers Spend Their Days?" *Matter of Fact*. Statistics Canada, Catalogue no. 89–630–X.

Hall, Jeffrey A., Namkee Park, Hayeon Song, and Michael J. Cody. 2010. "Strategic Misrepresentation in Online Dating: The Effects of Gender, Self-monitoring, and Personality Traits," *Journal of Social and Personal Relationships* 27, 1: 117–35.

Hantrais, Linda. 2000. *Social Policy in the European Union*, 2nd edn. London: Macmillan.

———. 2004. *Family Policy Matters: Responding to Family Change in Europe*. Bristol: Policy Press.

Harper, S. 2005. "Grandparenthood," in V.L. Bengston and M.L. Johnson, eds, *Cambridge Handbook of Age and Ageing*. Cambridge: Cambridge University Press, 422–8.

——— and L. Ruicheva. 2004. "Role and Relationships in Contemporary Grandparenting," Oxford Institute of Ageing Working Paper, University of Oxford.

Harrison, Margaret. 1993. "The Law's Response to New Challenges," in K. Funder, M. Harrison, and R. Weston, eds, *Settling Down: Pathways of Parents after Divorce*. Melbourne: Australian Institute of Family Studies, 33–55.

Health Canada. 2000. *Canadian Perinatal Health Report 2000*. Ottawa: Minister of Health. At: <www.hc-sc.gc.ca>.

Heitlinger, Alena. 1993. *Women's Equality, Demography, and Public Policy: A Comparative Perspective*. London: Macmillan.

Henman, Paul. 2006. "Updated Costs of Raising Children—March Quarter 2006," Social Policy Unit, School of Social Work and Applied Human Services, Brisbane, University of Queensland.

Hewitt, Belinda, Mark Western, and Janeen Baxter. 2005. "Who Decides? The Social Characteristics of Who Initiates Marital Separation," paper presented at Australian Sociological Association annual meeting, University of Hobart, Tasmania, 5–8 Dec.

Higgins, Jane, and Karen Nairn. 2006. "'In Transition': Choice and the Children of New Zealand's Economic Reforms," *British Journal of Sociology of Education* 27, 2: 207–20.

Hird, Myra, and Kimberley Abshoff. 2000. "Women without Children: A Contradiction in Terms?" *Journal of Comparative Family Studies* 31: 347–66.

Hobcraft, John, and Kathleen Kiernan. 2001. "Childhood Poverty, Early Motherhood and Adult Social Exclusion," *British Journal of Sociology* 52, 3: 495–517.

Hochschild, Arlie Russell. 1989. *The Second Shift: Working Parents and the Revolution at Home*. New York: Viking Penguin.

———. 1997. *The Time Bind: When Work Becomes Home and Home Becomes Work*. New York: Metropolitan Books.

Hoffman, S.D., and E.M. Foster. 1997. "Economic Correlates of Nonmarital Childbearing among Adult Women," *Family Planning Perspectives* 29, 3: 137–40.

Holstein, James A., and Gale Miller. 2006. *Reconsidering Social Constructionism: Debates in Social Problems Theory*. Piscataway, NJ: Aldine Transaction.

Hopkins, Susan. 2002. *Girl Heroes: the New Face in Popular Culture*. Sydney: Pluto Press.

Hou, Feng. 2010. *Homeownership over the Life Course of Canadians: Evidence from Canadian Censuses of Population*. Ottawa: Statistics Canada Analytical Studies Branch Research Paper Series. At: <www.statcan. gc.ca/pub/11f0019m2010325-eng.htm>.

Houston, Susan E., and Allison Prentice. 1988. *Schooling and Scholars in Nineteenth Century Ontario*. Toronto: University of Toronto Press.

Hughes, Karen. 2005. "The Adult Children of Divorce: Pure Relationships and Family Values?" *Journal of Sociology* 41, 1: 69–86.

Human Resources and Skills Development Canada (HRSDC). 2012. "Indicators of Well-Being in Canada, Family Life—Marriage." Ottawa: HRSDC. At: <www4.hrsdc. gc.ca>.

Humm, Maggie. 1995. *The Dictionary of Feminist Theory*, 2nd edn. London: Prentice-Hall/Harvester Wheatsheaf.

Hunsley, Terrance. 1997. *Lone Parent Incomes and Social Policy Outcomes: Canada in*

International Perspective. Kingston, Ont.: Queen's University, School of Policy Studies.

Hunt, J. 2003. *Family and Friends Carers*. Report prepared for the UK Department of Health. At: <www.doh.gov.uk/carers/familyandfriends.htm>.

Ihinger-Tallman, Marilyn, and David Levinson (revised by J.M. White). 2003. "Definition of Marriage," in Ponzetti (2003: 1094–8).

Ingraham, C. 2008. *White Weddings*, 2nd edn. New York: Routledge.

Inland Revenue Department (IRD). 2012. "Common Questions and Answers about Child Support for Paying Parents," Wellington, NZ. At: <www.ird.govt.nz>.

International Labour Organization. 2000. "International Labour Standards on Maternity Protection." At: <www.ilo.org>.

Jackson, A., and P. Roberts. 2001. "Physical Housing Conditions and the Well-Being of Children," background paper on housing for *The Progress of Canada's Children 2001*. Ottawa: Canadian Council on Social Development.

Jaffe, Peter, Nancy Lemon, and Samantha Poisson. 2003. *Child Custody and Domestic Violence: A Call for Safety and Accountability*. Thousand Oaks, Calif.: Sage.

———, Marlies Suderman, and Robert Geffner. 2000. "Emerging Issues for Children Exposed to Domestic Violence," in Jaffe, Suderman, and Geffner, eds, *Children Exposed to Domestic Violence: Current Issues in Research, Intervention, Prevention, and Policy Development*. New York: Haworth Press.

Jagger, Elisabeth. 2005. "Is Thirty the New Sixty? Dating, Age and Gender in Postmodern, Consumer Society," *Sociology* 39, 1: 89–106.

Jamieson, Lynn. 1998. *Intimacy: Personal Relationships in Modern Societies*. Cambridge: Polity Press.

———, M. Anderson, D. McCrone, F. Bechhofer, R. Stewart, and L. Yaojun. 2002. "Cohabitation and Commitment: Partnership Plans of Young Men and Women," *Sociological Review* 50, 3: 356–77.

Jenson, Jane. 2004. "Changing the Paradigm: Family Responsibility or Investing in Children," *Canadian Journal of Sociology* 29, 2: 169–92.

——— and Mariette Sineau. 2001a. "The Care Dimensions in Welfare State Design," in Jenson and Sineau (2001b: 3–18).

——— and ———. 2001b. *Who Cares? Women's Work, Childcare, and Welfare State Design*. Toronto: University of Toronto Press.

Johnson, Holly. 1990. "Wife Abuse," in C. McKie and K. Thomson, eds, *Canadian Social Trends*. Toronto: Thompson Educational Publishing, 173–6.

Johnson, Jennifer A., and Megan S. Johnson. 2008. "New City Domesticity and the Tenacious Second Shift," *Journal of Family Issues* 29, 4: 487–515.

Jones, Michael. 1996. *The Australian Welfare State: Evaluating Social Policy*. Sydney: Allen & Unwin.

Juby, H., J. Billette, B. Laplante, and C. Le Bourdais. 2007. "Nonresident Fathers and Children," *Journal of Family Issues* 28: 1220–45.

Kahneman, D., A. Krueger, D. Schkade, N. Schwarz, and A. Stone. 2006. "Would You Be Happier If You Were Richer? A Focusing Illusion," *Science* 312, 5782 (June): 1908–10.

Kamerman, Sheila B., and Alfred J. Kahn, eds. 1997. *Family Change and Family Policies in Great Britain, Canada, New Zealand and the United States*. Oxford: Clarendon Press.

Karney, B., and T. Bradbury. 1995. "The Longitudinal Course of Marital Quality and Stability: A Review of Theory, Method and Research," *Psychological Bulletin* 118: 3–34.

Kaufman, Gayle, and Frances Goldsheider. 2007. "Do Men 'Need' a Spouse More Than Women?: Perceptions of the Importance of Marriage for Men and Women," *Sociological Quarterly* 48, 1: 29–46.

Kedgley, Sue. 1996. *Mum's the Word: The Untold Story of Motherhood in New Zealand*. Auckland: Random House.

Kelan, Elisabeth. 2009. *Performing Gender at Work*. Basingstoke: Palgrave Macmillan.

Kelsey, Jane. 1999. *Reclaiming the Future: New Zealand and the Global Economy*. Wellington: Bridget Williams Books.

Kerr, Don, Melissa Moyser, and Roderic Beaujot. 2006. "Marriage and Cohabitation: Demographic and Socioeconomic Differences in Quebec and Canada," *Canadian Studies in Population* 33, 1: 83–117.

Kiernan, Kathleen. 1997. *The Legacy of Parental Divorce: Social, Economic, and*

Demographic Experiences in Adulthood. London: Centre for Analysis of Social Exclusion.

Kimmel, M.S. 2008. *The Gendered Society.* New York: Oxford University Press.

Kitterød, Ragni H., and Silje V. Pettersen. 2006. "Making Up for Mothers' Employed Working Hours?" *Work, Employment and Society* 20, 3: 473–92.

Knaak, Stephanie. 2005. "Breast-feeding, Bottle-feeding and Dr. Spock: The Shifting Context of Choice," *Canadian Review of Sociology and Anthropology* 42, 2: 197–216.

Kobayashi, Karen M. 2007. "'Mid-Life Crises': Understanding the Changing Nature of Relationships in Middle-Age Canadian Families," in David Cheal, ed., *Canadian Families Today: New Perspectives.* Toronto: Oxford University Press.

Koropeckyj-Cox, T., and V. Call. 2007. "Characteristics of Older Childless Persons and Parents: Cross-National Comparisons," *Journal of Family Issues* 28, 10: 1362–1414.

Krane, Julia. 2003. *What's Mother Got to Do With It? Protecting Children from Sexual Abuse.* Toronto: University of Toronto Press.

Krug, E., L. Dahlberg, J. Mercy, A. Zwi, and R. Lozano, eds. 2002. *World Report on Violence and Health.* Geneva: WHO.

Kruger, Colin, S. Peatling, and E. Jenson. 2008. "ABC Learning Closures Force 4000 to Move," *Sydney Morning Herald*, 11 Dec.

Kurdeck, L.A. 1998. "Relationship Outcomes and Their Predictors: Longitudinal Evidence from Heterosexual Married, Gay Cohabiting and Lesbian Cohabiting Couples," *Journal of Marriage and the Family* 60: 553–68.

———. 2001. "Differences between Heterosexual-Nonparent Couples and Gay, Lesbian and Heterosexual-Parent Couples," *Journal of Family Issues* 22: 728–55.

Land, Hilary. 1980. "The Family Wage," *Feminist Review* 6: 55–7.

Lapointe, Rita Eva, and C. James Richardson. 1994. *Evaluation of the New Brunswick Family Support Orders Service.* Fredericton: New Brunswick Department of Justice.

Lashewicz, Bonnie, Gerald Manning, Margaret Hall, and Norah Keating. 2007. "Equity Matters: Doing Fairness in the Context of Family Caregiving," *Canadian Journal on Aging* 26, supp. 11: 91–102.

Laslett, Peter. 1971. *The World We Have Lost.* London: University Paperbacks.

Laumann, E.O., G.H. Gagnon, R.T. Michael, and S. Michaels. 1994. *The Social Organization of Sexuality: Sexual Practices in the United States.* Chicago: University of Chicago Press.

Lauster, Nathan, and A. Easterbrook. 2011. "No Room for New Families? A Field Experiment Measuring Rental Discrimination against Same-Sex Couples and Single Parents," *Social Problems* 58, 3: 389–409.

Lavner, Justin A., and Thomas N. Bradbury. 2010. "Patterns of Change in Marital Satisfaction over the Newly Wed Years," *Journal of Marriage and Family* 72, 5: 1171–87.

Lawlor, Allison. 2003. "Births on the Rise," *Globe and Mail*, 12 Aug. At: <www. globeandmail.com>.

Lawton, J. 1991. "What Is Sexually-Transmitted Debt?" in R. Meikle, ed., *Women and Credit: A Forum on Sexually-Transmitted Debt.* Melbourne: Ministry of Consumer Affairs.

Le Bourdais, Céline, and Evelyne Lapierre-Adamcyk. 2004. "Changes in Conjugal Life in Canada: Is Cohabitation Progressively Replacing Marriage?" *Journal of Marriage and Family* 66 (Nov.): 929–42.

Lee, Amy Su May, and Maggie Kirkman. 2008. "Disciplinary Discourses: Rates of Caesarean Section Explained by Medicine, Midwifery, and Feminism," *Health Care for Women International* 29, 5: 448–67.

Legge, Jaime, and Anne Heynes. 2008. *Beyond Reasonable Debt.* Wellington, NZ: Families Commission and Retirement Commission Report.

Leibrich, Julie, Judy Paulin, and Robin Ransom. 1995. *Hitting Home: Men Speak about Abuse of Women Partners.* Wellington, NZ: Department of Justice.

Leira, Arnlaug. 2009. *Welfare States and Working Mothers: The Scandinavian Experience.* Cambridge: Cambridge University Press.

Leslie, Gerald, and Sheila K. Korman. 1989. *The Family in Social Context*, 7th edn. New York: Oxford University Press.

Letherby, G. 1999. "Other Than Mother and Mothers as Others: The Experience of Motherhood and Non-Motherhood in

Relation to 'Infertility' and 'Involuntary Childlessness'," *Women's Studies International Forum* 22: 359–72.

Lewis, Jane. 1992. "Gender and the Development of Welfare State Regimes," *Journal of European Social Policy* 2, 3: 159–73.

———. 1999. "Marriage and Cohabitation and the Nature of Commitment," *Child and Family Law Quarterly* 11, 4: 355–63.

———. 2003. *Should We Worry about Family Change?* Toronto: University of Toronto Press.

Lichter, D.T., and Z. Quian. 2008. *"Serial Cohabitation and the Marital Life Course,"* *Journal of Marriage and Family* 70, 4: 861–78.

———, ———, and L.M. Mellot. 2006. "Marriage or Dissolution? Union Transitions among Poor Cohabiting Women," *Demography* 43, 2: 223–40.

Liefbroer, Aart C., and Edith Dourleijn. 2006. "Unmarried Cohabitation and Union Stability: Testing the Role of Diffusion Using Data from 16 European Countries," *Demography* 43, 2: 203–21.

Lindsay, Colin. 2008. "Are Women Spending More Time on Unpaid Domestic Work Than Men in Canada?" *Matter of Fact*. Statistics Canada, Catalogue no, 89–630–X.

Lipman, Ellen L., David R. Offord, and Martin D. Dooley. 1996. "What Do We Know about Children from Single-Parent Families? Questions and Answers from the National Longitudinal Survey on Children," in *Growing Up in Canada: National Longitudinal Survey on Children and Youth*. Ottawa: Human Resources Development Canada.

Little, Margaret. 1998. *No Car, No Radio, No Liquor Permit: The Moral Regulation of Single Mothers in Ontario, 1920–1997*. Toronto: Oxford University Press.

Lopata, Helena Z. 1971. *Occupation: Housewife*. New York: Oxford University Press.

———. 1996. *Current Widowhood: Myths and Realities*. Newbury Park, Calif.: Sage.

Lundberg, Shelly, and Elaina Rose. 1998. "The Determinants of Specialization within Marriage," discussion paper, Department of Economics, University of Washington.

Lunt, Neil, Mike O'Brien, and Robert Stephens, eds. 2008. *New Zealand, New Welfare*. Auckland, NZ: Cengage Learning.

Lupri, Eugen, and James Frideres. 1981. "The Quality of Marriage and the Passage of Time: Marital Satisfaction over the Family Life Cycle," *Canadian Journal of Sociology* 6, 3: 283–306.

Luxton, Meg. 1980. *More Than a Labour of Love*. Toronto: Women's Education Press.

———. 2006. "Feminist Political Economy in Canada and the Politics of Social Reproduction," in K. Bezanson and M. Luxton, eds, *Social Reproduction: Feminist Political Economy Challenges Neo-Liberalism*. Montreal and Kingston: McGill-Queen's University Press, 11–44.

———. 2009. "Conceptualizing 'Families': Theoretical Frameworks," in Baker (2009a).

———. 2011. *Changing Families, New Understandings*. Ottawa: Vanier Institute of the Family.

——— and June Corman. 2001. *Getting By in Hard Times: Gendered Labour at Home and on the Job*. Toronto: University of Toronto Press.

McDaniel, Susan A. 2009. "The Family Lives of the Middle-Aged and Elderly in Canada," in Baker (2009a: 225–42).

——— and Lorne Tepperman. 2000. *Close Relations: An Introduction to the Sociology of the Families*. Toronto: Pearson/Prentice-Hall.

——— and ———. 2004. *Close Relations: An Introduction to the Sociology of the Families*, 2nd edn. Toronto: Pearson/Prentice-Hall.

——— and ———. 2010. *Close Relations: An Introduction to the Sociology of the Families*, 4th edn. Toronto: Pearson Education.

McDonald, Peter. 2000. "Gender Equity in Theories of Fertility Transition," *Population and Development Review* 26, 3: 427–39.

MacDorman, Marian F., Fay Menacker, and Eugene Declercq. 2010. "Trends and Characteristics of Home and Other Out-of-Hospital Births in the United States, 1990–2006," *National Vital Statistics Reports* 58, 11: 1–16.

McFadden, Suzanne. 2005. "Teen Money: Get Real," *Canvas, Weekend Herald* (New Zealand), 9 Apr., 10–12.

McGillvray, A., and B. Comaskey. 1998. "'Everybody Has Black Eyes . . . Nobody Don't Say Nothing': Intimate Violence, Aboriginal Women, and the Justice System Response," in K.D. Bonnycastle and G.S. Rigakos, eds, *Unsettling Truths:*

Battered Women, Policy, Politics and Contemporary Research in Canada. Vancouver: Collective Press.

McGilly, Frank. 1998. *An Introduction to Canada's Public Social Services: Understanding Income and Health Programs,* 2nd edn. Toronto: Oxford University Press.

McKay, S., and K. Rowlingson. 1998. "Choosing Lone Parenthood? The Dynamics of Family Change," in R. Ford and J. Millar, eds, *Private Lives and Public Responses: Lone Parenthood and Future Policy in the UK.* London: Policy Studies Institute, 42–57.

McKenna, K., A. Green, and M. Gleason. 2002. "Relationship Formation on the Internet: What's the Big Attraction?" *Journal of Social Issues* 58, 1: 9–31.

Mackey, R.A., and B.A. O'Brien. 1995. *Lasting Marriages: Men and Women Growing Together.* Westport, Conn.: Praeger.

McLaughlin, Diane K., and Daniel T. Lichter. 1997. "Poverty and the Marital Behavior of Young Women," *Journal of Marriage and the Family* 59: 589.

Maclean, M., and D. Kuh. 1991. "The Long Term Effects for Girls of Parental Divorce," in M. Maclean and D. Groves, eds, *Women's Issues in Social Policy.* London: Routledge, 161–78.

McMahon, A. 1999. *Taking Care of Men.* Cambridge: Cambridge University Press.

McNair, Ruth, Deborah Dempsey, Sarah Wise, and Amaryll Perlesz. 2002. "Lesbian Parenting: Issues, Strengths and Challenges," *Family Matters* 63: 40–9.

Madathil, Jayamal, and James M. Benshoff. 2008. "Importance of Marital Characteristics and Marital Satisfaction: A Comparison of Asian Indians in Arranged Marriages and Americans in Marriages of Choice," *Family Journal* 16: 222–30.

Madsen, Stephanie D. 2008. "Parents' Management of Adolescents' Romantic Relationships through Dating Rules: Gender Variations and Correlates of Relationship Qualities," *Journal of Youth and Adolescence* 37, 9: 1044–58.

Magarick, R.H., and R.A. Brown. 1981. "Social and Emotional Aspects of Voluntary Childlessness in Vasectomized Childless Men," *Journal of Biosocial Science* 13: 157–67.

Malin, M., E. Hemminki, O. Raikkonen, S. Sihvo, and M. Perala. 2001. "What Do Women Want? Women's Experiences of Infertility Treatment," *Social Science and Medicine* 53: 123–33.

Mann, Robin. 2007. "Out of the Shadows?: Grandfatherhood, Age and Masculinities," *Journal of Aging Studies* 21: 281–91.

Manning, W.D., M.A. Longmore and P.C. Giordano. 2007. "The Changing Institution of Marriage: Adolescents' Expectations to Cohabit and Marry," *Journal of Marriage and Family* 69: 559–75.

Marcil-Gratton, Nicole. 1998. *Growing Up with Mom and Dad? The Intricate Family Life Courses of Canadian Children.* Ottawa: Ministry of Industry.

Marshall, Katherine. 1993. "Employed Parents and the Division of Labour," *Perspectives on Labour and Income* 5, 3: 23–30.

———. 1994. "Balancing Work and Family Responsibilities," *Perspectives on Labour and Income* 6, 1: 26–30.

———. 1998. "Stay-at-Home Dads," *Perspectives on Labour and Income* 10, 1: 9–15.

Martin, Chantal, and Paul Robinson. 2008. *Child and Spousal Support: Maintenance Enforcement Survey Statistics, 2006/2007.* Statistics Canada Catalogue no. 85–228–XIE. Ottawa: Ministry of Industry.

Martin-Matthews, Anne. 2007. "Situating 'Home' at the Nexus of the Public and Private Spheres," *Current Sociology* 55, 2: 229–49.

———. 2011. "Revisiting 'Widowhood in Later Life': Changes in Patterns and Profiles, Advances in Research and Understanding," *Canadian Journal on Aging* 30, 3: 359–75.

——— and J.E. Phillips, eds. 2008. *Aging and Caring at the Intersection of Work and Home Life: Blurring the Boundaries.* New York: Taylor and Francis/Psychology Press.

——— and J. Sims-Gould. 2011. "My Home, Your Work, Our Relationship: Elderly Clients' Experiences of Home Care Services," in Cecilia Benoit and Helga Hallgrimsdottir, eds, *Valuing Care Work: Comparative Perspectives on Canada, Finland and Iceland.* Toronto: University of Toronto Press, 107–24.

Mason, Jennifer, Vanessa May, and Lynda Clarke. 2007. "Ambivalence and Paradoxes of Grandparenting," *Sociological Review* 55, 4: 687–706.

May, Elaine Campbell. 1995. *Barren in the Promised Land: Childless Americans and the Pursuit of Happiness.* New York: Basic Books.

May, Vanessa, ed. 2011. *Sociology of Personal Life*. London: Palgrave Macmillan.

Mead, George H. 1934. *Mind, Self and Society*. Chicago: University of Chicago Press.

Mead, Margaret. 1935. *Sex and Temperament in Three Primitive Societies*. New York: Dell.

Meezan, William, and Jonathan Rauch. 2005. "Gay Marriage, Same-Sex Parenting, and America's Children," *Marriage and Family Well-being* 15, 2: 97–114.

Merla, Laura. 2008. "Determinants, Costs, and Meanings of Stay-at-Home Fathers: An International Comparison," *Fathering: A Journal of Theory, Research and Practice about Men as Fathers* 6, 2: 113–32.

Michaels, M.W. 1996. "Other Mothers: Toward an Ethic of Postmaternal Practice," *Hypatia* 11, 2: 49–70.

Millar, Jane, and Karen Rowlingson, eds. 2001. *Lone Parents, Employment and Social Policy: Cross-National Comparisons*. Bristol, UK: Policy Press.

——— and Peter Whiteford. 1993. "Child Support in Lone-Parent Families: Policies in Australia and the UK," *Policy and Politics* 21, 1: 59–72.

Millett, Kate. 1970. *Sexual Politics*. New York: Doubleday.

Mink, Gwendolyn. 1998. *Welfare's End*. Ithaca, NY: Cornell University Press.

———. 2002. "Violating Women: Rights Abuses in the American Welfare Police State," in Sylvia Bashevkin, ed., *Women's Work Is Never Done*. New York: Routledge, 141–64.

Mitchell, Barbara A. 2007. *The Boomerang Age*. New Brunswick, NJ: Transaction.

Mitchell, Juliet. 1974. *Psychoanalysis and Feminism*. Harmondsworth: Penguin.

——— and Jack Goody. 1997. "Feminism, Fatherhood and the Family in Britain," in Ann Oakley and Juliet Mitchell, eds, *Who's Afraid of Feminism? Seeing Through the Backlash*. London: Hamish Hamilton.

Monari, F., S. Di Mario, F. Facchinetti, and V. Basevi. 2008. "Obstetricians' and Midwives' Attitudes toward Caesarean Section," *Birth* 35, 2: 129–35.

Mongeau, P.A., and C.M. Carey. 1996. "Who's Wooing Whom: An Experimental Investigation of Date Initiation and Expectancy Violation," *Western Journal of Communication* 60, 3: 195–213.

Montgomerie, Deborah. 1999. "Sweethearts, Soldiers, Happy Families: Gender and the Second World War," in Caroline Daley,

ed., *The Gendered Kiwi*. Auckland: Auckland University Press, 163–90.

Moore, Oliver. 2003. "Bush Wants to 'Codify' Heterosexual Unions," *Globe and Mail*, 31 July.

Morell, Carolyn M. 1994. *Unwomanly Conduct: The Challenges of Intentional Childlessness*. New York: Routledge.

Mullender, Audrey, G. Hague, U. Imam, L. Kelly, E. Malos, and L. Regan. 2003. "Could Have Helped but Didn't: The Formal and Informal Support Systems Experienced by Children Living with Domestic Violence," in C. Hallett and A. Prout, eds, *Hearing the Voices of Children: Social Policy for a New Century*. London and New York: RoutledgeFalmer.

Murdock, George. 1949. *Social Structure*. New York: Macmillan.

Myles, John. 1996. "When Markets Fail: Social Welfare in Canada and the United States," in Esping-Andersen (1996: 116–40).

Nanda, Serena, and Richard Warms. 2007. *Cultural Anthropology*, 9th edn. Belmont, Calif.: Wadsworth.

National Association of Child Care Resource and Referral Agencies (NACCRRA). 2011. *Parents and the High Cost of Child Care: 2011 Update*. Arlington, Va: NACCRRA.

National Council of Welfare (NCW). 2008. *Welfare Incomes 2006 and 2007*. Ottawa: Minister of Public Works and Government Services Canada.

National Longitudinal Survey of Children and Youth (NLSCY). 1996. *Growing Up in Canada*. Ottawa: Human Resources Development Canada and Statistics Canada.

Neal, Margaret B. 2007. *Working Couples Caring for Children and Aging Parents: Effects of Work and Well-Being*. Mahwah, NJ: Erlbaum.

Nelson, E.D., and Barrie W. Robinson. 1999. *Gender in Canada*. Scarborough, Ont.: Prentice-Hall Allyn and Bacon Canada.

Nelson, F. 1996. *Lesbian Motherhood*. Toronto: University of Toronto Press.

———. 2001. "Lesbian Families," in Bonnie J. Fox, ed., *Family Patterns, Gender Relations*, 2nd edn. Toronto: Oxford University Press.

Nett, Emily. 1981. "Canadian Families in Social-Historical Perspective," *Canadian Journal of Sociology* 6, 3: 239–60.

———. 1988. *Canadian Families Past and Present.* Toronto: Butterworths.

———. 1993. *Canadian Families Past and Present,* 2nd edn. Toronto: Butterworths.

New Zealand Housing Research Centre (NZHRC). n.d. "Homeownership in New Zealand," Dunedin: University of Otago. At: <www.otago.ac.nz>.

New Zealand Ministry of Social Development. 2008. *Children and Young People: Indicators of Wellbeing in New Zealand 2008.* Wellington: NZ. Summary Table of Indicators, at: <www.msd.govt.nz>.

———. 2010. *Sole Parenting in New Zealand: An Update on Key Trends and What Helps Reduce Disadvantage.* Wellington, NZ.

Neysmith, Sheila, Marge Reitsma-Street, Stephanie Baker-Collins, and Elaine Porter. 2012. *Beyond Caring Labour to Provisioning Work.* Toronto: University of Toronto Press.

Nguyen, Tuyen D., and Susan Larsen. 2012. "Prevalence of Children Witnessing Parental Violence," *Review of European Studies* 4, 1: 1–7.

Oakley, Ann. 1974. *The Sociology of Housework.* Oxford: Martin Robertson.

O'Connor, Julia S., Ann Shola Orloff, and Sheila Shaver. 1999. *States, Markets, Families: Gender Liberalism and Social Policy in Australia, Canada, Great Britain and the United States.* Cambridge: Cambridge University Press.

O'Leary, K.D., et al. 1989. "Prevalence and Stability of Physical Aggression between Spouses: A Longitudinal Analysis," *Journal of Consulting and Clinical Psychology* 57: 263–8.

Organisation for Economic Co-operation and Development (OECD). 2001. *Society at a Glance: OECD Social Indicators 2001.* Paris: OECD.

———. 2002. *OECD Employment Outlook July 2002.* Paris: OECD.

———. 2005a. *OECD Employment Outlook 2005.* Paris: OECD.

———. 2005b. *Society at a Glance: OECD Social Indicators.* Paris: OECD.

———. 2007a. *Babies and Bosses: Reconciling Work and Family Life, vol. 5, A Synthesis of Findings for OECD Countries.* At: <www.oecd.org/els/social/family>.

———. 2007b. *Society at a Glance: OECD Social Indicators, 2006.* Paris: OECD.

———. 2008a. *Growing Unequal? Income Distribution and Poverty in OECD Countries.* Paris: OECD.

———. 2008b. *OECD Employment Outlook.* Paris: OECD.

———. 2009a. *OECD Employment Outlook.* Paris: OECD.

———. 2009b. *Society at a Glance.* Paris: OECD.

———. 2010. *Employment Outlook 2010, Database on Earnings Distribution.* Paris: OECD.

———. 2011a. *Doing Better for Families.* Paris: OECD.

———. 2011b. *OECD Factbook 2011–12.* Paris: OECD.

———. 2011c. *Society at a Glance: OECD Social Indicators.* Paris: OECD.

———. 2011d. *Employment and Labour Markets: Key Tables from OECD.* Paris: OECD.

———. 2011e. *Country Snapshots on Family and Children Policies and Outcomes.* Paris: OECD.

———. 2012. *Towards a More Inclusive Labour Market.* Paris: OECD.

Oswald, R.F., and E.A. Suter. 2004. "'The Royal We': Heterosexist Inclusion and Exclusion during Ritual: A 'Straight versus Gay' Comparison," *Journal of Family Issues* 25: 881–99.

Otnes, C., and E.H. Pleck. 2003. *Cinderella Dreams: The Allure of the Lavish Wedding.* Berkeley, Calif.: University of California Press.

Pahl, Jan. 1995. "His Money, Her Money: Recent Research on Financial Organisation in Marriage," *Journal of Economic Psychology* 16: 361–76.

———. 2001. "Couples and Their Money: Theory and Practice in Personal Finances," in R. Sykes, C. Bochel, and N. Ellison, eds, *Social Policy Review 13.* Bristol, UK: Policy Press, 17–37.

———. 2005. "Individualisation in Couple Finances: Who Pays for the Children?" *Social Policy and Society* 4, 4: 381–91.

Papp, Lauren M., E. Mark Cummings, Marcie C. Goeke-Morey. 2008. "For Richer, for Poorer: Money as a Topic of Marital Conflict in the Home," *Family Relations* 58, 1: 91–103.

Parker, Robyn. 2002. "Why Marriages Last. A Discussion of the Literature," Research Paper #28. Melbourne: Australian Institute of Family Studies.

Parsons, Talcott, and Robert F. Bales. 1955. *Family Socialization and Interaction Process.* New York: Free Press.

Patterson, C.J. 2000. "Family Relationships of Lesbians and Gay Men," *Journal of Marriage and the Family* 62: 1052–69.

——— and R.W. Chan. 1997. "Gay Fathers," in M.E. Lamb, ed., *The Role of the Father in Child Development*, 3rd edn. New York: Wiley and Sons, 245–60.

Phillips, J. 1988. *The Mother Experience: New Zealand Women Talk about Motherhood.* Auckland: Penguin Books.

Phipps, Shelley, and Peter S. Burton. 1992. "What's Mine Is Yours? The Influence of Male and Female Incomes on Patterns of Household Expenditure," Discussion Paper #92–12. Halifax: Dalhousie University, Department of Economics.

Pierson, Ruth, Marjorie G. Cohen, Paula Bourne, and Philinda Masters, eds. 1993. *Canadian Women's Issues*, vol. 1. Toronto: James Lorimer.

Ponzetti, James J., ed. 2003. *International Encyclopedia of Marriage and Family*, 2nd edn. New York: Thomson Gale.

Poole, Marilyn, ed. 2005. *Family: Changing Families, Changing Times.* Sydney: Allen & Unwin.

——— and Susan Feldman, eds. 1999. *A Certain Age: Women Growing Older.* Sydney: Allen & Unwin.

Portanti, Martina, and Simon Whitworth. 2009. *A Comparison of the Characteristics of Childless Women and Mothers in the ONS Longitudinal Study.* London: Office for National Statistics.

Potuchek, J.L. 1997. *Who Supports the Family: Gender and Breadwinning in Dual-Earner Marriages.* Stanford, Calif.: Stanford University Press.

Probert, Belinda. 2005. "'I Just Couldn't Fit It In': Gender and Unequal Outcomes in Academic Careers," *Gender, Work and Organization* 12, 1: 50–72.

Pryor, Jan. 2004. "The Child–Stepparent Relationship: Its Fragility and Importance," paper presented at Australian Institute of Family Studies conference, 9–11 Feb., Melbourne.

———. 2005. "What Is Commitment? How Married and Cohabiting Parents Talk about Their Relationship," *Family Matters* 71 (Winter): 28–35.

———, ed. 2008. *The International Handbook of Stepfamilies: Policy and Practice in Legal, Research, and Clinical Environments.* Hoboken, NJ: Wiley.

——— and Bryan Rodgers. 2001. *Children in Changing Families: Life after Parental Separation.* Oxford: Blackwell.

Pulkingham, Jane. 1994. "Private Troubles, Private Solutions: Poverty among Divorced Women and the Politics of Support Enforcement and Child Custody Determination," *Canadian Journal of Law and Society* 9, 2: 73–97.

——— and Sylvia Fuller. 2012. "From Parent to Patient: The Medicalization of Lone Motherhood through Welfare Reform," *Social Politics: International Studies in Gender, State and Society* 19, 2: 243–68.

———, Sylvia Fuller, and Paul Kershaw. 2010. "Lone-Motherhood, Welfare Reform and Active Citizen Subjectivity," *Critical Social Policy* 30, 2: 267–91.

Qu, Lixia. 2004. "Children's Living Arrangements after Parental Separation," *Family Matters* 67 (Autumn): 4–7.

——— and Ruth Weston. 2008. "Snapshot of Family Relationships," *Family Matters* (May).

Queen, Stuart, Robert W. Habenstein, and J.S. Quadagno. 1985. *The Family in Various Cultures*, 5th edn. New York: Harper and Row.

Quinlan, Robert J. 2006. "Gender and Risk in a Matrifocal Caribbean Community: A View from Behavioral Ecology," *American Anthropologist* 108, 3: 464–79.

Raley, Sara, and Suzanne Bianchi. 2006. "Sons, Daughters and Family Processes: Does Gender of Children Matter?" *Annual Review of Sociology* 32: 401–21.

Ram, Bali. 1990. *New Trends in the Family: Demographic Facts and Figures.* Statistics Canada, Catalogue no. 91–535E. Ottawa: Minister of Supply and Services Canada, Mar.

Ramu, G.N., and Nicholas Tavuchis. 1986. "The Valuation of Children and Parenthood among the Voluntarily Childless and Parental Couples in Canada," *Journal of Comparative Family Studies* 17, 1: 99–115.

Ranson, Gillian. 2009. "Paid and Unpaid Work: How Do Families Divide Their Labour?" in Baker (2009a: 108–29).

Ravanera, Zenaida R., and Fernando Rajulton. 2007. "Changes in Economic Status and Timing of Marriage of Young Canadians," *Canadian Studies in Population* 34, 1: 49–67.

Research New Zealand. 2007. "Special Report on the 2006 Census of New Zealand's Population and Dwellings." Wellington: Research New Zealand. At: <www.researchnz.com>.

Reserve Bank of Australia. 2003. "Household Debt: What the Data Show," *Reserve Bank of Australia Bulletin* (Mar.): 1–11.

Reserve Bank of New Zealand. 2006. "Key Graphs—Household Debt." At: <www.rbnz.govt.nz>.

Rhoades, G.K., S.M. Stanley, and H.K. Markham. 2009. "Pre-engagement Cohabitation and Gender Asymmetry in Marital Commitment," *Journal of Family Psychology* 23, 1: 107–11.

Rich, Stephanie, Ann Taket, Melissa Graham, and Julia Shelley. 2011. "'Unnatural', 'Unwomanly', 'Uncreditable' and 'Undervalued': The Significance of Being a Childless Woman in Australian Society," *Gender Issues* 28, 4: 226–47.

Richardson, C. James. 2001. "Divorce and Remarriage," in M. Baker, ed., *Families: Changing Trends in Canada*, 4th edn. Toronto: McGraw-Hill Ryerson, 206–37.

Roberts, Helen. 1997. "Children, Inequalities and Health," *British Medical Journal* 314, 7087 (12 Apr.): 11–22.

Rodney, Patricia. 1995. "Domestic Violence in Vulnerable Populations: International Models Relevant to American Healthcare and Safety for Women." At: <www.i3m.org/main/pcpc/ppoint/ws6-rodney.pdf>.

Rolfe, Alison, and Elizabeth Peel. 2011. "'It's a Double-edged Thing': The Paradox of Civil Partnership and Why Some Couples Are Choosing Not to Have One," *Feminism and Psychology* 21, 3: 317–35.

Rosenfield, Michael J., and Reuben J. Thomas. 2012. "Searching for a Mate: The Rise of the Internet as a Social Intermediary," *American Sociological Review* 77, 4: 523–47.

Rowland, Donald T. 2007. "Historical Trends in Childlessness," *Journal of Family Issues* 28: 1311–37.

Sainsbury, Diane. 1993. "Dual Welfare and Sex Segregation of Access to Social Benefits: Income Maintenance Policies in the UK, the US, the Netherlands and Sweden," *Journal of Social Policy* 22, 1: 69–98.

———. 1996. *Gender, Equality and Welfare States*. Cambridge: Cambridge University Press.

Sanday, Peggy Reeves. 2002. *Women at the Center: Life in a Modern Matriarchy*. Ithaca, NY: Cornell University Press.

Sarantakos, Sotirios. 1996. *Modern Families: An Australian Text*. Melbourne: Macmillan Education Australia.

———. 1998. "Sex and Power in Same-Sex Couples," *Australian Journal of Social Issues* 33, 1: 17–36.

Sarfati, Diana, and Kate Scott. 2001. "The Health of Lone Mothers in New Zealand," *New Zealand Medical Journal* 114, 1133: 257–60.

Sassler, S., and A. Miller. 2011. "Waiting to be Asked: Gender, Power and Relationship Progression among Cohabiting Couples," *Journal of Family Issues* 32, 4: 482–506.

Sauvé, Roger. 2006. "The Effects of the Changing Age Structure on Households and Families to 2026." Ottawa: People Patterns Consulting. At: <www.vifamily.ca>.

———. 2009. "Family Life and Work Life: An Uneasy Balance." Ottawa: People Patterns Consulting, for Vanier Institute of the Family. At: <www.vifamily.ca>.

Saxton, L. 1993. *The Individual, Marriage, and the Family*. Belmont, Calif.: Wadsworth.

Scanzoni, John. 1982. *Sexual Bargaining: Power Politics in American Marriage*, 2nd edn. Chicago: University of Chicago Press.

Schecter, E., A.J. Tracy, K.V. Page, and G. Luong. 2008. "'Shall We Marry?' Legal Marriage as a Commitment Event in Same-Sex Relationships," *Journal of Homosexuality* 54, 4: 400–22.

Schodt, Paul. 2008. "Sex Differences in Stepchildren's Reports of Stepfamily Functioning," *Communication Reports* 21, 1: 46–58.

Schultz, James A. 2006. *Courtly Love, the Love of Courtliness, and the History of Sexuality*. Chicago: University of Chicago Press.

Sev'er, Aysan. 1990. "Mate Selection Patterns of Men and Women in Personal Advertisements," *Atlantis: A Women's Studies Journal* 15, 2: 70–6.

———. 1992. *Women and Divorce in Canada: A Sociological Analysis*. Toronto: Canadian Scholars' Press.

———. 2002. *Fleeing the House of Horrors: Women Who Have Left Abusive Partners.* Toronto: University of Toronto Press.

——— and Jan E. Trost, eds. 2011. *Skeletons in the Closet: A Sociological Analysis of Family Conflict.* Waterloo, Ont.: Wilfrid Laurier University Press.

Shapiro, D.N., C. Peterson, and A.J. Stewart. 2009. "Legal and Social Contexts and Mental Health among Lesbian and Heterosexual Mothers," *Journal of Family Psychology* 23: 255–62.

Sharlin, S.A., F.W. Kaslow, and H. Hammerschmidt. 2000. *Together through Thick and Thin: A Multinational Picture of Long-Term Marriages.* New York: Haworth Clinical Practice Press.

Shechory, Mally and Riva Ziv. 2007. "Relationships between Gender Role Attitudes, Role Division, and Perception of Equity between Heterosexual, Gay and Lesbian Couples," *Sex Roles* 56, 9 and 10: 629–38.

Shipman, Beccy, and Carol Smart. 2007. "'It's Made a Huge Difference': Recognition, Rights and the Personal Significance of Civil Partnership," *Sociological Research Online* (1).

Shorter, Edward. 1975. *The Making of the Modern Family.* New York: Basic Books.

Shriner, Michael. 2009. "Marital Quality in Remarriage: A Review of Methods and Results," *Journal of Divorce and Remarriage* 50: 81–99.

Shulman, Julie L., Gabrielle Gotta, and Robert-Jay Green. 2012. "Will Marriage Matter? Effects of Marriage Anticipated by Same-Sex Couples," *Journal of Family Issues* 33, 2: 158–81.

Sigal, A.B., S.A. Wolchik, J.-U. Tein, and I.N. Sandler. 2012. "Enhancing Youth Outcomes Following Parental Divorce: A Longitudinal Study of the Effects of the New Beginnings Program on Educational and Occupational Goals," *Journal of Clinical Health and Adolescent Psychology* 41, 2: 150–65.

Sims-Gould, J., and A. Martin-Matthews. 2010. "'We Share the Care': Family Caregivers' Experiences of Their Older Relative Receiving Home Support Services," *Health & Social Care in the Community* 18, 4: 415–23.

Singh, G.K., and R.M. Ghandour. 2012. "Impact of Neighborhood Social Conditions and Household Socioeconomic Status on Behavioral Problems among US Children," *Maternal and Child Health* 16: S158–69.

Singh, S. 1997. *Marriage Money: The Social Shaping of Money in Marriage and Banking.* Sydney: Allen & Unwin.

Skolnick, A. 1987. *The Intimate Environment,* 4th edn. Toronto: Little, Brown.

Smart, Carol. 2007a. *Personal Life.* Cambridge: Polity Press.

———. 2007b. "Same-Sex Couples and Marriage: Negotiating Relational Landscapes with Families and Friends," *Sociological Review* 55, 4: 671–86.

———. 2008. "'Can I Be Bridesmaid?' Combining the Personal and Political in Same-Sex Weddings," *Sexualities* 11, 6: 763–78.

——— and Bren Neale. 1999. *Family Fragments?* Cambridge: Polity Press.

——— and Selma Sevenjuijsen. 1989. *Child Custody and the Politics of Gender.* London: Routledge.

Smith, Marjorie. 2004. "Relationships of Children in Stepfamilies with Their Non-Resident Fathers," *Family Matters* 67 (Autumn): 28–35.

Smith, Raymond T. 1996. *The Matrifocal Family: Power, Pluralism and Politics.* New York: Routledge.

Smyth, Bruce. 2002. "Research into Parent–Child Contact after Separation," *Family Matters* 62 (Winter): 33–7.

———, ed. 2004. *Parent–Child Contact and Post-Separation Parenting Arrangements.* Research Report #9. Melbourne: Australian Institute of Family Studies.

———, G. Sheehan, and B. Fehlberg. 2001. "Patterns of Parenting after Divorce: A Benchmark Study," *Australian Journal of Family Law* 15, 2: 114–28.

——— and Ruth Weston. 2004. "The Attitudes of Separated Mothers and Fathers to 50/50 Shared Care," *Family Matters* 67 (Autumn): 8–15.

Solomon, S.E., E.D. Rothblum, and K.F. Balsam. 2005. "Money, Housework, Sex and Conflict: Same-Sex Couples in Civil Unions, Those Not in Civil Unions, and Heterosexual Married Siblings," *Sex Roles* 52, 9 and 10: 561–75.

Speirs, Carol, and Maureen Baker. 1994. "Eligibility to Adopt: Models of 'Suitable' Families in Legislation and Practice," *Canadian Social Work Review* 11, 1: 89–102.

Stanley, S.S., G.K. Rhoades, and H.J. Markham. 2006. "Sliding versus Deciding:

Inertia and the Premarital Cohabitation Effect," *Family Relations* 55 (Oct.): 499–509.

Statistics Canada. 2002a. "2001 Census: Marital Status, Common-law Status, Families and Households," *The Daily*, 22 Oct.

———. 2002b. "Changing Conjugal Life in Canada," *The Daily*, 11 July.

———. 2003. "Marriages," *The Daily*, 2 June.

———. 2006. "Concept: Census Family," *Definitions of Concepts and Variables*. At: <www.statcan.gc.ca/concepts/definitions/cfamily-rfamille-eng.htm>.

———. 2007a. "2006 Census of Population." At: <www12.statcan.ca/English/census06/analysis/farmhouse/tables/table1.htm>.

———. 2007b. "2006 Census: Families, Marital Status, Households and Dwelling Characteristics," *The Daily*, 12 Sept.

———. 2007c. "Marriages, 2003," CANSIM Table 101–1013. Ottawa: Statistics Canada.

———. 2007d. "Family Portrait: Continuity and Change in Canadian Families and Households in 2006: National Portrait: Individuals." Ottawa: Statistics Canada. At: <www12.statcan.ca/english/census06/analysis/famhouse/ind3.cfm>.

———. 2007e. *Report on the Demographic Situation in Canada: 2005 and 2006*. Ottawa: Statistics Canada. At: <www.statcan.gc.ca/91–209-x/2004000/5200779eng.htm>.

———. 2008a. "Census Snapshot of Canada—Families," *Canadian Social Trends* 39. Catalogue no. 11–008.

———. 2008b. "Live Births, by Geography—Marital Status of Mother," Table 2.5. At: <www.statcan.gc.ca/pub/84f0210x/2006000/5201681-eng.htm>.

———. 2011. *Family Violence in Canada: A Statistical Profile*. Ottawa: Minister of Industry.

———. 2012a. "2011 Census of Population: Families, Households, Marital Status, Structural Type of Dwelling, Collectives," *The Daily*, 19 Sept.

———. 2012b. "Data Tables for Families, Households and Housing," Table 14.7. At: <www.statcan.gc.ca/pub/11-402-x/2012000/chap/fam/tbl-eng.htm>.

———. 2012c. "Portrait of Families and Living Arrangements in Canada." At: <www12.statcan.gc/census-recensement/2011>.

Statistics New Zealand. 2004. "Family Types." At: <www.stats.govt.nz/ analytical-reports/looking-past-20th-century/changes-in-society/family-types.htm>.

Steele, F., C. Kallis, H. Goldstein, and H. Joshi. 2005. "The Relationship between Childbearing and Transitions from Marriage and Cohabitation in Britain," *Demography* 42, 4: 647–73.

Strohm, Charles, Judith A. Seltzer, Susan D. Cochran, and Vickie M. Mays. 2009. "'Living Apart Together' Relationships in the United States," *Demographic Research* 13 (Aug.): 177–214.

Strong-Boag, Veronica. 1982. "Intruders in the Nursery: Childcare Professionals Reshape the Years One to Five, 1920–1940," in Joy Parr, ed., *Childhood and Family in Canadian History*. Toronto: McClelland & Stewart, 160–78.

Summers, Anne. 2008. "A Sorry Way to Right a Terrible Wrong," *Sydney Morning Herald*, 12 Jan.

Sweeney, Megan M. 2004. "The Changing Importance of White Women's Economic Prospects for Assortative Mating," *Journal of Marriage and Family* 66, 4: 1015–28.

Swift, Karen. 1995. *Manufacturing "Bad Mothers"? A Critical Perspective on Child Neglect*. Toronto: University of Toronto Press.

Synnott, Anthony. 1983. "Little Angels, Little Devils: A Sociology of Children," *Canadian Review of Sociology and Anthropology* 20, 1: 79–95.

Tasker, Fiona. 2010. "Same-Sex Parenting and Child Development: Reviewing the Contribution of Parental Gender," *Journal of Marriage and Family* 72, 1: 35–40.

Taylor-Gooby, Peter, ed. 2004. *New Risks, New Welfare: The Transformation of the European Welfare State*. Oxford: Oxford University Press.

Tew, Marjorie. 1998. *Safer Childbirth? A Critical History of Maternity Care*, 3rd edn. London and New York: Free Association Books.

Thomas, Derrick. 2001. "Evolving Family Living Arrangements of Canada's Immigrants," *Canadian Social Trends* (Summer): 16–22.

Thorne, Barry. 1982. "Feminist Rethinking of the Family: An Overview," in Barry Thorne, with Marilyn Yalom, eds, *Rethinking the Family: Some Feminist Questions*. New York: Longman, 1–24.

Tombaugh, A. 2009. "Pretty Dresses and Privilege: Gender and Heteronormativity in Weddings," *Sociological Insight* 1: 106–23.

Torjman, Sherri, and Ken Battle. 1999. *Good Work: Getting It and Keeping It*. Ottawa: Caledon Institute of Social Policy.

Tough, S., K. Tofflemire, K. Benzies, N. Fraser-Lee, and C. Newburn-Cook. 2007. "Factors Influencing Childbearing Decision and Knowledge of Perinatal Risks among Canadian Men and Women," *Maternal and Child Health Journal* 11: 189–98.

Trapski, Judge, et al. 1994. *The Child Support Review*. Wellington: New Zealand Parliament.

Treas, Judith, and Tsui-o Tai. 2012. "How Couples Manage the Household: Work and Power in Cross-National Perspective," *Journal of Family Issues* 33 (Aug.): 1088–1116.

Tschann, Jeanne, Lauri Pasch, Elena Flores, Barbara Marin, E. Marco Baisch, and Charles Wibbelsman. 2009. "Nonviolent Aspects of Interparental Conflict and Dating Violence among Adolescents," *Journal of Family Issues* 30, 3: 295–319.

Turner, B.S. 1995. "Aging and Identity," in M. Featherstone and A. Wernick, eds, *Images of Aging*. London: Routledge, 245–60.

Ungar, Michael. 2008. "Resilience across Cultures," *British Journal of Social Work* 38: 218–35.

United Nations (UN). 2000. *The World's Women: Trends and Statistics*. New York: UN.

United Nations Children's Fund (UNICEF). 2000. *A League Table of Child Poverty in Rich Nations*. Florence: Innocenti Research Centre.

———. 2003. *A League Table of Child Maltreatment Deaths in Rich Nations*. Florence: Innocenti Research Centre.

———. 2005. *Child Poverty in Rich Nations 2005*. Report Card #6. Florence: Innocenti Research Centre.

———. 2008. *The Child Care Transition*. Report Card #8. Florence: Innocenti Research Centre.

United States Bureau of the Census. 2011. "Same-Sex Couple Households." At: <www.census.gov>.

United States Department of Health and Human Services. 2002. "Births: Final Data for 2001," *National Vital Statistics Reports* 51, 2: 1–103.

Ursel, Jane. 1992. *Private Lives, Public Policy: 100 Years of State Intervention in the Family*. Toronto: Women's Press.

Van den Berg, Axel, and Joseph Smucker, eds. 1997. *The Sociology of Labour Markets: Efficiency, Equity, Security*. Toronto: Prentice-Hall Allyn and Bacon Canada.

Vanier Institute of the Family (VIF). 1994. *Profiling Canada's Families*. Ottawa: VIF.

———. 2000. *Profiling Canada's Families II*. Ottawa: VIF.

———. 2004. *Profiling Canada's Families III*. Ottawa: VIF.

———. 2007. *Family Facts*. Ottawa: VIF. At: <www.vifamily.ca/library/facts/facts.html>.

———. 2008. "Fertility Intentions: If, When and How Many?" *Fascinating Families*. Ottawa: VIF.

———. 2009. "Becoming a 'Lone-Mother'," *Fascinating Families*. Ottawa: VIF.

———. 2010. *Families Count: Profiling Canada's Families*. Ottawa: VIF.

———. 2011. "Child Abuse and Neglect," *Fascinating Families* Issue 38 (15 May). Ottawa: VIF.

———. 2012. "Four in Ten Marriages End in Divorce," *Fascinating Families* Issue 41 (26 Oct.). Ottawa: VIF.

van den Hoonaard, D.K. 2009. *"Experiences of Living Alone: Widows' and Widowers' Perspectives,"* *Housing Studies* 24, 6: 737–53.

———. 2010. *By Himself: The Older Man's Experience of Widowhood*. Toronto: University of Toronto Press.

Van Laningham, J., D.R. Johnson, and P. Amato. 2001. "Marital Happiness, Marital Duration and the U-shaped Curve: Evidence from a 5-Wave Panel Study," *Social Forces* 78, 4: 1313–41.

Veblen, T. 1953 [1899]. *The Theory of the Leisure Class*. New York: Mentor.

Veevers, Jean E. 1980. *Childless by Choice*. Toronto: Butterworths.

Vogler, C., and J. Pahl. 1994. "Money, Power and Inequality within Marriage," *Sociological Review* 42: 263–88.

Vogler, Carolyn, Clare Lyonette, and Richard D. Wiggins. 2008. "Money, Power and Spending in Intimate Relationships," *Sociological Review* 56, 1: 117–43.

Voicu, M., B. Voicu, and K. Strapcova. 2008. "Housework and Gender Inequality in European Countries," *European Sociological Review*, 21 Sept. (online publication).

Vosko, Leah F. 2000. *Temporary Work: The Gendered Rise of a Precarious Employment Relationship.* Toronto: University of Toronto Press.

———. 2002. "The Pasts (and Futures) of Feminist Political Economy in Canada: Reviving the Debate," *Studies in Political Economy* 68 (Summer): 55–83.

———. 2009. "Precarious Employment and the Challenges for Employment Policy," in M. Cohen and J. Pulkingham, eds, *Public Policy for Women.* Toronto: University of Toronto Press, 374–95.

Wadsworth, J., I. Burnell, B. Taylor, and N. Butler. 1983. "Family Type and Accidents in Preschool Children," *Journal of Epidemiology and Community Health* 37: 100–4.

Waite, Linda. 2005. "Marriage, Family and Health," keynote address to the Australian Institute of Family Studies Conference, 9–11 Feb., Melbourne.

Walker, R., D. Turnbull, and C. Wilkinson. 2002. "Strategies to Address Global Caesarean Section Rates: A Review of the Evidence," *Birth* 29 (1 Mar.).

Walker, Seb. 2005. "Divorce Makes Women Happier Than Men," *The Guardian*, 5 July. At: <www.guardian.co.uk>.

Wall, Glenda. 2004. "Is Your Child's Brain Potential Maximized? Mothering in an Age of New Brain Research," *Atlantis* 28, 2: 41–50.

———. 2005. "Childhood and Child Rearing," in Baker (2005a: 163–80).

———. 2009. "Childhood and Child Rearing," in Baker (2009a: 91–107).

——— and Stephanie Arnold. 2007. "How Involved Is Involved Fathering? An Exploration of the Contemporary Culture of Fatherhood," *Gender & Society* 21, 4: 508–27.

Wallace, P. 1999. *The Psychology of the Internet.* Cambridge: Cambridge University Press.

Wallerstein, J., and S. Blakeslee. 1996. *The Good Marriage.* New York: Warner Books.

Walsh, Rebecca. 2005. "Obesity To Shorten Many Lives," *New Zealand Herald*, 19 Mar., 1.

Walsh, Sara M. 2008. "Kathleen A. Bogle, *Hooking up: Sex, Dating and Relationships*," *Journal of Youth and Adolescence* 37, 6 (July).

Ward, Peter. 1990. *Courtship, Love, and Marriage in Nineteenth-Century English Canada.* Montreal and Kingston: McGill-Queen's University Press.

Weedon, J., M. Abrams, M. Green, and J. Sabini. 2006. "Do High-Status People Really Have Fewer Children?" *Human Nature* 17, 4: 377–92.

Weeks, Jeffrey. 2002. "Elective Families: Lesbian and Gay Life Experiments," in A. Carling, S. Duncan, and R. Edwards, eds, *Analysing Families.* London: Routledge, 218–28.

Weir, L. 1996. "Recent Developments in the Governance of Pregnancy," *Economy and Society* 25, 3: 372–92.

West, C., and D.H. Zimmerman. 1987. "Doing Gender," *Gender and Society* 1, 2: 125–51.

Westad, Callie, and David McConnell. 2012. "Child Welfare Involvement of Mothers with Mental Health Issues," *Community Mental Health Journal* 48: 29–37.

Weston, Ruth, and Robyn Parker. 2002. "Why Is the Fertility Rate Falling? A Discussion of the Literature," *Family Matters* 63 (Spring/Summer): 6–13.

———, Lixia Qu, Robyn Parker, and Michael Alexander. 2004. "'It's Not for Lack of Wanting Kids . . .': A Report on the Fertility Decision Making Project." Melbourne: Australian Institute of Family Studies, Research Report #11.

Whitehead, Margaret, Bo Burström, and Finn Diderichsen. 2000. "Social Policies and the Pathways to Inequalities in Health: A Comparative Analysis of Lone Mothers in Britain and Sweden," *Social Science and Medicine* 50, 2: 255–70.

Whitehouse, E.R., and A. Zaidi. 2008. "Socio-Economic Differences in Mortality," OECD Social Employment and Migration Working Papers #71.

Whitty, Monica T. 2007. "Revealing the 'Real' Me, Searching for the 'Actual' You: Presentations of Self on an Internet Dating Site," *Computers in Human Behaviour* 24, 4: 1707–23.

Willen, Helena, and Henry Montgomery. 1996. "The Impact of Wish for Children and Having Children: Attainment and Importance of Life Values," *Journal of Comparative Family Studies* 27: 499–518.

Willoughby, Brian J., Jason S. Carroll, Jennifer M. Vitas, and Lauren M. Hill. 2012. "'When Are You Getting Married?' The Intergenerational Transmission of Attitudes Regarding Marital Timing and Marital Importance," *Journal of Family Issues* 33, 2: 223–45.

Wilson, M., and M. Daly. 1994. *Spousal Homicide*. Ottawa: Canadian Centre for Justice Statistics.

Winch, Robert. 1955. "The Theory of Complementary Needs in Mate Selection: A Test of One Kind of Complementariness," *American Sociological Review* 20 (Oct.): 552–5.

Winterich, Julie A. 2007. "Aging, Femininity, and the Body: What Appearance Changes Mean to Women with Age," *Gender Issues* 24: 51–69.

Wister, Andrew. 2005. *Baby Boomer Health Dynamics*. Toronto: University of Toronto Press.

Wolfe, David, and Peter Jaffe. 2001. "Prevention of Domestic Violence: Emerging Initiatives," in S. Graham-Bermann and J. Edleson, eds, *Domestic Violence in the Lives of Children: The Future of Research, Intervention and Social Policy*. Washington: American Psychological Association.

———, Claire Crooks, Debbie Chiodo, and Peter Jaffe. 2009. "Child Maltreatment, Bullying, Gender-Based Harassment, and Adolescent Dating Violence: Making the Connections," *Psychology of Women Quarterly* 33, 1: 21–4.

Woodward, Lianne, David M. Fergusson, and Jay Belsky. 2000. "Timing of Parental Separation and Attachment to Parents in Adolescence: Results of a Prospective Study from Birth to Age 16," *Journal of Marriage and the Family* 62: 162–74.

World Health Organization (WHO). 1998. *The World Health Report 1998: Life in the Twenty-First Century: A Vision for All*. Geneva: WHO.

———. 2010. *World Health Statistics 2010*. Geneva: WHO.

——— and UNICEF. 1990. *Innocenti Declaration on the Protection, Promotion and Support of Breastfeeding*. At: <www.unicef. org>.

Worrall, Jill. 2008. "Kin Care—Understanding the Dynamics," *Social Work Now* (Dec.): 4–11.

Worth, H.B., and K.E. McMillan. 2004. "Ill-Prepared for the Labour Market: Health Status in a Sample of Single Mothers on Welfare," *Social Policy Journal of New Zealand* 21 (Mar.): 83–97.

Wu, Zheng. 1996. "Childbearing in Cohabitation Relationships," *Journal of Marriage and the Family* 58: 281–92.

———. 2000. *Cohabitation: An Alternative Form of Family Living*. Toronto: Oxford University Press.

——— and Christoph Schimmele. 2005. "Divorce and Repartnering," in Baker (2005a: 202–28).

Zelizer, V. 1994. *The Social Meaning of Money*. New York: Basic Books.

Zhang, Xuelin. 2009. "Earnings of Women with and without Children," *Perspectives* (Mar.): 5–13.

Index